I f you picked up this copy of **Edge** in a shop, if your experience of the magazine trails all the way back to October 1993, and if your memory remains sharp even after having 16 years of gaming sieved through it, perhaps you noted similarities to the package pictured below. (If your copy arrived by subscription, focus instead on the fact that the edition in your hands, pictured left, is unavailable in the shops.) Since this is our 200th issue, we thought it only right to salute our origins.

Looking back, **Edge**, a magazine whose original mission statement was 'The future of interactive entertainment', could not have been launched at a more appropriate time. In 1993, CD-ROM media for PCs and consoles was in the process of transforming gaming as a whole, not only in terms of the amount of data that could be shipped on single discs but what optical storage could do for the streaming of soundtracks and (shouldn't we have worried more?) video. In the arcade, Sega's AM2 division redefined realtime 3D graphics with the release of the astonishing *Virtua Fighter*. In the home, the 3DO console promised a multimedia future filled with riches beyond anything being offered by Sega, Nintendo or Atari. And what were these things we were hearing about Sony making a bold entry into the videogame hardware market? In comparison to the changes afoot when **Edge** launched, the videogame industry's recent move into the HD era registers little more than a flicker on the grand evolutionary scale.

In issue 200 we talk to some of the people who were working at the heart of the mid-'90s videogame revolution to discover the real stories that shaped an industry. We also take a trip through Sega's colourful history with *Sonic The Hedgehog* coder Yuju Naka (p88), and delve further back in time to tell the story of Atari's forgotten co-founder (p94).

But we look to the future, too, by asking four leading game developers what we might be discussing in issue 300 of **Edge** (p82). If you don't find anything to disagree with there, you'll no doubt be able to find something in our 100 best games feature (p46). If you don't already subscribe, take up the offer on p160 and drop us a line using one of your 200 cover postcards to let us know what you think in appropriate style.

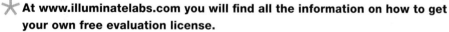

Future Publishing, 30 Monmouth Street, Bath, BA1 2BW
Telephone: +44 (0)1225 442244
Fax: +44 (0)1225 732275
Email: edge@futurenet.com
Edge website: www.edge-online.com

PEOPLE ON EDGE
Tony Mott editor-in-chief
Alex Wiltshire deputy editor
Ian Evenden production editor
Martin Davies writer
Richard Stanton writer
Christophe Kagotani Tokyo bureau
Darren Phillips art editor
Andrew Hind deputy art editor
Colin Campbell online editor

CONTRIBUTORS
Brick Bardo, Jon Blyth, Nick Cox, N'Gai Croal,
Matthew Castle, Chris Dahlen, Nathan Ditum,
Christian Donlan, Tony Ellis, Tom Francis, Duncan Harris,
Phil Haycraft, Leonard Herman, Leon Hurley, Jon Jordan,
Harry Malt, Charlotte Martyn, Alec Meer, Michael
Moneypenny, Craig Pearson, Simon Parkin, Steven Poole,
Paul Roberts, Randy Smith, Rob Smith, Terry Stokes

Ian Miller group art director
Robin Abbott creative director
Matthew Williams design director
Jim Douglas editorial director

ADVERTISING
Julian House advertising manager
Mark Hanrahan advertising director
Jude Daniels advertising director,
central agency team (0207 042 4105)
Kerry Nortcliffe agency sales manager,
central agency team (0207 042 4153)
Advertising phone 01225 442244

MARKETING
Tom Acton marketing campaign manager
Matt Woods brand marketing director

CIRCULATION
Stuart Agnew trade marketing manager
Matt Cooper trade marketing executive
Rachael Cock trade marketing director
John Lawton international account manager
(john.lawton@futurenet.com)

PRINT & PRODUCTION
Frances Twentyman production co-ordinator
Rose Griffiths production manager
Richard Mason head of production
Colin Polis Future Plus buyer

LICENSING
Tim Hudson head of international licensing

FUTURE PUBLISHING LIMITED
James Binns publishing director
Simon Wear chief operating officer
Robert Price chief executive

SUBSCRIPTIONS
Phone our UK hotline on 0844 848 2852
Subscribe online at www.myfavouritemagazines.co.uk

Printed in the UK by William Gibbons.
Covers printed by Midway Colour Print, Holt, Wilts.
Distributed in the UK by Seymour Distribution Ltd
2 East Poultry Avenue, London, EC1A 9PT.
(0207 429 4000)

Edge is the registered trademark of Future
Publishing Limited. All rights reserved.

"Together we will cross the reality datum!"

THE BEST 100 GAMES...   46
...to play today. We compile a list uncluttered by nostalgia.
(Warning: certain sacred cows have become burger meat)

MASTER OF THE ARTS   66
Entrepreneur, visionary and... failure? EA and 3DO founder
Trip Hawkins on the dangers of thinking too far ahead

AGES   88
Prope's Yuji Naka talks through his extraordinary career at
Sega (and might just mention a particular blue hedgehog)

THE UNTOLD ATARI STORY   94
Thirty-five years on, Ted Dabney is ready to share his
experiences of co-founding one of gaming's classic brands

CONTENTS
APRIL

This month

CONTENTS
CONTINUED

Hype

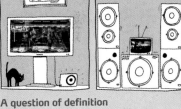
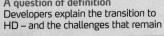

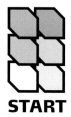

START

The 200 covers of E200

Unlike Nintendo's Pokémon, we're not expecting you to catch them all

When you're a making a music magazine celebrating a landmark issue and offering multiple cover options featuring separate gurning-mug portraits of John, Paul, George and Ringo, it's probably fine to encourage your readers to collect the set. When you're offering 200 unique designs, it's a bit different. If you're committed to collecting a number of these covers, however, we've broken down the 200 into categories (see right). Some groups are defined by genre, some by simply being a selection of our favourite genre-defining series. One game

even has a collection all to itself, for reasons that will become clear on page 58.

For some of these cover choices we opted for games with universal appeal; with others we were more indulgent. Many games are old, some are recent, a few aren't yet released. Out of the 200 designs, though, we're confident that every **Edge** reader will find something from the world of gaming that means something to them.

If you're still keen to collect the entire set, albeit in arty postcard form, turn to the subscription offer on page 160.

1. Mario
Super Mario Galaxy

2. Agent 47
Hitman series

3. Manuel 'Manny' Calavera
Grim Fandango

4. Kratos
God Of War series

5. Sir Arthur
Ghosts 'N Goblins

6. Gordon Freeman
Half-Life series

7. Gum
Jet Set Radio series

8. Link
Zelda: A Link To The Past

9. Armakuni
The Last Ninja series

10. Ken Masters
Street Fighter II series

11. Ebisumaru
Mystical Ninja series

12. Miner Willy
Manic Miner

13. Samus Aran
Metroid Prime series

14. Mr Game & Watch
Game & Watch series

15. Wander & Agro
Shadow Of The Colossus

16. Nathan Drake
Uncharted: Drake's Fortune

17. The Prince
Prince Of Persia: SOT

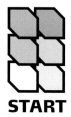

18. Amaterasu
Okami

19. Sonic
Sonic The Hedgehog series

20. Solid Snake
Metal Gear Solid series

21. Ryo Hazuki
Shenmue series

22. Lara Croft
Tomb Raider series

23. Bayonetta
Bayonetta

24. Lester Knight Chaykin
Another World

25. Batman
Batman: Arkham Asylum

26. Bub
Bubble Bobble series

27. Bob
Bubble Bobble series

28. Simon Belmont
Castlevania series

29. Earthworm Jim
Earthworm Jim series

30. Space marine
Doom series

31. Conrad B Hart
Flashback

32. Mega Man
Mega Man series

33. Adam Jensen
Deus Ex 3

34. Richard B Riddick
Riddick series

35. Marco Rossi
Metal Slug series

36. Marcus Fenix
Gears Of War series

37. Parappa
Parappa The Rapper

38. Reiko Nagase
Ridge Racer series

39. Pikachu
Pokémon series

40. Altaïr Ibn La-Ahad
Assassin's Creed

41. Sam Fisher
Splinter Cell series

42. Yoshi
Yoshi's Island

43. Paul Phoenix
Tekken series

44. Tom-Tom
Wonder Boy

45. Jackie Estacado
The Darkness

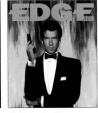
46. Jade
Beyond Good & Evil

47. James Bond
GoldenEye

48. Red Harlow
Red Dead Revolver

49. Donkey Kong
Donkey Kong series

50. Tiki
New Zealand Story

51. Strider Hiryu
Strider

52. Joe
Viewtiful Joe series

53. Q*Bert
*Q*Bert* series

54. Stranger – *Oddworld: Stranger's Wrath*

55. Toku
LostWinds

56. Nariko
Heavenly Sword

57. Zeke – *Zombies Ate My Neighbours*

58. Agent
Crackdown

59. Pac-Man
Pac-Man

60. Charlie Fotheringham-Grunes – *Nodes Of Yesod*

61. Luke Skywalker
Lego Star Wars

62. Travis Touchdown
No More Heroes

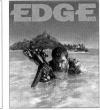
63. Taki
Soul Calibur IV

64. Jack Carver
Far Cry

65. Mario & Luigi
Mario Bros

66. Sparrow
Fable II

67. Isaac Clarke
Dead Space

68. Little Computer Person
Little Computer People

69. Guybrush Threepwood
Monkey Island series

70. Dizzy
Dizzy series

71. Vibri
Vib Ribbon

72. Laharl
Disgaea series

73. Jake Dunn
Crysis

74. *Mini Ninjas*

75. *BioShock*

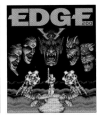
76. *Paradroid*

77. *Actraiser*

78. *Elite*

79. *Exile*

80. *Fallout 3*

81. *Adventure*

82. *Gunstar Heroes*

83. *Contra III: The Alien Wars*

84. *Killer 7*

85. *Bomberman*

86. *The Chaos Engine*

87. *APB*

88. *Gods*

 89. *Shadow Of The Beast*
 90. *Cave Story*
 91. *Atic Atac*
 92. *Sabre Wulf*
 93. *Shinobi*
 94. *Mario Bros*
 95. *Gauntlet*
 96. *Arkanoid II: Revenge Of Doh*

 97. *Dig Dug*
 98. *Dragon's Lair*
 99. *Spy Hunter*
 100. *I, Robot*
 101. *Rolling Thunder*
 102. *Green Beret*
 103. *Bomb Jack*
 104. *Marble Madness*

 105. *720°*
 106. *Tron*
 107. *Commando*
 108. *Tetris*
 109. *Advance Wars*
 110. *Lords Of Midnight*
 111. *Sensible Soccer*
 112. *Hyper Sports*

 113. *Speedball 2*
 114. *World Games*
 115. *Katamari Damacy*
 116. *Pilotwings 64*
 117. *Pikmin*
 118. *Skool Daze*
 119. *Wario Ware Inc*
 120. *Guitar Hero*

 121. *Secret Of Mana*
 122. *EarthBound*
 123. *World Of WarCraft*
 124. *Eve Online*
 125. *Chrono Trigger*
 126. *Head Over Heels*
 127. *Knight Lore*
 128. *Super Mario 64*

 129. *Super Mario World*
 130. *Rainbow Islands*
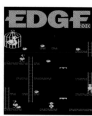 131. *Chuckie Egg*
 132. *Dead Rising*
 133. *Manhunt*
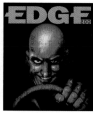 134. *Carmageddon*
 135. *Silent Hill 2*
 136. *Mortal Kombat*

 137. *Barbarian*
 138. *Left 4 Dead*
 139. *Kung-Fu Master*
 140. *Karate Champ*
 141. *Yie Ar Kung-Fu*
 142. *Street Fighter II*
 143. *Super Punch-Out*
 144. *Streets Of Rage*

 145. *Virtua Fighter 5*

 146. *Way Of The Exploding Fist*

 147. *Final Fight*

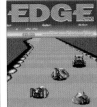 148. *F-Zero*

 149. *Super Mario Kart*

 150. *Wipeout*

 151. *Pole Position*

 152. *OutRun*

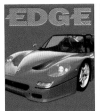 153. *OutRun 2006: Coast 2 Coast*

 154. *Super Sprint*

 155. *Galaxian*

 156. *Gradius*

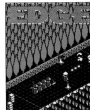 157. *Highway Encounter*

 158. *Jetpac*

 159. *Wing Commander*

 160. *Xevious*

 161. *Space Invaders*

 162. *Missile Command*

 163. *Rez*

 164. *Robotron*

 165. *R-Type*

 166. *Space Harrier*

 167. *Star Wars*

 168. *Starfox*

 169. *Team Fortress 2*

 170. *Uridium*

 171. *1942*

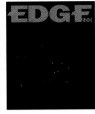 172. *Battlezone*

 173. *Axelay*

 174. *Asteroids*

 175. *Defender*

 176. *Einhänder*

 177. *Ikaruga*

 178. *Geometry Wars Retro Evolved 2*

 179. *Parodius*

 180. *Bangaio Spirits*

 181. *Locke Cole* *Final Fantasy VI*

 182. *Edgar Roni Figaro* *Final Fantasy VI*

 183. *Celes Chere* *Final Fantasy VI*

 184. *Kefka Palazzo* *Final Fantasy VI*

 185. *Ashelia 'Ashe' B'nargin Dalmasca – Final Fantasy XII*

 186. *Halo*

 187. *Halo 2*

 188. *Halo 3*

 189. *Tommy Vercetti* *GTA Vice City*

 190. *The Truth* *GTA San Andreas*

 191. *Vladimir Glebov* *Grand Theft Auto IV*

 192. *Resident Evil*

 193. *Resident Evil 2*

 194. *Resident Evil 4*

 195. *Resident Evil 5*

 196. *Link* *Zelda: Ocarina Of Time*

 197. *Ganondorf* *Zelda: Ocarina Of Time*

 198. *Stalfos* *Zelda: Ocarina Of Time*

 199. *Zelda: Ocarina Of Time*

 200. *LittleBigPlanet*

HARDWARE

Are you HD ready?

Four years into the HD era, how well do gamers know their tech?

Despite general consensus that gamma controls should be kept to the darkest regions of the frontend, its priority in *Killzone 2 is* perhaps essential. The average player may not understand the science behind it, but the results of poor screen calibration can mar anyone's game

L ess than half a year before J Allard took the stage at GDC 2005, sharing with an audience of 3,000 his vision of 'the HD era', The Hollywood Reporter tried to predict, in anticipation of the 2006 FIFA World Cup, how many TVs would be presenting it in high definition. It hit a snag: sales of HD equipment in Europe were so nominal that no figures existed. The best estimate of one market researcher: "It's certainly less than one per cent". No wonder Allard's speech was so conspicuously inclusive, taking into account everything from ubiquitous 5.1 audio to 'polymorphic' IP and connected communities.

In his defence, few of those sweeping statements remain unfulfilled. Early this year, broadcaster Sky estimated that seven million UK households now have an HD television set, forecasted to reach 14 million in 2010. According to a YouGov survey in January, 96 per cent of people are aware of HDTV, while 74 per cent are keen to watch their favourite programmes on it. How many are gamers? Not, you'd hope, the 40 per cent who still believe that to watch HD programming, all you need is the right symbol on the box.

You may laugh, but ask yourself this: how many of us, gamer or otherwise, know HD like we knew CRT? In a field known for its imperceptible details, do we actually know yet which is better out of 720p and 1080p? Do the TVs bought last year deliver on the promise, regardless of factors like viewing angle or refresh rate? Are our settings optimal for the darkest FPS, or just the SD broadcasts that still dominate the airwaves? To put it another way, is the image seen on a developer's monitor, described in glowing terms by a review, the same when it appears in your living room? Or even that seen by a reviewer? Four years on, are any of us really 'HD ready'?

For a developer, explains Codemasters producer **Clive Moody**, finding out is a vital but inexact science. "We can't give you figures, but we do a lot of home tests to make sure we look great on all types," he says. "That basically means travelling around Warwickshire looking at different TVs. To sum it up in one line, we make it less of an issue just by hard work and making sure we've covered all the bases." What stats there are, says **Daniel Oxford**, principal artist on games like *Colin McRae: Dirt* and *Race Driver: Grid*, are eye-opening. "We did a quick straw poll this morning and a surprising amount of us still only have SD TVs. There are an awful lot still out there."

Even in the US, where an HD broadcast of the Super Bowl fatefully caught Allard's eye, many consumers are still stuck not just at the HD hurdle, but at the one that came before it: widescreen. **Tim Willits**, co-owner and creative director of id Software, jokes: "It's because Americans aren't smart enough to realise that the black bars at the top and bottom are not actually making the picture smaller. Everything's got to be *big* over there because it's the US; people have big living rooms and big houses, so they want to those huge square television sets to watch their football on." But Wal-Mart, he notes, one of America's largest retailers, no longer sells 'square tubes' in any of its stores. "That was a major change."

Was gaming too quick to embrace HD? On the contrary, he declares: "It didn't come soon enough. PCs have always run in 1280x1024 and such, so for us the transition was smoother. But when we did work with partner developers on older consoles such as Sega Saturn, it was always a struggle. If we could get everyone on LCD or plasma it'd make designing the interfaces, HUDs and refresh rates so much easier. One of the great things about *Rage* [id's upcoming game of Mad Max-inspired running, gunning and vehicular mayhem] is the unified code base, with the same assets going on all platforms."

Nathan Fisher, art director at Codemasters, agrees: "We were aware of it coming thanks to the console vendors and getting early development kits. I don't know whether we could have squeezed any more out of SD, but we always want to push things visually and HD was a great way to do it." And Codemasters, Moody reminds us, is a PC developer as well. "We're looking at stuff on PC that's way ahead of anything else out there, stuff that's not in the marketplace. I guess that'll come down to the next generation of consoles."

For studios like these, though, HD readiness can be a double-edged sword. The further you push into the realms of 720p and beyond, the more you have to consider the HD unready – the millions still out there, many of them current-gen gamers looking to play *Rage* or *Dirt 2*, who plan to do so in 4:3. Woe betide anyone who forgets *Dead Rising's* brush with the SD militia. Having failed to see the pitfalls of using a microscopic font for its

LIFE

PP   Lv: 10

Steven

100%

MEATS

X : Attack   RT + X : Throw   LB or RB : Change Item   ◯ : Discard Item   ● : Unequip Item

Codemasters producer Clive Moody (left) and art director Nathan Fisher concede that, while HDTV is fine right now, it will be replaced by better tech – but not for a while yet

OUT THERE

MEGGY DRIVE

Ladies and gentlemen, the Meggy Jr RGB: an 8x8 LED display with big chunky buttons that's smaller than a PSP and looks absolutely adorable. Don't all rush, though, because you need to be willing to do some self-assembly (including soldering) and wait for the games – or program them yourself. It uses the open source Arduino development environment and programming language, and there's a specific Meggy Jr RGB library you can download in advance to get started. The basic kit clocks in at $75 (£52), comes with a preinstalled shooter, and there's a video of a prototype *Rogue*-like doing the rounds, with doubtless many more productions to follow.

● www.evilmadscience.com/tinykitlist/100-meggyjr

first HD title, Capcom filled its game with so much text that players cried out for a patch, but none came. In hindsight, director **Yoshinori Kawano**'s response to one interviewer could have been better pitched. "People should definitely have an HDTV," he said, "before buying a 360."

Codemasters is a bit more careful, says Moody. "Fonts is the obvious one, so we take extra care in making everything readable – and in all languages as well. Because when you're localising to Japanese the font is quite complicated. But we've never had to patch to make stuff like that work."

"We have certain templates and guidelines for font sizes at certain resolutions," adds Fisher, "so we'll always keep to what we know will work." And 4:3? "We have a screen area that caters to both, so we have an area around the screen for vital information, and even the widescreen stuff fits into that 4:3 bounding area."

"That's the biggest challenge – staying within the safe zone," says Willits. "We actually want to use more of the real estate but we can't because there are still those people using CRT sets." It sounds frustrating. "I wouldn't say that, but there are challenges. If we knew the consumer had one type of TV and one aspect ratio, it'd make our lives much easier. At least with the consoles we just have the one system to deal with; it's not as bad as the old days when we had infinite types of PCs. So HD's easier than we've had in the past."

It falls to everyone at id, he continues, to

make sure SD gamers don't miss out. Even John Carmack, who you might think would isolate himself from such peripheral technologies, naturally considers them. Then again, says Willits, "he thinks of everything." Eric Wills, the company's UI designer, sits behind two TVs at his desk, a square CRT and a widescreen. And if someone else needs to see things through square eyes, strips of cardboard are always on hand. "So it's the artist and John who make sure that when the pixels go from square to long, it all kinda jives; and it's the designer's job too," says Willits. "Even where the weapon goes makes a difference. Then it goes to Microsoft, or EA for *Rage*, and their testing group makes sure we don't screw up."

Willits doesn't skip a beat when confirming that *Rage* runs at 720p, the same thing true of *Dirt* and *Grid*. It begs the question: are we missing something here? Didn't Phil Harrison advise that claims of an HD era were, prior to the arrival of PS3 and 1080p, 'premature'? Why, then, are we here, somewhere between *Wipeout HD* and *Gran Turismo 5*, wondering where 'True HD' has gone?

Programmer Sean Davies at Sheffield studio Sumo Digital became one of the first coders to achieve actual 1080p on Xbox 360 with *Virtua Tennis 3*. Not the first, he admits – that would be *NBA Street Homecourt*, which beat Sumo by a week. But make no mistake, we're talking *actual* 1080p, not the dynamic framebuffer shenanigans of *Wipeout* or the upscaling trickery that goes on elsewhere. "I can't speak for the PS3 market, where Sony made it a requirement for some submissions," he says, "but there are very few Xbox 360 games out there that actually render to a 1080p buffer. Off the top of my head, *Virtua* and *NBA* are the only ones I can name, and *NBA* dropped to 30fps to support the fillrate. There is actually a surprising amount that don't even render to a 720p buffer."

It takes a lot of balancing, he continues, for a game to run smoothly at 1080p on current console hardware, and it changes decisions about optimisation dramatically. "Things which would otherwise make much more sense to do on the

Banjo-Kazooie: Nuts & Bolts is the latest game to suffer illegible text in SD. Rare's initial response was that it'd be too expensive to fix, but a backlash prompted a patch to increase the font size

Willits believes that the visual style of games like *FEAR 2* (right) represent a niche, or fad, that asks for trouble when it comes to players' TVs. Perhaps it's early shadow tech that begged for such extreme lighting. *Rage* (above) shows off rather more subtle ambient lighting

graphics hardware – soft skinning, for instance – suddenly need moving to the CPU because of the sheer work the GPU has to do. It's having to output two million pixels a frame; by comparison, 720p is just under a million. Even if it takes three to four times as long on the CPU, the time saved elsewhere is necessary to meet your frame goals." A lot of current-gen effects, he adds, such as bloom and depth of field, become "cripplingly expensive" when the framebuffer is so big.

Perhaps more importantly, is 1080p even noticeable? Not really, he says. "In fact, since 1080p essentially precludes proper antialiasing, I always think that good-looking four-times-antialiased 720p looks better, especially on this hardware where other compromises need to be made." Are publishers aware of this? "We had some pressure to do it for *Virtua Tennis 3*," he says, "just because it was a marketing bullet-point on the PS3 version and feature parity was important. But my general impression is that it's not a feature most publishers demand. Considering the market penetration of 1080p TVs is still pretty low, it's probably a wasted effort."

This all assumes, of course, that the sumptuous HD experience that goes into your console is coming out properly in the first place. Thanks in part to the hurriedness of the HD era and its multifarious, rapidly evolving displays, this is arguably more uncertain than during the dark ages of 50Hz PAL. If it's not the blacks being too grey,

Which version of *Doom 3* did you play? The cutting-edge, artfully gloomy one, or the grey washout with the muddy textures? Few games have been quite so susceptible to such fine calibrations

it's the greys being too black – hazards which prompted two of last issue's biggest games, *Killzone 2* and *Fear 2*, to open with screens devoted to that dreariest of settings, the gamma slider. It's a problem Willits has known only too well since the earliest forms of 'HD'.

"One of the things we learned is that you can't really make a game too dark. Yes, you can put gamma sliders in for people to adjust, but you should really make it look as good as possible on most systems. You don't need to make gamma the very first thing that people see; the average consumer doesn't even understand it, they just put the game in and play. It was one of the biggest frustrations working on the Xbox version of *Doom 3*; we'd put it on different TV sets and it'd

"At least with consoles we just have the one system to deal with; it's not as bad as the old days when we had infinite types of PCs"

just look like crap. All you had was 480p, but most TV sets just didn't do it. And the way people had their TVs set up was troubling. Even when people buy 'high-end' sets today, the factory defaults are horrible. Most manufacturers put them on high vibrant settings to get them looking all right in a retail environment, then you get them home and the picture's oversaturated."

Things have improved considerably, though, says Moody, before conceding that while technology marches on, the majority of gamers won't change so easily – nor should they be expected to. "Ultimately, you have to work to something," he says, "which is why all of our lighting's tested under factory settings. And right now, something better is always coming along." Not, we shudder, *another* HD era? "You've got to have a fair old lifecycle for that to come in," says Fisher. "There's a huge amount of investment needed just to support a given broadcast standard. So the manufacturers will be out there trying to push the next big thing, but what we've got now won't be going away for some time."

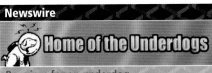

Lore enforcement

How Blizzard's win against a cheat bot could challenge user rights

F or two years, Blizzard Entertainment – maker of the enormously popular *World Of WarCraft* – has fought a legal battle with MDY Industries, maker of a program that lets people advance their characters without actually playing the game. After granting a summary judgment against MDY last July, on January 28 a judge ruled that MDY is guilty of copyright infringement. The decision troubles some critics who see a dangerous precedent that could harm user rights and give unintended powers to software licences.

The ruling is the latest blow to MDY Industries and its owner, **Michael Donnelly**. Donnelly is the inventor of Glider, a piece of software commonly called a bot – a simple artificial intelligence that will play a character in place of a live human being. Glider works by studying the game's data from memory, and then plugging in keystrokes to control the player's character.

While simple bots are jerky, repetitive and easily caught, advanced ones like Glider smoothly navigate rough terrain; kill, loot and even skin their prey; perform quests; and seek out and sell to vendors. A player can sleep or go to work while Glider earns experience and money, grinding through the hundreds of hours it typically takes to reach the game's highest level.

Donnelly, a 37-year-old programmer who lives in Phoenix, Arizona, originally coded Glider for his own use. He was playing *WOW* with a level-45 character, while his friends in-game had moved on to level 60. Looking for a quick and easy way to catch up, Donnelly considered buying a bot online,

Michael Donnelly claimed his Glider bot was meant to overcome design flaws in *WOW*. Sadly for him, Blizzard and the US Federal Court disagreed

but, "They all looked like spyware, and I was too scared to install any of them on my machine."

Instead, he wrote his own. It worked so well that he decided to sell it, thinking he might move one or two copies a day. Today, Donnelly's company has two other employees and at least 130,000 paying customers, and continues to sell Glider for $25 (£17) a copy.

Some argue that bots are perfectly legitimate because they don't enhance a player's skill; they just save hours of time. "I never considered it cheating, as long as it's passive and just injects keystrokes," says Donnelly. "It does the same things you can get your nephew to do."

Many *WOW* players disagree and, more importantly, so did Blizzard. On October 25, 2006, three representatives of Blizzard and its parent, Vivendi Games, came to his house and stated they would file a complaint the next day unless Donnelly agreed to stop selling Glider and surrender his profits. Donnelly contacted a lawyer, and this led to the case MDY Industries vs Blizzard.

Blizzard's chief operating officer, **Paul Sams**, is vehement about catching and stopping bots. "We simply have to protect the integrity of the game experience, so as to ensure the gameplay is exactly as it was intended," he says. "We absolutely, positively protect the user experience and the game experience."

In a multiplayer community such as *WOW*, bots can ruin the experience of other players. Bot-run characters can hog crucial locations in the game or hover to grab rare goods. The players who use them can ruin the in-game economy by causing inflation or dumping valuables in auction halls.

Sams points to the decline of Blizzard's earlier hit, *Diablo II*, as a case study in how rampant cheating can bring a thriving game to its knees.

Blizzard COO Paul Sams. The Warden software scans the RAM of the user's computer and compares programs found there with a database of known cheats

Continue

The next 200
"Edge said *what* in 2009?" We can't wait

Playing the 100
Well, clearly someone has to do this stuff

Street Fighter IV
If only we could focus-cancel sleep and work

Quit

Blue meanie
Seth is annoying enough without his belly vortex

Sega retro unlockables
Shouldn't the hard work be paying for it, not playing?

T-Dog
Who's going to put chilli in our tea now he's gone?

"We spent inordinate amounts of money, time and energy trying to deal with people that were cheating and hacking. And ultimately it destroyed the in-game economy. I think [*Diablo II*] would still have legs had it not been absolutely annihilated by folks that are doing the same types of things that we're talking about here."

Blizzard dedicates a team of employees to chasing and banning bot-users, gold-sellers, power-levellers and other violators of the game's licence. *World Of WarCraft* also includes a piece of software called Warden that tries to detect and block illicit programs. These efforts are expensive – and every time a bot is blocked, its coder can just look for a new way to sneak through the door. Glider, for example, was first blocked by Warden as early as 2005; since then, it has evolved to the point where it is practically undetectable.

However, even some of the gamers who

> **Unlike a physical product that can be used any way the buyer wishes, *World Of WarCraft* can only be played the way Blizzard demands – under penalty of copyright infringement**

support Blizzard's position have criticised its legal strategy. The decision against MDY, reached by Judge David G Campbell in a federal court in Arizona, rests on a non-intuitive use of the Digital Millennium Copyright Act, a 1998 US law that expands copyright protection. Among other things, it bans the circumvention of the locks and protections that companies apply to their media – for example, the copy protection attached to an iTunes download or a DVD. Blizzard's case was built on the principle that a user 'copies' its

software by merely loading it into their computer's memory. *WOW*'s EULA allows this under normal circumstances, but as it prohibits bots, it considers loading the game and running Glider as breaking those terms and therefore infringing Blizzard's copyright.

The worst-case implications reach beyond the gaming industry. Critics warn that the decision gives software producers much more power to write restrictions into their EULAs and terms of service, and then enforce them with the serious charge of copyright infringement. A company may choose to ban users from running a competitor's software with their own; for example, the maker of an operating system could dictate which software users run on it. And nothing protects users from being charged for breaking the licence in trivial ways: *WOW*'s EULA also prohibits users from choosing 'leetspeak' names like 'ROFLcopter'.

The Electronic Frontier Foundation has also criticised the ruling for reinforcing the idea that users don't actually own the software they bought. Under this reasoning, the user who runs a piece of software doesn't own the copy that sits in their computer's memory; instead, they have purchased a licence to use that software under the terms dictated to them by the producer. Unlike a physical product that can be used and abused any way the buyer wishes, *World Of WarCraft* can only be played the way Blizzard demands – under penalty of copyright infringement.

"While nobody appears to have a terrible amount of sympathy for Mr Donnelly, it's the decision itself people seem to have problems with," says **Gillian Cordall**, a partner with law firm Maclay Murray & Spens, which specialises in IP and technology.

"The question arises as to when a breach of the EULA or terms of use amounts to copyright infringement, and when it only gives rise to a claim for breach of contract."

As Cordall explains, "There's a battle royale between rights owners, users and third parties over control, access and liability. I see this as being another step in the battle going on at the moment over how much protection and control rights owners have and can exercise over their works."

Blizzard remains comfortable with the strategy. "We think that it was within our reasonable rights to seek a ruling on that particular item," says Sams. "I recognise that some folks writing about this feel like it's a slippery slope, but in this particular circumstance and based upon the facts of the case, we felt that it was the right decision."

MDY has appealed the decision and, at the time of going to press, its website is still trading. If the appeal fails, Glider will be finished and MDY will have to cough up US$6 million in damages. "I don't have $6 million. I don't have $1 million," says Donnelly. "It's going to wipe the company out, it's going to wipe me out."

But whatever happens to Glider, bots will still thrive – some open source, some for sale. Donnelly says a Chinese company has already started posting on his forums, telling his customers: 'Once Glider's gone, we'll still be here!'

Out damn spot

IO Interactive cleans up its act and swaps brutal gun crime for pocket-sized guerrilla tactics

Moving from hitmen to ninjas may not sound like the largest of leaps, but in the case of IO Interactive it marks a brave broadening from a gritty, gruesome past to a family-friendly future. The crime and grime of *Hitman* and *Kane & Lynch* couldn't be further from the bright, minimalist cartoon of *Mini Ninjas'* world – a place where, for all the flying shuriken and whirling kendo sticks, the player doesn't actually kill anyone. We talked to the game's director, **Jeremy Petreman**, about why IO decided to wash the blood from its hands.

> **"We have drawn on a lot of platform conventions and there are a lot of tributes to older games – definitely the old Nintendo games, even right back to the NES *Zelda*"**

This is quite a shift in tone for IO, isn't it?
I think when a studio is first starting out it's easy to get pigeonholed because people have a confidence in you to build a certain type of game. But as we've got larger and proven ourselves over time, we've always wanted to break out and do other things. It's a misconception that we're only into hardcore games here. We are all sorts of game fanatics – I think everyone who has worked on *Mini Ninjas* has a pretty broad spectrum of games that they're into, and I'm the same. But there are lots of other reasons – we're getting older, too.

Some of us have kids, and we want to be able to go home and tell our kids what we do without having to say, "Daddy's been blowing someone's head off with a sniper rifle."

Is *Mini Ninjas'* family-friendly direction a reaction to the negative press surrounding *Kane & Lynch*?
No, I don't think so – we were working on this before *Kane & Lynch* came out. We have a couple of guys who were involved in *Kane & Lynch* on our team, but for the most part we're separate teams working on separate projects in the studio. In the beginning it was just me and Henrik Hansen working out the concept. He's the art director now, but originally he was the only concept artist on the project, so he's had a lot of control of what's gone into the game. Back then, *Kane & Lynch* was finishing up and we were starting out, so we've always been fairly separate.

Is there a palpably different atmosphere on the *Mini Ninjas* team compared to elsewhere at IO headquarters?
It's certainly lighter – I guess when you're working on something you take on a bit of its mood. So when you're working on *Hitman* things get a little gloomy and dark and you can't help but get into it. *Mini Ninjas* is a much lighter project to work on for sure. It feels good to work on something like this. In a weird way we've been a really happy

START

Though *Mini Ninjas* isn't an explicit reaction to the violence of IO's previous games, the change of tone draws a line under the debacle surrounding Kane & Lynch, when Eidos was accused of pulling advertising following unfavourable reviews. "It was just bizarre for us," recalls Petreman. "We're not really connected to it – we work really hard on games and when controversy breaks out, it's just like, well, another world to us"

team. We started off small – we were only about ten people for quite a while, and we've only grown up to 28 now at the maximum. That's small for us. We go out for sushi together a lot.

Are these mostly IO old hands or have you needed to bring in new talent to pull off a platform-brawler?
Oh, I wouldn't call it a platform game. That's probably misleading. You really have a lot of freedom in your movement through the environment – so you can climb on any surface, hang from ledges and run on rooftops – but it's not really a platformer. We have drawn on a lot of platformer conventions and there are a lot of tributes to older games – definitely the old Nintendo games, even right back to the NES *Zelda*. I was playing *Shadow Of The Colossus* when we first started out, so a big thing for me is exploration – that's like a cornerstone of the game. And it's been challenging for sure, but we have a

lot of talent from a broad area. We've had a few new additions to the company and the team, but the rest of our team is made up of people from IO's previous games. One of my conditions when we were starting off was that if we were going to make a game with a small team then we'd put really experienced people in all the key positions. And we have people on the team who have worked at other companies so it's not like we're confined to the experience that IO has.

The art in *Mini Ninjas* has an elegant simplicity – how much of that is born from a need to be scalable between consoles?
It helps – but it wasn't the driving reason behind the art. It all stemmed from the fact that Henrik had these kickass designs from the beginning, and we tried a lot of ways of replicating his 2D art in 3D, and after months of prototyping we settled on a style that was minimalistic – but not for the sake of squeezing it on to lower-end consoles. We were just trying to capture the look we saw in his paintings. You know, it's like now that all of these consoles have got all this technology, with all the hi-res super-realistic graphics, to me the last frontier is style. It doesn't have to be photorealistic for you to have a good-looking game. You just have a brilliant art direction. The first goal is to push the hardware to the limit, and after that you're like, "Oh, man, everybody's doing that, what can we do?"

Prior to taking the reigns of *Mini Ninjas*, Petreman has been a stalwart on many of IO's projects, having been at the company for a little over eight years: "I worked on *Freedom Fighters* first, did a lot of the level designs, and I helped with some of the pre-production on *Kane & Lynch*. I've worked for most of the *Hitman* games in some capacity – level design, graphic work or voice-acting. I'm Canadian so I was an easy pick for some roles"

Virtua Tennis 2009
FORMAT: 360, PC, PS3 PUBLISHER: SEGA

The rally may have slowed, but *Top Spin* and *Virtua* keep on swinging, Sumo's latest adding a Davis Cup licence and a certain Scot riding high in the world rankings. Oh, and stumbling feet

Red Dead Redemption
FORMAT: 360, PS3 PUBLISHER: ROCKSTAR

If this is the same game as the 'Untitled Western' demo at E3 2005, Rockstar San Diego has had all the time in the world to make a worthy sequel. "Breathtaking beauty," says **Sam Houser**

Alien Vs Predator (working title)
FORMAT: 360, PS3 PUBLISHER: SEGA

From the visionary creators of *Shellshock 2* – not. Apparently in capable hands, Rebellion's return to one of the greatest shooters of its age is set for 2010. *Colonial Marines* slips, meanwhile

Brütal Legend
FORMAT: 360, PS3 PUBLISHER: EA

EA Partners scores another potential hit with Tim Schafer's latest, a thirdperson romp starring *Psychonauts* fan Jack Black. Inspired by Danzig, among others, it's a heavier metal than *Guitar Hero*

Fallout 3: The Pitt
FORMAT: 360, PC, PUBLISHER: BETHESDA

Just when you thought the outlook couldn't get any bleaker, here comes the age of steel. Factories galore await you in Pittsburgh, along with a raider settlement split between haves and have-nots

Battlefield: Bad Company 2
FORMAT: 360, PC, PS3 PUBLISHER: EA

A few months after the downloadable *1943*, a second salvo from the reinvigorated Frostbite engine. B Company's mission, as ever: drive anything, destroy everything, then go online and repeat

Battlestations: Pacific
FORMAT: 360, PC PUBLISHER: EIDOS

A new website opens for Eidos' action/strategy game, the tour giving you a choice of sides during missions including Pearl Harbour. This time, make sure Japan blows up the aircraft carriers

The Witcher: Rise Of The White Wolf
FORMAT: 360, PS3 PUBLISHER: ATARI

If CD Projekt tackles its console adaptation with the same heroic grit that transformed the PC version, Atari could have a champion for its autumn line-up. "Rebuilt pixel-by-pixel," says the studio

Need For Speed World Online
FORMAT: PC PUBLISHER: EA

While franchise title *Shift* flees the scene of *NFS: Undercover*, EA's busy Singapore studio takes the Play 4 Free model out for a spin. Expect the 'free' bit to be a Trebant with fluffy dice

---

□ INTERNET GAME OF THE MONTH
Chain Factor
www.chainfactor.com □

It's been around on the web for a while now, but the recent £3 appearance on iPhone of *Drop7* sent us back to its Flash (and free) forebear, *Chain Factor*. Don't let its unpromising lineage as part of an ARG that publicised the CBS crime show *Numb3rs* put you off. Area/Code's self-contained puzzler needs no special knowledge of ludic theory, plot points or higher maths, and its existence goes a long way toward justifying both over-involved viral marketing and slightly wonky CSI knockoffs.

A block-dropper at heart, which tasks you with matching the number on a ball with the number of balls in the column or row you're placing it in, once you realise *Chain Factor* isn't as dauntingly educational as it might seem it's hard to pull yourself away from the frenzied score-chaining, especially when it's delivered with dainty pastels and a wonderful soundtrack. If so inclined, fans of *Numb3rs* itself can immerse themselves in the wider hassle of hidden passwords and intertextual twists hovering around the game, all of which relate back to the TV series.

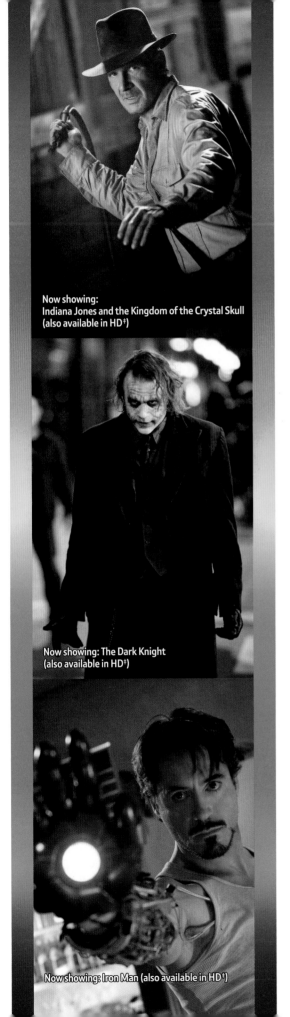

Now showing:
Indiana Jones and the Kingdom of the Crystal Skull
(also available in HD‡)

Now showing: The Dark Knight
(also available in HD‡)

Now showing: Iron Man (also available in HD‡)

With BT Vision's huge film library, just sit back and shout 'Action!'

BT Vision† is the digital TV service for BT Total Broadband customers, powered by Microsoft® Mediaroom.™ With over 500 great films available on demand it's like having a huge DVD library in your living room, so whatever you fancy watching the action won't start until you're ready. What's more, with increasing numbers of titles available in breathtaking HD you'll see everything as the director intended.

With no compulsory TV subscription and new releases from just £3.37, only pay for what you want to watch, not what you don't.

Call 0800 678 1944
bt.com/edge

Microsoft® Mediaroom™

DOLBY DIGITAL

BT
Bringing it all together

Industry
FOCUS

In association with Screen Digest

The difference between the haves and have-nots

Screen Digest analyst Piers Harding-Rolls looks at market and industry performance in 2008

During 2008, more money than ever before flowed through the tills and on to credit cards having been spent on videogames. The market for packaged games reached a colossal $30.5 billion (£20.7 billion) and is expected to represent the peak of this current cycle of sales. There's still more to come, of course, from the latest generation of home consoles, but the handheld cycle is expected to enter a transition period and game sales for PS2 are in rapid decline. This, combined with falling sale prices for console software, means that the value of the market in 2009 will be less than last year. The 2008 performance is way ahead of the previous peak

in 2004, when the competitive climate was completely different to the Nintendo-dominated landscape the industry is faced with today. The 2004 peak saw game sales of $19.2 billion (£15.4 billion) and therefore, peak to peak, the market has grown by 59 per cent, an impressive feat for a sector many feared had reached saturation with the installed base of the PS2. The handheld market, the rise of peripheral-based games and Nintendo's Wii strategy have changed the market potential of the games sector for good.

Nintendo software, including those on older handheld platforms, accounted for over 40 per cent of all software value sales in 2008, more than half of which came from Wii game sales. The DS, now in its fifth year, recorded over $5 billion of sales from games. Wii titles bundling peripherals such as *Wii Fit* (Balance Board) and *Mario Kart* (steering wheel) as well as thirdparty music titles (*Guitar Hero* and *Rock Band* titles with musical instrument-based peripherals) maintained average software prices during a period when numerous budget-packaged releases for the Wii threatened to drive ASPs downwards.

Nintendo, which rarely puts a foot wrong as far as its eager fans are concerned, saw strong sales of peripheral-based games

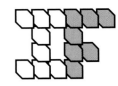

screen**digest**

www.screendigest.com

Microsoft's console split the year between so-called casual titles, such as *Lips* and *Guitar Hero*, and 'hardcore' examples like *Fable II* and *Gears Of War 2*. The flurry of big releases in the run-up to Christmas led to a strong finish to the year in terms of sales

Just as in 2007, the Xbox 360 started the year slowly, but the hardware price drop in September improved demand considerably; its situation was also assisted by weaker competition in the peak season as the PS3 was left out in the cold with a significant price premium over the competition. Xbox 360 finished the year strongly, driven by a number of big firstparty releases led by *Gears Of War 2* and *Fable II*. In addition, Microsoft endeavoured to appeal to more mainstream classes of gamer with *You're In The Movies*, *Scene It?* and the introduction of a new karaoke franchise, *Lips*.

The 2004 peak saw game sales of $19.2 billion and therefore, peak to peak, the market has since grown by 59 per cent, an impressive feat for a sector many feared had reached saturation

Sony platforms provided just under a third of total software sales in 2008. The PS3 had a few hits in 2008 but, with no price reduction on the hardware, became less desirable as the economic recession worsened and the price differential between its lowest-priced SKU compared with the Xbox 360 Arcade increased significantly. The PSP continues to display admirable longevity and is proving more resilient than some commentators expected at the start of the year. Indeed, in Japan it was the best-selling gaming device for most of the year on the back of just a few titles: *Monster Hunter Portable 2nd G* (the best-selling game in Japan in 2008) and *Final Fantasy: Dissidia*.

So has the record consumer spend been reflected in record profits for thirdparty publishers? In fact, quite a few publishers suffered pretty disappointing December quarters. In the Christmas quarter, EA reported heavy GAAP net losses of $641m as its major titles underperformed, and some game releases were delayed; THQ reported GAAP net losses of $192m; Atari's sales were down 23 per cent year-on-year as the company reported difficult trading conditions, while Capcom's net profits dived 95 per cent year-on-year. On the flip side, Activision Blizzard (taking into account charges associated with the merger earlier in the year) and Ubisoft both performed well.

These poor results were due to some internal mismanagement and a lack of releases on a case-by-case basis, and also due to the combined impact of two major external factors: heavy competition and the macro economic environment. The Christmas sales season for games represented one of the most competitive markets seen in recent times with 264 game SKUs released for current generation consoles alone. This high volume of releases meant that retailer shelf-space was at a premium and that some lesser SKUs were not even stocked.

Although all established franchises and well-reviewed titles were often stocked, the high volume of good quality titles available to consumers also resulted in some weaker than expected performances for key titles as consumers were forced to pick their one or two must-haves from the numerous titles available. The competitive climate was compounded by prevailing economic conditions. This saw action from both the consumer – some of whom were prompted to buy fewer games – and from the retailers – who managed their inventory levels very closely due to the squeeze on credit and the overall macro economic uncertainty. The competitive climate has forced a number of publishers into a strategic rethink, with more emphasis on fewer, established and predictable, high-quality titles and a retreat from high-risk new intellectual property. From a publisher perspective, 2008 was most definitely a year of the haves and the have-nots.

People in glass houses, throwing stones
Brick Bardo takes a look at stereotyping outside and inside gaming

Back in a previous column I discussed – no, I laughed heartily about – *Command & Conquer: Red Alert 3* and its incredible depiction of Japan. Recently, something has cropped up that serves to perfectly illustrate the other side of that rather unpleasant coin, and is gaining in popularity: it's the Hetalia Axis Powers problem.

What is HAP? It's a webcomic, created by Himaruya Hidekazu, constructed around jokes about World War II, with characters representing the various nations. If the manga is 'about' anything, it's the cultural difference between nations, playing stereotypes and caricatures against each other.

Here's a brief idea of how a few nations are represented:

Italy – a bit of a crybaby who cheers up when eating some delicious pasta or when around beautiful girls.

Japan – a noble warrior, very quiet and serious, but so serious he's often mislead (if not ridiculed) by his entourage. Basically, what he thinks is normal is often anything but for others.

England – a former bad boy who is stubborn and quite sarcastic. He doesn't take his alcohol well and behaves very badly when drunk. He also loves tea and needlework.

Ever since the first Resident Evil 5 videos, people have been waiting for this game for one particular reason: racism. You feel there's a portion of commentators who actually want it to fall flat on its face

So why do you need the basics? Hetalia Axis Powers has been turned into an animation series, and the first story was recently broadcast and caused major (and violent) uproar in South Korea. Why? Because of the description of a Korean character in the manga: South Korea – a young man filled with energy and a 'going my own way' attitude, he tends to see everything as originating

from his own country and loves the internet.

There's more detail, but that's the broad outline. This image has been seen by parts of South Korean society as an insult, and the complaints recently reached the National Assembly. A petition has been initiated and insults have flooded in via mails and faxes to the companies involved in the animation series. As well as this,

Himaruya Hidekazu has been sent death threats. But this Korean character has never appeared in the anime, and isn't currently expected to.

Although Hetalia Axis Powers mocks the nations it includes, the reason for the Korean sensitivity is a historical one related to the setting – there are still tensions between Japan and South Korea that centre on WWII. Because

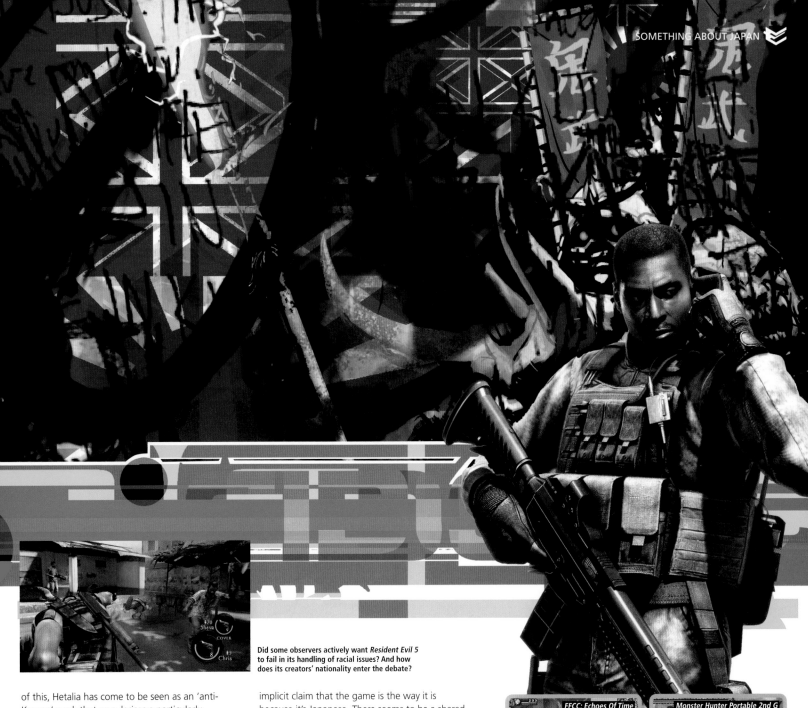

Did some observers actively want *Resident Evil 5* to fail in its handling of racial issues? And how does its creators' nationality enter the debate?

of this, Hetalia has come to be seen as an 'anti-Korean' work that popularises a particularly Japanese brand of racism.

I'm not sure which perspective is right, but I do think Hetalia has become the focal point for an argument that won't have much to do with the work itself. And this brings me to *Resident Evil 5*, which I think is about to suffer something of the same. Ever since the first videos, people have been waiting for this game for one particular reason: racism. You feel there's a portion of commentators who actually want it to fall on its face. But I want to take issue with a particular point about how this debate has been framed.

I've been re-reading a lot of posts on the topic, and many mention that the game is being developed in Japan, or by a Japanese company, or by Japanese developers. It's obviously felt that *Resident Evil 5*'s Japanese origin is relevant to the debate. Otherwise, why mention it?

My point of contention is, of course, the

implicit claim that the game is the way it is because it's Japanese. There seems to be a shared assumption that Japan is a nation that it's acceptable to stigmatise as racist: I could spell out the irony of well-meaning commentators doing this while criticising the stereotyping of Africa, but I guess it should be pretty clear by now.

I'm not trying to say that Japanese creators shouldn't be scrutinised and criticised for anything that does stem from their own set of cultural assumptions. But, equally, I feel a lot of comments on Japanese culture are impossibly generalised, based on second-hand knowledge. Certainly, the idea that we're a nation of inveterate racists looking to have a dig at Africa in a big international release is just a tiny bit offensive. If *Resi 5* does turn out to have a strain of racism, I hope it's looked at and criticised properly. But I also hope this happens to the game itself, and not to the country from which it hails.

Weekly Famitsu (Enterbrain)
Japanese sales: January 5–February 2

1. *Tales Of The World Radiant Mythology 2* (BNG, PSP): 210,297 (NE)
2. *Wii De Asobu Mario Tennis GC* (Nintendo, Wii): 105,608 (NE)
3. *Winning Eleven 2009* (Konami, PSP): 102,221
4. *Final Fantasy Crystal Chronicles: Echoes Of Time* (Square Enix, DS): 101,989 (NE)
5. *Winning Eleven 2009* (Konami, PS2): 101,857
6. *Dissidia Final Fantasy* (Square Enix, PSP): 83,106 (857,059)
7. *Monster Hunter Portable 2nd G PSP The Best* (Capcom, PSP): 81,939 (366,905)
8. *Rhythm Tengoku Gold* (Nintendo, DS): 79,488 (1,539,725)
9. *Devil Survivor* (Atlus, DS): 79,308
10. *Wagamama Fashion Girls Mode* (Nintendo, DS): 77,097 (723,064)

Everything you need for

0871 641 21 21 Calls cost 6p per minute from a BT landline, calls from other operators and mobiles may be higher.

a successful website

DOMAINS

Reserve your unique web address now. 1&1 offers simple and efficient domain name registration at great prices – plus loads of FREE features.

.biz domains now £3.99* per year!

Now 50% off

WEB HOSTING

.uk domains included!

Design your professional looking website. 1&1 Hosting Packages are ideal for creating an attractive internet presence without the need of specialist skills.

Business Packages now from only £3.99* per month!

Now 50% off

SERVERS

Our new range of feature packed AMD Opteron™ servers give you ultimate processing performance and unparalleled reliability with cutting-edge, energy-efficient technology. 100% of the energy consumed in 1&1 data centres is renewable energy.

Dedicated Servers now from £49.99* per month and VPS Servers from only £11.99* per month!

Now 50% off

E-COMMERCE

1&1 eShops are eCommerce simplified. Use setup wizards to build your shop, include the payment option to suit your needs and start selling your products online.

eShops now from only £4.99* per month!

Now 50% off

Limited time offer: Get 50% or more off for the first 6 months (first 12 months for .biz domains) when you sign up for a 1 year package! Visit www.1and1.co.uk for details!

1&1

* Terms and conditions apply, please see website for further details. Special offer for a limited time only. Prices exclude VAT.

www.1and1.co.uk

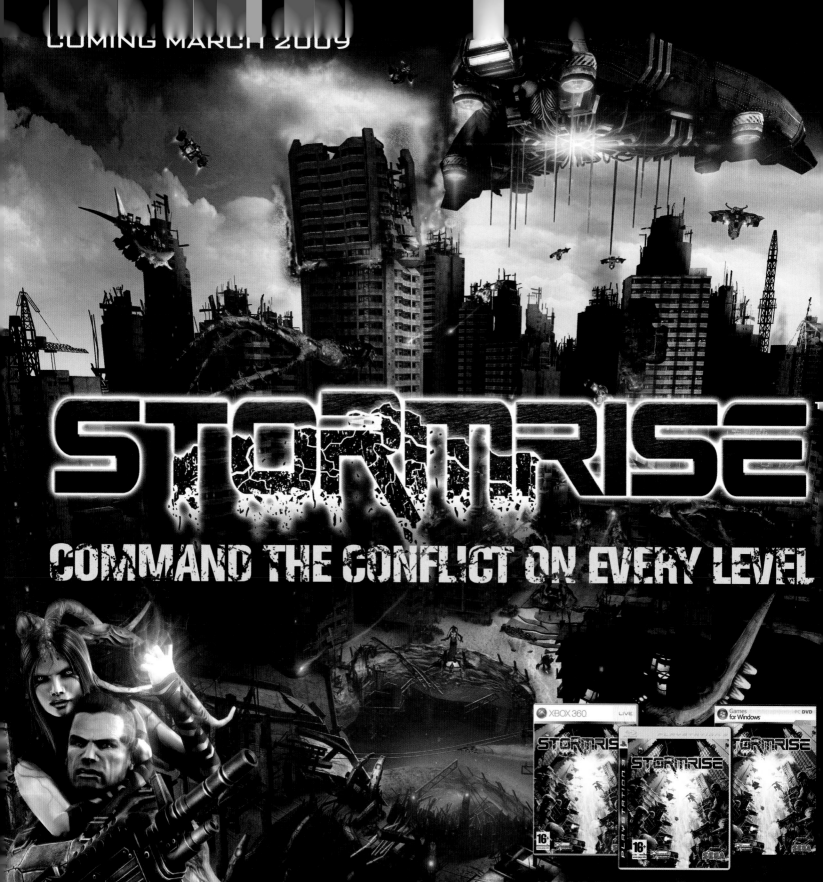

Hype

The future of electronic entertainment

Edge's most wanted

Dante's Inferno

Turning Italy's greatest poet into a halberd-wielding ninja is an odd move, but we are people of Catholic tastes. Or maybe we just enjoy a good train wreck.
360, PC, PS3, EA

Professor Layton And The Demon's Box

An ode to brilliant puzzlers:
He's Professor Hershel Layton,
He has an awesome name.
We don't like his assistant,
But can't wait to play his game.
DS, NINTENDO

Mass Effect 2

The teaser trailer implies a gloomy fate for our favourite ET-romancing Spectre – but we refuse to give up on Shepherd until we get to take Urdnot Wrex for a candlelit meal.
360, PC, EA

Grating expectations
The bigger the licence, the harder they fall

Terminator Salvation decides not to recreate the action of the film, instead following events that predate it – perhaps a cunning plan that limits just how far it can fail to match up to expectations generated by its big-screen sibling

Some time ago, we had a short and fruitless debate with one of the developers behind *Star Wars: The Force Unleashed*. We asked him, perhaps a little pointedly, about the presence of blue, fizzing special effects that emanate from the Apprentice every time he uses Force powers. He was nonplussed by our objection – this is a game, not a film, he explained; they could operate under different rules. George Lucas said so. Not that we are sticklers for canon, you understand, but surely one point of a Star Wars videogame is to transport players into the universe made familiar by the films? Eventually, we agreed to disagree, if only because the inside of our Boba Fett helmet had misted up.

Converting subject matter from film to videogame is not a lossless process. Nonetheless, the use of brands generates expectations regarding the content. Will those who automatically sweep the latest *Need For Speed* game off the shelf expect *Shift* to be a hardcore racing sim? And what gameplay do people assume could be wrung out of The Godfather series? Do players really anticipate single-handedly carving their way through a heavily defended drugs factory before subjecting the proprietor to lethal wing chung in a back room full of topless women?

Violence was always the punctuation of The Godfather, but not its verbs, and yet the bloodbath seen in EA Redwood Shores' game is only so troublesome because it is compromised, simultaneously attempting to fit into a version of the films' plot and yet deviating from Coppola's work in tone and action. You can't help but think that Rocksteady's approach to the Batman licence promises to be far more successful – choosing to build a game that is loyal to the feel of Batman rather than adhering to any one narrative.

Then again, maybe EA Redwood Shores' twisted experiments with *The Godfather* are simply in preparation for its grand act of cultural sabotage with *Dante's Inferno*. You can only stifle a horrified giggle at the brashness with which EA has reduced the much-worshiped literary behemoth into an unapologetic *God Of War* clone. Is this intentional irreverence or brain-dead name-dropping? It's hard to say, but one thing's for sure – we should be prepared to reset our expectations.

FORMAT: **360, PC, PS3**
PUBLISHER: **DISNEY INTERACTIVE STUDIOS**
DEVELOPER: **BLACK ROCK STUDIO**
ORIGIN: **UK**
RELEASE: **2010**

Split/Second

Why master a track when you can blow it to pieces instead?
Pure's developer comes down from the clouds with a bang

Take out a rival and the camera cuts back to show them getting buried under rubble. Making sure such moments don't jar you out of your racing line will require careful balancing by Black Rock Studio in the months ahead

S o, if videogames are art, what kind of art are they? If Black Rock Studio is to be believed, the industry can currently be found somewhere out past the Renaissance and headed straight for Baroque, powersliding away from a period of austere graphics fidelity on a collision course with wilful, exaggerated nuttiness. If that's not the kind of insight you expect from an arcade racer, it's probably because *Split/Second*'s not the kind of experience you expect from one, either.

Yet it's hardly the first time the Brighton-based studio has shifted gears so rapidly. *Pure*, the company's previous offering, had concept art that initially suggested a ploddingly refined *MotorStorm* clone – a trip around some rugged textures accompanied by the farmyard sexlessness of an ATV – and that turned out to be a million miles away from the over-ramped trick racer the game actually was. So when *Split/Second*'s pre-teaser teaser uses 30 seconds of fender-bending sparks and TV static to suggest something that looks a lot like a doomed trip into Criterion territory, it pays to remind yourself that the truth probably isn't that straightforward. And it isn't. Once again, initial impressions can be misleading: the trick is to ignore the sparks entirely – it's the static that seems likely to define this game.

Split/Second cheerfully co-opts reality television – this century's premise-justifier of choice – to explain away its deranged concept: this is a metropolis racer in which

the metropolis itself has been wired up to heavy explosives in the name of brutal last-man-standing entertainment. It's *Smash TV* meets *Burnout*, then, or in the words of franchise design director **Paul Glancey**: "*Split/Second*'s what might happen if NASCAR viewing figures started to drop, and the sport asked Jerry Bruckheimer for help in making it popular again."

But while it fills the screen with lavish swathes of HD anarchy, the game's

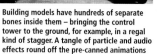

Building models have hundreds of separate bones inside them – bringing the control tower to the ground, for example, in a regal kind of stagger. A tangle of particle and audio effects round off the pre-canned animations

> The explosions keep getting bigger. Once the Power Bar is filled, players can trigger a more powerful tier of effects: huge bursts of damage that fundamentally alter the track

The game's frontend plays up the gameshow elements, with a range of different CCTV monitors revealing little windows of chaos. Even the shimmery metallic font used for the logo exudes just the right kind of cable TV naffness

mechanics remain anything but chaotic, and the clockwork heart of Black Rock's game ticks along with strategic potential. Taking a cue from Criterion's classic title, skilful driving in *Split/Second* – chaining near misses, drifts, drafts or jumps – slowly fills your Power Bar. But rather than rewarding you with a simple boost, Black Rock then plays its trump card: each topped-off segment of the meter allows you to trigger one of the level's dozens of bombs. Targets are automatically highlighted in blue, one potential victim at a time, as you zip around the track, and there's a strong tactical element to your choices: do you opt to simply blast through a wall to open up a shortcut, or instead hold on in order to blow up a crane and thus drop steel girders on your enemies in a bend's time?

The game's already-fearsome audio is being endlessly tweaked: engine sounds have been broken down to split-second loops, and the rumble of a bridge collapsing is subtly blended with the roar of a lion to give it that extra edge

Down in flames

The walls of most specialist racing developers' studios are covered with nothing but car art, and while it's still there at Black Rock, it's sitting alongside giant stills from Transformers, blurred demolition film screengrabs and numerous renderings of flaming wreckage. *Split/Second* will succeed or fail on the appeal of its explosions as much as its vehicles, then, and the team is after something it is calling 'cinematic realism'. That means obsessing over brave new ways of lighting dust clouds, bringing in deferred rendering to cope with fire effects, and triggering the game's giant explosions in discrete phases, to draw the eye through the wreckage.

Watching a playthrough on a course set inside an airport, this potentially complex idea quickly becomes effortlessly simple. Partly it's down to the presentation – despite the bloodthirsty themes, this is an endlessly upbeat game, filled with huge blue skies, bleached utopian architecture and rows of bobbing palm trees cheerily lining the tracks – but it's also a result of the ever-escalating pace of play, dictated by Hollywood, and playing out in a drumbeat of weighty explosions. Sweeping through the large environments allows you to flick through a surprising range of targeting choices as you drive, each lap turning as much on a handful of tricky decisions as it does on your cornering ability. And the complete chaos that ensues when an explosion goes off – the massive clouds of dust rolling across the road as the player blasts a luggage truck to pieces, or the flaming wreckage of a monorail trail falling from its perch – seems ripe with carefully weighted potential. The animations themselves may be canned, but their effects certainly aren't, and whether a rigged wall takes out one enemy or five is entirely down to nailing the timing.

And the explosions keep getting bigger. Once the Power Bar is entirely filled, players can trigger a more powerful tier of effects: huge bursts of damage that fundamentally alter the racetrack, mixing murderous instinct with breezy spectacle and blowing out the entire front of the airport terminal so that the path threads through the departure lounges,

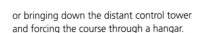

The team is promising visual effects that "chase" the player down the track. Clouds of dust hang in the air long after the initial explosion, and most rubble seems to be persistent

or bringing down the distant control tower and forcing the course through a hangar.

In among the fury erupting around the course, it's hard to judge the competence of the enemy AI, but much of the game's success will hang on the mixture of aggression and fairness with which rivals fling the environment against you. Another potential question hangs over replayability once a level's been beaten and the cinematic excess has lost its appeal. But *Pure* has already proved this studio's dedication to balancing, and with *Split/Second* still a year away from release, Black Rock is well on its way to creating an addictive tension between the track and the scenery that most other racers simply can't match.

Each track will be replayed at various stages of the game's campaign, but with more explosive trigger points. The serene airport is soon turned into a charred wreckage, with a flaming jumbo coming into land

FORMAT: **PC**
PUBLISHER: **K2 NETWORK**
DEVELOPER: **ACONY GAMES**
ORIGIN: **GERMANY**
RELEASE: **2009**

Parabellum

The initialism war intensifies as Acony Games
sets its sniper sights on an F2PMMOFPS

Players won't be able to tweak facial features, instead choosing from a range of about 12 presets –
all of whom look rather grumpy at the moment. Taunts will also be available in the finished game

Free2play is more than just a revenue structure shrouded in textspeak: it's development seen through the strangest of looking glasses, where financial rewards increase, rather than diminish, over time, games are launched rather than shipped, and titles are sold based on what they will become as much as what they are.

And it's a wild west, too – even by PC standards – with thousands of RPGs, kart-racers and deathmatches competing for the attention span of the most nebulous of global audiences. Stars have already emerged – it's almost impossible to discuss the free-to-play market without name-dropping Korea and, by extension, *Maple Story* and its publisher Nexon. But just as many titles fade without a trace, unwept, unhonoured and unsung. Because of the brutal failure rate,

The team promises 1.2 million combinations of character
assets at launch, with more available at the in-game shop

The sweet spot for team size in *Parabellum* is said to be five against five, with the various maps designed accordingly,
but the game will support up to 24 players in total. The game gives away its engine with its chunky Unreal 3 look

technology tends to be basic and budgets tend to be small. That's what makes *Parabellum*, the first title from Germany-based Acony Games, so surprising. Acony has chosen not to follow the traditional, pared-down model, instead bringing in the considerable bulk of Unreal Engine 3, a development team of over 30, and a towering ambition to become the first triple-A free-to-play title available.

While the long-term plan is to blend together the persistent worlds and levelling of an MMO with the headshots and close-combat maps of *Counter-Strike*, for the game's release the developer has wisely focused on getting the core shooting mechanics nailed down. When *Parabellum* launches later this year on K2 Network's elegant Gamers First portal – a site that brings together numerous free-to-play titles

including Nexon's own quite basic, yet entertaining FPS, *War Rock* – it will have 12 maps, 12 weapons (ranging from sniper rifles and SMGs to shotguns and pistols) and a handful of team-based multiplayer modes to play through.

Parabellum's campaign offers a taste of what's to come. The game's story revolves around a plot to trigger a nuclear warhead in New York City and, with one team trying to find and disarm the bomb while the others try to stop them, the game takes place across a series of interconnected deathmatch maps that can be linked together to create non-linear campaigns. It's a tantalising prospect, bringing a touch of strategy and narrative purpose to what is essentially a convoluted take on capture the flag, but it would all be for nothing if the simple business of shooting someone in the head fails to convince.

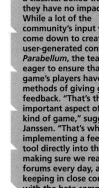

Acony has split its studio into two internal groups – a live team that keeps the game running, fighting balancing issues and hacking, plus a little short-term planning, and a core team that works on expansions and features. Visual changes to characters and equipment are purely cosmetic – you can have Hello Kitty stencilled on your gun, but it won't make it more powerful

Happily, that doesn't seem to be a problem: playing a handful of skirmishes on a claustrophobic residential map reveals a game that's confident, uncomplicated and moreish. Respawns are quick, weapons have a strong sense of personality, and the map's initially confusing mass of alleyways and parking garages soon reveals a clever internal framework of unexpectedly good sight-lines and secret ledges that mix tactical strength

clans can interact and, most intriguingly, user-generated maps and missions.

That's the plan, anyway. *Parabellum* doesn't look like it's been cheap to make, and Acony's pinning its revenue hopes on the playerbase's willingness to shell out for new costumes and soft-advantage items like levelling boosts (tailored for clan members who can't put in as much time as everyone else, but don't want to be left behind), rather

and character models, and only the slight flatness of the environmental textures revealing any hint of compromise. With a release planned for the first half of 2009, Acony has the technology in place and a fully fledged vision to deliver; all that remains to be seen is if there's a worldwide audience willing to repay the team's generosity with patience and a desire to buy a lot of downloadable clown costumes.

Care in the community

"It's not a product, it's a service," says Acony's product manager **Lars Janssen**. "We want to look at it as a platform where the user can change the basis of the game, and not a classical boxed title where they have no impact." While a lot of the community's input will come down to creating user-generated contact for *Parabellum*, the team is also eager to ensure that the game's players have lots of methods of giving general feedback. "That's the most important aspect of this kind of game," suggests Janssen. "That's why we're implementing a feedback tool directly into the beta, making sure we read the forums every day, and keeping in close contact with the beta community after the release. Instead of 'fire and forget', this is 'launch and learn'."

> The team is currently working on chipping away at the download size – Acony is adamant that one gigabyte is the maximum players can be expected to put up with

with weakness. The environments are surprisingly detailed and pretty for a free-to-play title, with pigeons taking off from rooftops, convincing draw distances and some truly excellent character animation – a mix of in-house key-framing and outsourced motion capture.

The MMO elements are currently restricted to fairly extensive character customisation (alongside a range of fatigues and balaclavas, there's already a fine line in Viking helmets ready to equip, and weapons can be retextured alongside clothes) and persistent levelling, but it will eventually expand to encompass what appears to be a Risk-like over-world view revealing all available campaigns, large social areas where

than risk unbalancing the game by allowing for the sale of more powerful weapons. Aside from virtual-asset purchase, Acony's also working on integrated billboard adverts, which should make sense in the urban maps revealed so far, but may prove harder to explain away as the game eventually moves beyond the confines of New York City and out into the rest of the world.

The team is currently working on chipping away at the download size – Acony is absolutely adamant that one gigabyte is the maximum that players can be expected to put up with for a free online game – and it's surprising how good *Parabellum* looks running on a heavily pared-down Unreal Engine 3, with normal-mapped weapons

Parabellum is being developed with a five-year content plan. After that? "Doing a sequel means you have to build a new community," says Janssen. "Our approach is: why lose the community you have? Sequels in MMOs are like big expansions if you do them well. Is *Wrath Of The Lich King* a sequel or an expansion? It's hard to say"

Mini Ninjas

IO Interactive puts the 'cute' in 'cut everybody's heads off'

The samurai enemies you face in the game were originally animals, corrupted and enslaved by the evil warlord's magic. As Hiro beats the enemy hordes in combat, they are returned to their animal form and not a drop of blood has to be spilled

Should redemption be too strong a word, then the colourful cartoon adventure of *Mini Ninjas* certainly offers IO Interactive something like catharsis. After the macabre pleasures of four *Hitman* games, IO took a nasty tumble with *Kane & Lynch: Dead Men*. Bickering, perma-swearing protagonists, a vicious-because-we-can plot and taboo-baiting scenes of torture did little to endear; the buggy implementation only further soured what was already an unpalatable prospect. Now, IO has put its bloody past to one side and, in *Mini Ninjas*, is making a game as sweet and innocent as preceding titles were mean and mature.

Taking on the role of tiny proto-ninja Hiro, the player is dispatched to rescue the world from the shadowy tyranny of an evil warlord, who has magically transformed the local animal life into an army of samurai.

"It's very much a journey game," says **Jeremy Petreman**, the game's director.

"You're setting off at the beginning of the game on this epic, Lord of the Rings-y adventure. It's linear in the sense that you're travelling across the land to defeat this evil samurai warlord – the gameplay changes between wandering the wilderness to coming into these big castles – but along the way, I want people to step off the path. Exploration is a big part of the game. If you explore off the path in the bamboo forest, you might come into a little clearing, find an ancient shrine, figure out how to unlock it and learn a magic ability."

In some ways, *Mini Ninjas'* clean-cut caricature, with its brash, flat colours, suggests a simplicity to the action that is perhaps misleading. The game's aesthetic

may strike all the right notes to appeal to a young audience, but dig a little further and there is a wealth of systems that offer players optional access to a much deeper experience. An RPG levelling process accompanies a rich possibility space that echoes *Hitman's* sandbox assassinations.

"When we started out, we wanted to make a game that was attractive and fun for eight- to 14-year-olds, but to have several layers of complexity to satisfy older players," says Petreman. "On the surface, it's really accessible. You aren't stressed out all of the time – there are points of real intensity followed by more relaxed exploratory moments. But there are other layers to the game, too, such as the magic system or the

> "You could attack a bridge held by enemies with a meteor storm, or hack and slash your way through, or possess an animal to scare them all away, or simply sneak past"

ability to enter the spirit world and possess any animal you see."

Entering said spirit world sees Hiro become a translucent spectre and, upon leaping into the body of an animal, is granted a different view on the world, coloured smoke revealing the location of herbs that can be combined into potions.

"Each animal has their own thing they can do," says Petreman. "All of them can sniff out ingredients. And some of them, such as the bear, can attack enemies or scare them away with a roar."

In addition to controlling animals, the game extends the player's repertoire of abilities through extra playable characters, who are unlocked as the game progresses.

As well as forming a makeshift shield, Hiro's hat can be deployed in other context-sensitive circumstances. In what will surely be one of the leading contenders for 2009's **Edge** award for Wettest Hat In A Game, it can even be used as a makeshift boat

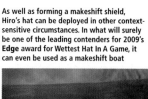

Although the level design offers a degree of non-linearity, a quick spot of meditation will set players on the right path should they get lost, bringing up a large arrow to point the way as well as sucking in all the surrounding XP, left to litter the ground following combat

Petreman counts the *Zelda* series as a chief inspiration for *Mini Ninjas* – although clearly that is a more full-fledged RPG experience – as well as less obvious touchstones like *System Shock* and *Outcast*, chosen less for their aesthetic qualities as for the way they involve the player in a world that invites and rewards exploration

Freeform fighters

Hiro follows in the footsteps of his less successful superiors, each of whom has been captured. Upon saving them, the player can switch to them in a puff of ninja smoke and gain access to their unique talents. From the outset, the player can flip between Hiro and Futo, a lumbering lunk with an oversized hammer who is capable of sending enemies tumbling like skittles as he rolls towards them. Later they are joined by Suzumi who, somewhat charmingly, can play the flute to temporarily hypnotise surrounding foes.

"It'll seem like a simple game on the surface, but as you get into it you'll realise how big the toolbox is," says Petreman. "In any given situation you might be able to attack a bridge held by enemies by conjuring a meteor storm on top of them, or hack and slash your way through it, or possess an animal to scare them all away, or simply sneak past. Obviously we're a company

infatuated by stealth, and there's a fairly detailed stealth system built into the game. You're not forced to use it but it's there. So should you come up to an enemy camp in the wilderness, you can sneak up through the grass and systematically take out all the enemies without alerting the other guards. It's an integral part of the ninja fantasy."

The nitty-gritty of combat itself remains unproven, but although the game clearly pitches for accessible rather than *Gaiden*-level gruel, there are hints at a level of tactical depth. Enemies possessing ranged weapons are best evaded by crafty means of cover, or their arrows blocked with the context-sensitive deployment of your handy conical straw hat as a shield. A high-powered special attack sees you leap into the air and, as time slows down, whisk a reticule over multiple opponents, selecting them for a dose of lightning-fast punishment.

Though there's potential for *Mini Ninjas*' combat to elevate itself from button-mashing, in some other respects the game doesn't attempt to stray from convention. There are heaps of collectibles of questionable value and we experience a disheartening moment of déjà vu when Hiro finds himself in a QTE-based boss-battle – you'll remember it from several other games: it's the one where the oversized brute somehow gets his weapon lodged in some scenery and you run up his arm.

Nonetheless, *Mini Ninjas* claims to put a good deal of choice at your disposal – multiple paths, multiple protagonists, magic, animal powers, stealth. Their combination could empower the player, making the game only as simplistic as you allow it to be. *Mini Ninjas*' protagonists may be only knee-high to the average game hero, but IO's ambition here is far from diminutive.

Non-linearity has been a staple of many of IO's games, and, just as *Hitman* offered multiple routes to a kill, *Mini Ninjas* gives the player a degree of power over the path they take through the world. Castle walls become opportunities to exploit Hiro's fine acrobatic skills rather than obstacles, while canal systems open up keeps to amphibious assaults. "Maybe you're travelling through a forest," says Petreman. "The road bends away to the left but you can see a river going off to the right – you might be able to navigate that river and go way off in the other direction, loop round some rapids and find yourself coming back to a common point later in the game."

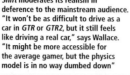

Shift moderates its realism in deference to the mainstream audience. "It won't be as difficult to drive as a car in *GTR* or *GTR2*, but it still feels like driving a real car," says Wallace. "It might be more accessible for the average gamer, but the physics model is in no way dumbed down"

It's unlikely that we've seen the last of the arcade racing *Need For Speed – Shift* certainly isn't a reaction to *Undercover*'s poor critical reception, having started development the better part of a year before its release. But can the *Need For Speed* brand really cope with such disparate products?

FORMAT: **360, PC, PS3**
PUBLISHER: **EA**
DEVELOPER: **SLIGHTLY MAD STUDIOS**
ORIGIN: **UK**
RELEASE: **AUTUMN**

Need For Speed: Shift

EA changes gears from arcade to sim,
but can it leave its past in the dirt?

No cops, no open world, no bling-studded fluorescent green pimpmobiles – EA's arcade racing licence has done something of a U-turn. By placing British-based *GTR* creator Slightly Mad behind the wheel, EA is hoping to turn the former steroidal street-racing cargasm into something like a respectable, but massmarket, driving sim. It's even got the adrenalising one-word subtitle grunt of latter-day successes *Grid* and *Dirt*.

You wonder if this might be the tyre iron to the back of the head that kills the series off altogether – the competence of the game aside, one hell of a marketing push is needed to bring the hardcore racing nut within a dipstick's length of a *Need For Speed* title. And won't the loyal *NFS* fanbase be alarmed at the need to brake every now and again?

"It'll be really interesting to see how the fans handle it," says *Shift*'s lead producer

Suzy Wallace cautiously. "But for us and for most people, we believe that driving a real car is so much fun that the more realistic the driving game, the better. The more accurate the driving model, and the more effects that go on to make the player feel like they're driving a real car – that's all good to us."

But though *Shift* eschews preposterous police chases in favour of track racing, Slightly Mad will pay its dues to accessibility.

"Damage is a tricky one," says Wallace. "Obviously there are games where you can come off at the first corner and completely total your car. That's not fun. All it forces the player to do is to hit the restart button. It kills immersion. But at the same time we want the player to be afraid of crashing – it should be a scary experience. So our crash feature is to really disorient the player as you would be in a real crash. We have lots of visual effects going on, and there's feedback from your car

as well – you can scrape your car up and knock bits off it, but that'll have an effect on the handling and performance as well. But though you can damage your car, we want you to be able to finish the race."

Just when we thought fidelity had reached its generational plateau, *Shift* ups the stakes by simulating the driver's sense of embodiment. It is remarkably affecting – accelerate and the perspective warps as though your head is being pressed back into the seat. Swing round a corner and the G-forces will tug and skew the screen. Plough into a tree and the viewpoint rattles around, blurs, smears and desaturates; the sound of your heart rises as you try to get your hyperventilation under control. Even when using the external camera, the game mimics these sensations, stretching the dials of the HUD as you screech forward.

This focus on the driver may be the unique bullet-point on the back of the box, but it's clear that Slightly Mad has ample talent to create something of standout value. The engine it has been creating over the last three years is pristine – heat hazes ripple in the air above engines and brake discs; the sidelines at Brands Hatch clamour with life; advanced multi-body physics and simulated grip levels ensure that petrolhead pedants get their fill. But the question remains: will all the advanced multi-body physics in the world be enough for the series to turn a corner?

Through Grid'd teeth

While *Grid* is regarded with some fondness in the **Edge** office, it is not held as the competitive standard of simulation by Wallace: "I don't get on with the driving model at all. I'm a big driver in real life and I play lots of racing games. The first thing I do is turn off the traction control and aids. Every car I drove in *Grid* – and maybe I was just picking the wrong ones – was oversteering manically and almost completely uncontrollable. I've driven loads and loads of hardcore sims before with the aids off, but I couldn't drive *Grid*'s cars with the aids off; to me that doesn't feel like driving a real car. I might be a bit outspoken about that, but I have to like the driving model in a racer."

Tying the camera to G-forces is intended to "impart the worry of a crash to the player." It's a smart compromise – but one that will have to be just as smartly balanced between the viewing modes

Though it's equivalent in size to San Esperito, the island of Panau has a more diverse geography than the tropical paradise of the first game. Rico can now cause mayhem in mountains, deserts and snowy plains, and fight through weather conditions that conform to the cloud formations above

Sadly, Johansson stubs out our hopes for co-op: "We've thought a lot about multiplayer, but there were so many things we felt we needed to do first. We have a lot of ideas – but we'll only do it when we think we can integrate it perfectly into the core experience. But it's not likely that we'll do it as a downloadable content"

Just Cause 2

Now with even more things to blow into millions of tiny pieces

Within the vast spectrum of open-world games that lie between *Crackdown*'s frivolous sandbox mayhem and *GTAIV*'s supportive narrative, *Just Cause* occupied a sometimes uncomfortable patch of ground somewhere left of centre. It obligated you to fulfil a storyline, but not an especially provocative or engaging one. It offered freedom, but the ambitions for self-expression were limited to what you blew up.

For the sequel, Avalanche has done some soul-searching. It's perhaps aware that reproducing a similar compromise won't cut it now that the open world has fledged, heralding a generation of games that have shrugged off the *GTA*-clone moniker.

"The important thing is that each of these [open-world] games finds their own identity," says lead designer **Peter Johansson**. "We've asked what the core

The technology underpinning Avalanche's depiction of Panau allows for an island-spanning draw distance and a near-seamless loading of textures and changes in the level of detail – features that perfectly complement the ability to skydive from several thousand feet up

experience of *Just Cause* is – it's the stunts. You should be able to play around a lot and not be too concerned about whether it's based in reality. *GTAIV* does its city thing really well – but it's a different experience."

There may still be a story of sorts – CIA operative Rico Rodriguez is dispatched to the island of Panau to take down his old mentor Tom Sheldon – but Avalanche has tweaked the structure to mesh plot progression with the basic action of the game.

"That's where the chaos system comes in," says Johansson. "The island's a pressure cooker ready to blow, and Rico's there to push it over the edge – causing chaos is the standard agency method to initiate regime change. So he might work with factions or simply cause destruction or do whatever he wants to do, but he does it to provoke a certain reaction in the world – key missions which are unlocked as he causes chaos."

It's not clear just how dramatic these changes are, how significant and permanent they feel, but Johansson is keen to stress that Avalanche's major consideration with *Just Cause 2* was how to populate the world with meaningful tasks. But even if the game fails to meet this promise and falls back on bedlam as its raison d'être, players should still expect some high-calibre carnage.

The game thrusts a basic toolset of

considerable power into the player's hands, taking in Rico from *El Mariachi*, *Bionic Commando* and beyond. Combining his collapsible parachute with a more easily accessible grappling hook, Rico is as agile as any avatar in an open world has been – surpassing *Crackdown*'s skyscraper-vaulting super-soldier and rivalling anything from the Marvel or DC universes. Rico grapples the ground in front of him, tugging himself forward to give lift to his quickly opened parachute. He soars into the air, only to loop about and plant himself on the roof of a car, boot out its driver and drive off a bridge. The car pirouettes, smoking, into the riverbank below. Rico has already ejected, and sails between the branches to find himself in an airbase. A moment later he surfs the wing of a plane as it climbs, and tugs open the cockpit before sending its pilot tumbling.

Describing any one sequence from *Just Cause 2* seems to defy punctuation – sliding dangerously towards a string of breathless 'and then' statements. There's always a risk that this brand of explosive wish-fulfillment and spectacle may only manage to keep our interest for so long, but by putting such power at the player's disposal, *Just Cause 2* threatens to make the transition from flash-in-the-pan pastime to bottomless box of delights.

FORMAT: **360, PC, PS3**
PUBLISHER: **EIDOS**
DEVELOPER: **AVALANCHE**
ORIGIN: **SWEDEN**
RELEASE: **2009**

Boys 'n' the hood

While civilian vehicles can easily be commandeered, enemy vehicles must have their multiple occupants subdued before they can be jacked. In one sequence we see, Rico battles with an APC's guards as he clambers around its hood and roof, articulating himself into positions where his enemies can't shoot him as they lean out of the windows. Taking cover by clinging on to the bumper and sinking down behind the car's boot, Rico pops a few of his adversaries, before deciding to take the last out in style. A new feature of the grapple is the ability to tether things together – such as hapless guards and pursuing vehicles, sending one flying after the other.

The early setting means that the only plasma weapons you'll see are mounted on Hunter Killers, so those hoping to re-enact the battles seen in the earlier Terminator films might be disappointed. The game's visualisation of a destroyed LA is convincing, with broken flyovers, plants growing through cracks and bowing palms proving powerfully evocative

Terminator Salvation

It can't be bargained with. It can't be reasoned with.
It is, after all, a videogame based on a motion picture

FORMAT: **360, PC, PS3**
PUBLISHER: **EVOLVED GAMES**
DEVELOPER: **GRIN/HALCYON GAMES**
ORIGIN: **US/SWEDEN**
RELEASE: **MAY**

Rez of the machines

The game will feature several on-rails sequences. One is a breakneck arrangement in which your ramshackle pickup, similar to those seen in the earlier films, flees from a Hunter Killer. With you spraying bullets from a gun mounted on the back, it proceeds over jumps and along highways, but it's actually very arcadey. Aerostats appearing in tight formations for your bullets to tear into sparking explosions and clearly marked weak points on the HK's exhaust points and engines. Though dramatically staged, it does look a little gimmicky and could prove a challenge to convincingly fit alongside the methodical nature of the main game.

T hough the calibre of its cast and the weight of the series' stature belie it, Terminator Salvation is an independent film. Produced by The Halcyon Company, the summer blockbuster has a game tie-in being developed for it by the company's newly minted game division, Halcyon Games, working alongside Grin. It's a setup that has great potential for movie-based games: Halcyon's VP of development, Cos Lazouras, is keen to emphasise the closeness with which the game and film makers worked together, with game artists working directly alongside film artists for a couple of months during preproduction.

Promisingly, the game is not an attempt to recreate the film but about, in Lazouras' words, "expanding the universe". As such, it doesn't follow the movie's story. Rather, it's set two years before it, in 2016, with John Connor still just a footsoldier in the human resistance against Skynet. And they're dark days indeed – Skynet's decimating the

Cover is destructible, though the extent to which this will force players to move around areas under fire is unclear in the early sections of the game we've seen

humans, and the game is keen to impress players with the sense that every solider is vital to the cause and yet extremely vulnerable in the face of the titanium-clad robot hordes that oppose them.

The setting also allows the game to add new enemies into Terminator canon, including the T-600, a precursor to Arnie's T-800 that's one of Skynet's first attempts at a humanoid robot. Fearsomely bulky and ugly, it makes its first appearance bursting through a wall in the opening section of the game, splitting the player, playing as John Connor, from his squadmates. Other new enemies include the less exciting T-70, a crab-legged robot from a previous generation of Skynet design, and an adapted version of the Aerostat, a small flying enemy that tends to attack in swarms. The need to credibly adhere to the Terminator universe hasn't resulted in vastly imaginative enemy design.

Indeed, Lazouras concedes that despite the closeness of the film and game teams and how early on in the production cycle they managed to start, they've still had less time to work on it than developers of most videogames are used to. After all, Halcyon only took the rights to the Terminator licence in May 2007 and the film didn't begin production until early 2008.

At any rate, the result is a *Gears Of War*-style thirdperson shooter in which players must traverse and exploit cover alongside an autonomous squad of friendlies. Those noticing similarities between this and

Squadmates are talkative with the usual peppy yet gritty war dialogue. Gruff soldiers bitch at the lady who gives radio orders, reasonable ones testily restore the peace

Wanted, another Grin film tie-in currently in development, can rest assured, however. This is a far more ponderously paced game, even if it is focused on movement and the idea of 'three-dimensional battlefields'. *Terminator Salvation*'s hook is that much combat strategy is down to players working their way around outlying cover to attack the relatively undefended rears of enemies while allies plug away from the front, so the areas we've seen feel very much like arenas, with their centres ripe for robots to obediently roll into.

It's hard at this point to feel inspired by what we've seen of *Salvation*, though what appears rather formulaic also appears quite workably implemented. The proof will be in how it feels to play, of course. Given the circumstances behind its production, it'll be interesting to see if independence can help give *Terminator Salvation* something more than just the licence.

ONLINE

"...more intense than World of
Warcraft or other MMOs."

Seth Schiesel
The New York Times ™

>> IN STORES NOW <<

$7,444

You need to hire people with certain abilities for your squad. Medics and stick-up men prove useful when the going gets rough, while demo experts and engineers can sabotage competing rackets. You'll need a demo man's skills to blow up rival families' compounds

SaniCo Dump and Disposal New York

Manhandling the owner of a business can persuade them to give you a cut of their action. But people are fragile, so be careful how hard you push them. Kill a man and his business will close for a time, preventing a takeover

The Godfather II

EA could do well to follow Clemenza's advice: leave the gun, take the cannoli

FORMAT: **360, PC, PS3**
PUBLISHER: **EA**
DEVELOPER: **IN-HOUSE**
ORIGIN: **US**
RELEASE: **APRIL 7 (US), APRIL 10 (EUROPE)**
PREVIOUSLY IN: **E193**

Remember that part in The Godfather Part II where Fredo and Michael blast their way out of Cuba, gunning down rebels left and right as they make their way through a sequence of exploding alleys? How about the bit in the armoured car, when it flies in slow-motion off a ramp, its occupants laying down hellfire with their Tommy guns? Not ringing any bells?

To be fair to EA, a Godfather game that was loyal to the action of the films might never work. Sitting in melancholy contemplation with the shutters closed isn't the kind of core gameplay that makes for snappy sales pitches. But this fact doesn't make the game's mix of filmic simulacra and GTA-style, gun-toting hoo-hah any less unsettling. Chunks of the film's script are left intact, albeit redistributed among the game's characters to make way for the entry of your protagonist into the storyline, and the game

employs spongy, awkward likenesses of some, but not all, of the film's cast. But at every point at which the game's creators have contributed to the fiction, the tone veers off straight into the seedier, ribald realms of GTA, creating a truly bizarre tug of war. "It's not personal, it's business," your character quotes as he crams a baseball bat into someone's mouth before slamming their skewered head into the floor.

Ultraviolence abounds, but it's just one of the many ways in which EA has confused being mature with getting a mature certification. Jokes about the clap, profuse swearing and the happy depiction of nipples are the kind of things that Coppola's sombre, realist approach could have rendered with artistic validity; here they seem like boorish giveaways to the Saints Row crowd.

But the frequently ludicrous disjunct in tone does at least raise a laugh, and the

action, while it defers to GTA for the style and quantity of its gunplay, has a very interesting trick up its sleeve. Management of the family and its businesses becomes a strategy game of some complexity: hiring soldiers and capos and upgrading their skills; distributing your men among your rackets to protect them; attempting to monopolise particular flavours of crime. And as you expand, your rivals push back, looking for places to hurt you most. It immediately feels like a more apt fit for the licence, and its integration with the open-world actioning is made reasonably fluid thanks to the Don's View mode (see 'Let me wet my beak').

It is this feature alone that promises to mitigate the clumsiness of the storytelling and make the game stand out from other city-based actioners. The visual standards certainly don't help to distinguish it, and the world is executed with a level of flimsiness familiar to GTA clones of yesteryear – cars and pedestrians pop in beside you; vehicles handle with neither credibility nor flair; AI is gallingly basic. All of this would be a lesser concern in a game as yet unreleased, but the code we've played was at one point considered complete: The Godfather II had been previously scheduled to reach store shelves in February. Its delay until April is, we've been told, a juggling of the release schedule for fiscal convenience rather than the result of quality concerns. We hope EA doesn't stop working on it just yet. Although the much-needed polish won't persuade the epic Godfather licence to squeeze itself into an action framework, there's a strong strategy angle here that, if bolstered by solid execution, could finally pay the Don the respect he's due.

Let me wet my beak

The Don's View mode combines a map with all the information you need about the current state of your family, and that of your competitors. Businesses are marked, and in a few clicks you can send the boys round to take them over, sabotage competing rackets to break other families' monopolies, set guards to protect your existing interests, or deploy reinforcements to fend off attacks. In fact, if you fancy yourself more of a Tom Hagen than a Sonny Corleone, you need do little fighting yourself and can instead concentrate on the strategy.

$2,215   Norman Visconti

Richie's Tavern New York

Bat

The films never shied away from the brutal depiction of violence but nor did they revel in it. EA's game, on the other hand, delights in having you execute enemies in laughably violent ways: snapping arms, pummelling faces with bats and stomping on heads

FORMAT: **360, PS3, PC**
PUBLISHER: **EA**
DEVELOPER: **DICE**
ORIGIN: **SWEDEN**
RELEASE: **2009**

Battlefield 1943: Pacific

DICE rekindles familiar old flames with 350Mb of Battlefield multiplayer

While we shudder at producer Patrick Liu's deployment of the term 'zany', it's clear that DICE's latest bite-sized *Battlefield* is intended to bring back some of the knockabout team-shooter silliness of the first game. This is confirmed the second that the press are allowed to hold the controller: immediately one straps det-packs to his own plane, flies it upwards until it stalls, then leaps out, exploding his tumbling craft as he parachutes into the glittering blue sea below.

A download-only title, *Battlefield 1943: Pacific* marks EA's increasing interest in digital distribution, following *Burnout Paradise*'s experiments in the online space and the company's endorsement of Steam.

Pacific takes you back to three of the series' best loved arenas: Iwo Jima, Guadalcanal and, from *1942*'s ludicrously popular demo, Wake Island. Along with destructible scenery to the crisply realised atoll, DICE has undertaken some other, potentially controversial, reformulations. The classes have been cropped back to just three, divided by range. Health and ammo replenishes over time, a little clock-face appearing when you fire your last round.

Our brief hands-on with the game gives little sense of the immediacy and hasty pace that such changes are intended to make as the servers are sadly depopulated. But at least this gives us the chance to try vehicles and planes without fear of being bayoneted en route – and, as you might hope, these handle with the kind of lenient physics that

Wake Island now has bunkers that enable players to remotely commandeer a squadron of bombers. Planes only offer players a degree of control to modify their path, but can deliver an almighty explosive payload

tempt players into tree-top trimming aerobatics, or ramp-propelled ram-raids.

It's easy to worry if and how DICE will manage piecemeal payments for content. But with private matchmaking seeing some improvements since *Bad Company*'s release, it's inevitable that *Pacific* will reignite the enthusiasm that set downloads of the original *1942* demo alight.

Batman: Arkham Asylum

We find out what it's like to beat a clown at midnight

FORMAT: **360, PC, PS3**
PUBLISHER: **EIDOS**
DEVELOPER: **ROCKSTEADY STUDIOS**
ORIGIN: **UK**
RELEASE: **2009**
PREVIOUSLY IN: **E196**

Beneath the ears, Bruce Wayne is still the world's greatest fighter – add a cape, gadget belt and body armour and he is every bit the shadowy, elemental force that his enemies most fear. Even so, his skull will crack just like anyone else's when subjected to the force of a 10mm bullet. *Arkham Asylum* yokes its central action to this delicate balance – Batman's peerless combat abilities don't make him unassailable; his greatest weapon is discretion, ensuring that, with careful planning, every attack is conducted on his terms.

Study, plan, attack: this is the mantra for what appears to be an oft reoccurring set-piece in Rocksteady's game. Perched in the darkened rafters, Batman watches the movements of the Joker's thugs below, before swooping silently down to pick them off one by one. Later we see Bats in less subtle form, gliding from some high perch into a gang of unarmed thugs, demolishing them with wince-inducing violence. The combat has something of *Assassin's Creed* in its eager use of countermoves, but Batman is more inclined toward offence than the parry-happy Altaïr. Tougher enemies must be stunned before they can be brought down – knife-carrying lunatics are disorientated by a swish of Batman's cape, before being brutally disarmed and bodyslammed through scenery.

As powerfully kinetic and empowering as such sections are, they seem a little inorganic in their introduction. There is a risk that

Switching into his analytical 'detective mode', the caped crusader can see enemies' heat signatures, scan walls for points that will be susceptible to explosive charges, and pick up clues, allowing him to follow paths of tobacco left by the kidnapped Commissioner Gordon

Arkham Asylum's rambling, crumbling environs could too transparently become a series of interconnected chambers: this one a stealth room, this one a fisticuffs arena. Gameplay by rote, padded by perfunctory puzzling. Batman's 'detective mode', in which green-hued vision offers up breadcrumb trails of DNA to his next objective or reveals breakable walls, has yet to impress its necessity. Nonetheless, the potential freedom within Arkham island's hub, and Batman's competence at navigating it with grapples and glides, could yet lead to sprawling, dynamic action that's impossible to convey in brief demonstrations. Rocksteady has nailed the tipping point between the bat and the man – will *Arkham* itself prove as deftly defined?

Our first glance at the eerie exterior of Arkham island suggests that Rocksteady has created something hauntingly unique: a sinister, decaying timepiece

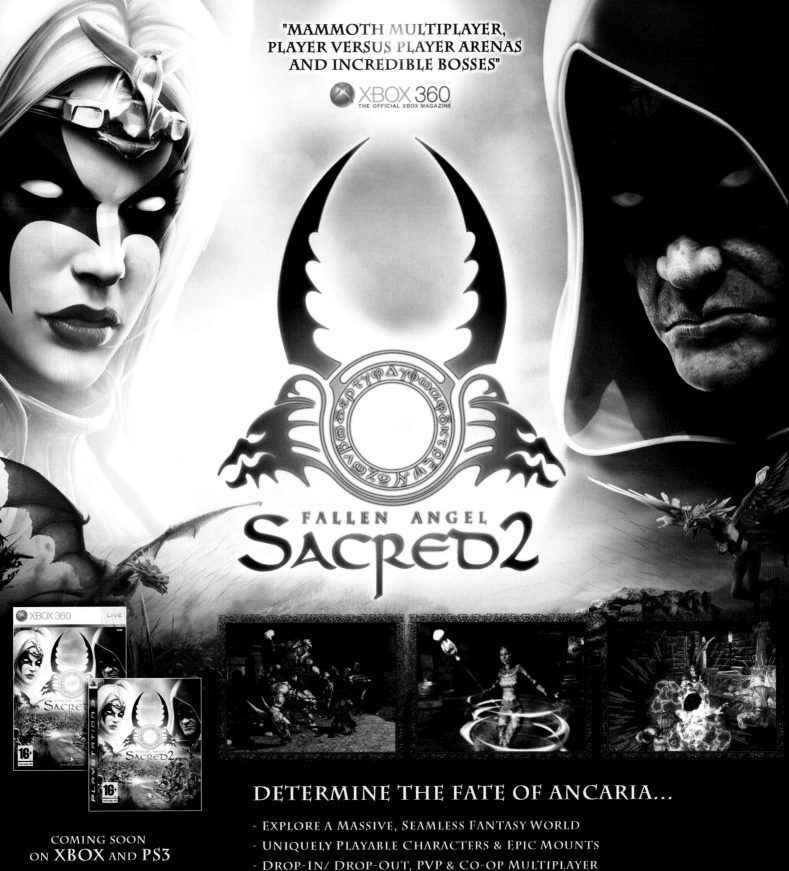

FORMAT: **WII**
PUBLISHER: **RISING STAR GAMES**
DEVELOPER: **MARVELOUS**
ORIGIN: **JAPAN**
RELEASE: **APRIL 24**

Little King's Story

Swap a shovel for a sceptre as Marvelous takes over the world

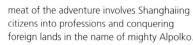

Considering *Little King's Story*'s developmental pedigree – a dream team boasting *Dragon Quest VIII*, *Final Fantasy XII*, *Harvest Moon* and *Mario And Luigi RPG* across their CVs – it's interesting to see Marvelous's monarch 'em up borrow most from a title absent from that list, Nintendo's *Pikmin*. You make kingly decrees to direct town management, but the meat of the adventure involves Shanghaiing citizens into professions and conquering foreign lands in the name of mighty Alpolko.

Tagging along like Olimar's vegetable army, your chosen professionals are not directed with the precision of a tossed Pikmin. Instead, the game employs a context-sensitive line of sight. Order a soldier towards a monster and he'll know to fight. Likewise, farmers, woodcutters and carpenters will know to dig, chop and build. Where swarming tactics sufficed in *Pikmin*, this focuses on judicious use of retreats, strategic depth found in navigating attack patterns.

While mechanically sound, it's the queer sense of humour that will undoubtedly woo players onwards. Under the twee character designs lie jabs at the unemployed masses (these 'carefree adults' clog up the village as professionals go about their jobs) and a church dedicated to Ramen noodles. A brilliant localisation holds it all together, one rival king setting the tone with smack talk aimed at the 'Kingdom of Al-jerk-o'.

In time spent away from the battlefield, Marvelous's rural *Harvest Moon* roots are

As Alpolko expands, so does your castle, from shack to respectable future tourist attraction – where else are you going store the princesses swiped from rival kingdoms?

Carefree adults can be put to basic digging duties, but applying spade-trained farmers to the same task will see the work pass faster, increasing your earthy reward

felt. There are funds to be raised, minerals to be mined and problems to be solved. The toil is toned down a notch – there's no way to lose, progress simply stalls – but it's good to see these ideas outside of a *Moon* spinoff. Most impressively, it arrives at a time when new Wii IP tiredly veers between family fare and snaring the disenfranchised 'core' gamer. Charming and cheery, but never at the cost of scope, *Little King's Story* proves these worlds needn't be exclusive.

Valkyrie Profile: Covenant Of The Plume

Feathers fly as tri-Ace's Valkyrie Profile ditches its RPG roots to turn tactics game

FORMAT: **DS**
PUBLISHER: **SQUARE-ENIX**
DEVELOPER: **TRI-ACE**
ORIGIN: **JAPAN**
RELEASE: **APRIL 2009**

As development houses go, tri-Ace is 'respected', according to the strangely muted press release that accompanies the preview build of *Valkyrie Profile: Covenant Of The Plume*. It's a peculiarly modest judgement coming from a sales pitch, but it happens to be true: tri-Ace's work tends not to set forums ablaze or send queues threading through the streets of Akihabara, but the company has made a name for itself over the years by being meticulous, level-headed and diligent.

The team also has a habit of bringing a quiet creativity to its work, not that that's immediately noticeable in this title. Like *Blue Dragon Plus*, *Valkyrie Profile*'s appearance on DS has heralded an identity crisis, culminating in the ageing RPG's transformation into a tactics game, ditching side-scrolling exploration in favour of a series of discrete encounters that play out on a standard battlefield grid.

Playing through the title's opening hour suggests that *Plume* is sturdy if slightly uninspired, with the rigid tactics template removing some of the series' more imaginative ideas, while the tiny sprites rein in any visual flights of fancy. In fact, while the game retains the *Valkyrie* standard of mapping each party member's attacks to a specific face button, the most enjoyable aspect initially comes in a straight lift from *Disgaea*, with enemies' lengthy health bars encouraging you to gang up for combo attacks by strategic placement of your various team members.

Further down the road, *Plume* hits its stride with a clever idea of its own, in the form of the eponymous feather, which bestows a stat boost on any chosen unit for a single battle, but comes at the price of their death immediately afterwards. Adding a welcome mercenary twist to proceedings, it remains to be seen whether the game can learn from genre brethren *Fire Emblem* and create the kind of characters that make such life-or-death decisions meaningful. Without a clear answer at this point, *Valkyrie Profile* suggests that, while tri-Ace is more than capable of joining the TRPG battle currently raging on DS, it's unlikely we'll see it landing a killer blow.

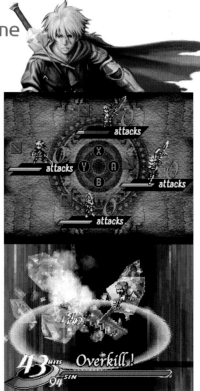

Offering no stylus controls, the isometric viewpoint plays straight into this handheld's weaknesses, with the mapping of diagonal movements to the limited D-pad of the console taking a while to get used to

Battles are solid, but the sprites are blotchy, while maps can be generic and ugly. The narrative unfolds in the sort of faux-olde-worlde couplets that sound like the dialogue you might get from a hotdog seller at a medieval fayre

THE 100 BEST GAMES TO PLAY TODAY

PRESENTED WITH EVERY VIDEOGAME SINCE SPACEWAR, WHICH EXAMPLES ACTUALLY MAKE THE GRADE IN 2009?

With another **Edge** anniversary comes another deliberation over the best games of all time. But we didn't want to think about the indisputable classics all over again. This time we wanted to make it personal by asking the question, if you had every game ever made at your fingertips, which would we play right now? What are the games, shorn of nostalgia and presumption, that we would actually want to spend time playing?

It means that you'll find many games that did so much to inspire and direct videogame culture and design missing. Our selection process quickly made clear the effect of the insatiable march of progress, new titles building upon the successes of older ones to better effect. That's why you'll find few 8bit games in the list. *Elite*, which this year celebrates its 25th birthday, isn't present, for example, but *Eve Online* is. Which is not to say that all old games are out of the picture. Certain games are remarkably resilient to time, with the *Zelda* series in particular proving its exceptionally consistent quality.

(We also invited a number of industry types to pick their all-time favourites, but, fortunately for them, they didn't have to stick to the new rules.)

We hope we've come up with a snapshot of the titles that define modern videogaming as it stands in March 2009. Turn over to begin the countdown.

100: R4: RIDGE RACER TYPE 4
NAMCO: PS1

The game that shrugged off the 'coin-op conversion' tag and turned a swirly mass of recycled roads into Ridge City. Home to the series' finest tracks, even its aircraft enter and exit the corners with perfect timing. Difficult jumps to PlayStation 2 and Xbox 360 dulled *Ridges V* and *6*, leaving this the most feature-rich and focused of the series; its soundtrack more explorative, its drift styles more deliberate, its singleplayer mode more complete, and its introduction of Gouraud shading more transformative.

99: FAR CRY
CRYTEK/UBISOFT: PC

An inexplicably accomplished first effort for a small German developer, *Far Cry* at release was remarkable for its tech. Today, after *Crysis* failed to recapture its raw thrills, it's remarkable for its mechanics. Rather than grant or deny total situational awareness within its opaque jungles, it asks players to acquire it themselves. After scouting with slightly magical binoculars, you have enough information about the enemy to plan angles of attack, or avoidance. It encourages clarity of tactics within its freely explorable islands that feels both hard-won and thoroughly satisfying.

98: STAR FOX 64
NINTENDO: N64

Or, the day Nintendo went Hollywood. From its opening bars, *Starfox 64* bellows "EPIC", ripping off movies from Independence Day to (of course) Star Wars, and delivering in spades. That's what gets the blood pumping, but the most memorable moments are the small things: the chatter between the pilots, branching difficulty routes, and Easter eggs dotted throughout its stages. With Miyamoto on development duties, it's also one of the finest on-rails shooters ever made – so good, actually, that the fact it introduced rumble feedback to videogames is just a footnote.

97: RESIDENT EVIL
CAPCOM: GC

It's now commonly shrugged away as decrepit and clumsy, and solely taking the lumbering controls, confined inventory and arbitrary puzzles, it's hard to argue. But the vividly realised mansion of the GC remake still galvanises attention, the puzzles and scant storage intricately threading your superbly paced progress through corridors infested with lethal crimson zombies and dreaded Hunters. By now, you'd have thought you knew what to expect, but it still makes you stop and desperately listen before turning any corner, every sense tuned into its weird rhythm of moans and scuffles.

96: ZELDA: TP
NINTENDO: WII

That it's a great adventure should be taken for granted but *Twilight Princess* is perhaps the most polarised *Zelda*, with series-best moments grinding against those that are close to mundane. But Link's lame wolf form and the incoherent overworld are mitigated by labyrinthine dungeons in which Link's actions are the stuff of spectacle: hookshotting on to the back of a giant fish, hopping from wall to wall on a spinning disc, battling a dragon on a tiny platform suspended in the sky. The scale of the biggest *Zelda* of them all almost makes Link seem small, and that's no inconsiderable achievement.

94: SPACE GIRAFFE
LLAMASOFT: 360, PC

Gaming Marmite? Only if you lack taste. This maligned title is Llamasoft's attempt to revitalise the tube shooter, and it's a searing masterclass in updating old-school rules. It tests players' ability to tune in to its warbles, bleats and psychedelic visuals as much as it does their trigger fingers with uncompromising visual design that turns off most new players, but that tie-dyed aesthetic hides a system of rare simplicity that balances risk and reward so finely that few shooters can hold a candle to it. Destined for oblivion, perhaps, but the very definition of a blaze of glory.

93: THE SIMS 2
MAXIS/EA: PC

The original *Sims* created a new genre, people simulation, but the sequel made the characters human. *The Sims 2* sticks to the open-ended model of the original but adds aspirations for each individual, small details that make them much more engaging to interact with and provide a much-needed extra layer of motivation for the player. Even more crucial, perhaps, is its modelling of six stages of life, allowing Sims to age. The enduring depth and warmth of this living dollhouse often goes unnoticed, but it makes *The Sims 2* one of the great accomplishments of modern game design.

95: FOOTBALL MANAGER 2009
SPORTS INTERACTIVE/SEGA: MAC, PC

Those that dismiss *Football Manager* as just being a game of numbers presumably haven't heard the epic rags-to-riches stories any player is keen to tell of their games. Involving dramas are ten a penny: a new and expensive signing winning a promotion against the odds, a change of tactics sending fortunes into freefall and causing a sacking. Whether they mirror or contrast with them, *FM*'s alternative versions of real-life football seasons are endlessly fascinating. Numbers might be abstract, but *FM* pops them into reality.

92: ANIMAL CROSSING WII
NINTENDO: WII

Animal Crossing's daily drip-feed is still magical: the turn of seasons, of special holidays, of shop opening times. Yes, it's very low-tech magic, and *Animal Crossing* still hasn't really ventured into the wilds of online. But then speeding it up to the rate things churn on the internet might erode some of the anticipation of the mundane: the thrill of completing a fossil collection, of getting a new line of conversation from the coffee shop pigeon. After all, *Animal Crossing* is a celebration of the magic of patience.

91: SPLINTER CELL: CHAOS THEORY
UBISOFT MONTREAL/UBISOFT: GC, PC, PS2, XB

Amon Tobin's soundtrack gets the nod, but, really, *Chaos Theory*'s music is half the game, creating synaesthesia usually reserved for art-house rail shooters. It exactly echoes Sam Fisher's feline movements, passing from foreboding noir to heart-rattling action as you dart from the shadows. Fisher gives Snake a run for his money in the sneaking stakes. It's not about gadgets or guns – *Chaos Theory* is a playground for Fisher's physical gifts and mastery of discretion: warfare, one broken neck at a time.

90: BRAID
NUMBER NONE: 360

Braid certainly has aspirations, and indeed its narrative has been championed, regardless of its flaws, by gamers anxious to prop up their hobby with credentials borrowed from other media. But cast all that away and you're still left with a puzzle game of startling imagination and invention. Each consecutive level brings a torrent of new ideas to further contort the game's internal time-bending logic. Sumptuous in both visual and audio design, the proof of *Braid* is in its many moments when a conundrum unravels before you, its elegance prompting an exultant "Oh!".

89: FINAL FANTASY VI
SQUARE ENIX: GBA, PS1, SNES

The delicately exquisite art style of Yoshitaka Amano hinted at what should be expected from *Final Fantasy VI* in the months leading up to its Japanese launch, and yet the game's ambition managed to surpass the wishes of even the keenest fans of Square's 2D RPG series. Rooted in a steampunk world whose industrial edges do not prevent it from being one of the most characterful entries in the series, *FFVI* has gameplay depth that transcends its limited presentation. And, yes, *that* sequence still holds up today.

88: PANEL DE PON
INTELLIGENT SYSTEMS: VARIOUS

The butterfly effect: the idea that a single, small action has unforeseeable and devastating consequences. *Panel De Pon* first flapped its wings on the SNES, and has found a home on every subsequent Nintendo system. The first 'match three' game, designed around switching two blocks horizontally to create chains of the same colour, its enduringly irresistible touch is the ability to 'chain' clearances with a single switch. It's as simple as that, yet the tiniest ripples on its playscreen produce moments of chaotic beauty that few games, never mind puzzlers, can match.

85: THE SECRET OF MONKEY ISLAND
LUCASFILM GAMES: PC

Do you want to know the true secret of *Monkey Island*? It's this: other games may have better puzzles and pacing, but none have Melee Island, with its wandering tricksters, grog-swilling pedants and rickety lantern-lit shacks artfully pin-pricking the thick black Caribbean night. Guybrush's forlorn quest to become a pirate refuses to turn stale, even almost 20 years after its release. You'll come for the jokes, and you'll stay for the sword fighting, but you'll return just to revisit its midnight shores.

87: DOOM II
ID SOFTWARE/GT INTERACTIVE: PC

Few sequels achieve it so well: *Doom II* nailed everything that the original game did right, and then expanded on it intelligently. Not through technical improvements, but through stronger design. The descent into Hell was more dramatic and on a larger scale, and it took place through a series of wide-open levels and huge multi-stage puzzles that are still fun to unravel today, especially in co-op. *Doom II* is still compulsive played alone: fluid, well-paced and balanced, and the double shotgun remains one of videogames' greatest weapons.

84: GOD OF WAR
SCEA/SCE: PS2

The masterstroke was to treat myth not as a museum piece but as the Saturday night entertainment that it really is, and to know that legends are enlivened, not insulted, by fresh interpretations. The result is a game where cheap spectacle blends perfectly with histrionics, where heroic suicide sits comfortably next to an orgy minigame. But while it gleefully defies taste, it never defies the fact that it's a straightforward combo-charged bloodbath – before the sequel's taste for exhibitionism started to turn a little of Kratos' lean muscle into fat.

86: SINGSTAR
LONDON STUDIO/SCE: PS3

The rest of the world views Europe's *SingStar* fixation with the uneasy confusion reserved for such oddities as cockfighting. So be it: they don't understand the duet of preparation and performance lurking at the heart of Sony's casual classic, and the entertaining possibilities when you hand level design over to Blondie and Elvis. The most transformative of all games, capable of yanking stellar recitals from the least likely of players, *SingStar*'s interface is a modest wonder, and the game's appeal is as timeless as that of singing itself.

83: PEGGLE
POPCAP: PC

Detractors who say it's just random miss the point. You'd think the Ode To Joy might give them a hint as where to find it. Always rewarding you, always cheering you on, *Peggle* may just sway favour by charm alone – but beneath the purposeful goofiness of unicorns and rainbows lies an undeniable compulsion. Yes, chance plays a large part, but it is precisely the struggle to impose your will over the random that forms its deadly addiction. It plays to the gambler in us, and be it by luck or judgement, triumph rarely feels as good.

82: SAM & MAX HIT THE ROAD
LUCASARTS: PC

Monkey Island titles may bookend the point-and-click genre's decade of high popularity, but nestled in the middle is its most persisting pleasure. The recent tepid continuations lack the original scabrous wit of *Hit The Road*. So, too, its wild imagination, voice talent and, vitally, the elastic flair with which Sam and his manic rabbitoid pal were drawn and animated. Still as hilarious today, *Hit The Road*'s non sequitur puzzle design is unusually forgivable thanks to the consistent, brilliant lunacy of its world.

80: QUAKE III
ID SOFTWARE/ACTIVISION: PC

Id's minimalist cyber-gothic deathmatch game remains at the summit of the studio's multiplayer achievements. The taut, balanced shooting leans heavily on unrealistic acrobatics and is all the more interesting for it. While Carmack's technology was a large part of the appeal when it first arrived, the true value of *Quake III* was in crowning the deathmatch with a game of unwavering precision. It was down to modders to complete the vision, however; it's unclear whether their multifarious insights will be put to work in *Quake Live*, a browser-based version of the game now in beta.

81: SILENT HILL 2
TEÁM SILENT/KONAMI: PS2

Surviving the horror in this drunken nightmare of a game is less about ammo than peeking through your fingers and managing to sleep through the night. With Francis Bacon scenes shot from demented alternatives to *Resident Evil*'s camera angles, and an extraordinary soundscape by composer Akira Yamaoka, it lives in a world of pain. Survival horror is not a matter of working perfectly but being broken in the right ways. A pain to navigate, daftly voiced and entirely ponderous, *Silent Hill 2* achieves its malevolent, dreamlike quality despite those flaws, and often because of them.

79: PAC-MAN CE
NAMCO-BANDAI: 360

There's nothing wrong with plain old *Pac-Man*, but it took *Championship Edition* to show us just how right he still is. The basics stay – Pac-Man, ghosts, dots, power pills, fruit and a maze – but it's all about how *CE* toys with them. Mazes morph, paths of dots grow, ghosts accelerate, power pill patterns change – all governed by collecting fruit. Every game begins with a mind to the hi-score by chaining ghosts and ends with the panic of sheer survival. The best thing about *Pac-Man: CE* isn't the sense you're playing with a classic, it's that designer Toru Iwatani was doing the same.

78: UFO: ENEMY UNKNOWN
MYTHOS GAMES/MICROPROSE: PC

Base building, turn-based strategy, RPG-like squad development, resource management – *UFO: Enemy Unknown* could have been sprawling, but smartly interlocks it all into singularity. Building the base that houses the squad that's equipped to attack the alien base to capture the commander to research him to advance the story – *UFO* puts you in charge of everything. Such involvement lends missions great consequence and enthralling tension, with every solider both vital and mortally vulnerable.

77: ZELDA: MAJORA'S MASK
NINTENDO: N64

The first time Link screams in agony, you know this is different. In staging the last three days of Termina, the face of the moon leering overhead, Nintendo took the opportunity to build *Zelda*'s most intricate town, so you can watch it fall apart over and over. Or you could learn what people are going to do before they do it and accompany them on their lonely vigils. Of course there's a bigger picture, but this is the only *Zelda* that isn't so much about saving the world as it is about saving its people.

76: PLANESCAPE: TORMENT
BLACK ISLE STUDIOS/INTERPLAY: PC

Sometimes, you'll try to zoom out to alleviate the pixellated graphics. Nothing happens, and now you know the only way in which this spellbindingly original RPG has been superseded by today's games. Words don't age like graphics engines, and it is out of words that Sigil is woven – exploring through dialogue a dusty, bustling city baking under an alien sun at the nexus of life, death and a million different planes besides, each far from the medieval realms of conventional fantasy. Stories, nightmares and mysteries unfold, and the greatest mystery of all turns out to be you.

75: F-ZERO GX
AMUSEMENT VISION/NINTENDO: GC

Newcomers can be forgiven for being terrified by their first go. Extraordinarily twitchy and fast, *F-Zero GX* is all about holding the thumb rigid on the GC stick, only allowing it to move in the most minutely controlled increments. It's only then that you can pull off the smooth cornering required to truly compete on its spectacular tracks. And, even then, the speed at which the courses wheel from horizontal to vertical and then about upon themselves, all at 1,000kph, means you're still far from feeling comfortable. But that's exactly what you're here for. *F-Zero GX*'s flashing neon and hairsbreadth between success and failure are some of gaming's greatest thrills.

74: PUZZLE QUEST: COTW
INFINITE INTERACTIVE/D3: VARIOUS

There's a lot standing in the way of *Challenge Of The Warlords* being any good – the menus are cheap, the artwork and story cheaper still, and it's blessed with more than its share of bugs – but it can nevertheless suck you in for entire days at a time. This weird chimera, the result of shoving a match-three game into an RPG world, may not initially seem likely to be a viable plan for world domination, but when the powerful addiction of moving blocks meets the class-A narcotic of level grinding, it's clear that humanity never had much of a chance. A work of twisted genius.

70: DAYTONA USA
SEGA: COIN-OP

Anyone turned off by the artificiality of videogames need only look to the reflected clouds in the rear window of a *Daytona USA* Hornet. Utterly unreal, they're a perfect expression of 60 frames-per-second and the sharp, bright Sega air you're cutting through. Though an early venture into the verisimilitudes of 3D racing, Sega kept true to its singular imagination by infusing its tracks with the surreal: Three Seven Speedway's giant slot machine, which doles out extra time if you can match reels, and Seaside Street Galaxy's moving statue of *Virtua Fighter*'s Jeffry. A pure expression of arcade racing, *Daytona USA* hasn't lost its capacity to entertain on every level.

73: FREQUENCY
HARMONIX/SCE: PS2

The plastic guitar is a great way to draw people in, but it's also an obstruction. Take it away, multiply the phrases by eight and dive headlong into darkest electronica and you have *Frequency*, Harmonix's answer to *Tempest*. Hypnotising the eyes, ears and fingers in equal measure, it's a sharper and more expansive beast than sequel *Amplitude*. The moment that earns its place here: when you realise your conscious mind stopped matching the beats 30 seconds ago, handing over to your all-too-seldom-tapped inner gamer.

69: SUPER SMASH BROS BRAWL
SORA LTD/NINTENDO: WII

Four Nintendo characters walk into a bar. A pint gets spilled. Fight! Yet *Smash Bros*' status as pure beat 'em up is doubtful. Instead, it's the closest thing to sumo that the west has seen, its system dependent on controlling space, pressure and knocking foes out of the level. *Brawl* is the most chaotic and feature-packed of the series, endless in its goodies yet restrained in its refusal to alter the concept of the N64 original. Why mess with a game that lets you batter Kirby?

72: SKATE 2
BLACK BOX/EA: 360, PS3

With quiet confidence EA brought polite revolution to the world of skating games, effortlessly upstaging *Tony Hawk's*, a series steadily ground down by a punishing schedule of yearly iterations. *Skate 2* may not have added any new twists to the original, but it does have the good grace to double the available tricks, with the result of the analogue Flickit system bringing a potent sense of physicality to the controls, while the mature presentation ensures you'll never land your ollie in a grimy puddle of focus-grouped youth-culture posturing.

68: SHADOW OF THE COLOSSUS
TEAM ICO/SCE: PS2

You are a lone, bedraggled man on a futile quest in a desolate wasteland. Even the exhilaration of defeating the colossi is matched by disquiet at murdering the few living things in this forgotten land. Few games could take such a bleak premise and compel you to continue, but *Shadow* so envelops you in its fiction that you relish its haunting and powerful melancholy. The battles with its epic foes inspire awe, but as a tribute to despair this remains a unique experience.

71: OUTRUN 2006 COAST 2 COAST
SUMO DIGITAL/SEGA: VARIOUS

It was the game everyone wanted until the moment came and the party moved elsewhere. Arcade perfect and decked in red, white and blue that only Sega and Ferrari could dream up, *OutRun 2* was left in *Burnout*'s wake. But it didn't hamper the stunning PC version and the best reason to mod a PSP to full clock-speed – *Coast 2 Coast* refused to be ignored. Sun seekers and joyriders call it home, its crystal lakes and epic drifts an escape from war-torn deserts and space marines.

67: CHRONO TRIGGER
SQUARE ENIX: DS

It's good to know that a game has its eye on you. By effecting surprising change in the world based on what you do, *Chrono Trigger* gives your every action great significance. With no random battles or grinding and being able to walk away during conversations, it allows nothing to come in the way of you and its touching, evocative and personal story. This stripping down of hoary JRPG tradition remains fresh – it might not reflect well on the form but does on *Chrono Trigger*.

66: PRINCE OF PERSIA: SOT

UBISOFT MONTREAL/UBISOFT: VARIOUS

You won't find yourself attempting backflips, but it's not uncommon to get up after playing *Sands Of Time* and feel you've become a little more graceful. That alone would be enough for most games, but this also layers in storybook visuals and a Möbius-strip narrative that wraps itself tightly around the gymnastics, while time-manipulation allows you to sidestep the frustrations of falling. If only the Sands of Time also allowed you to unstitch any memories of the increasingly misjudged sequels.

63: LEMMINGS

DMA DESIGN/PSYGNOSIS: VARIOUS

Lemmings concocts a curious mix of cunning double-thinking and deep simplicity from its save 'em up formula. Although the floppy-haired presentation may make the game seem trivial, anyone who's watched in horror as their tiny charges make it to the end of a gigantic deathtrap only to plummet into a forgotten canyon will know that this, over many more serious titles, is truly a matter of life and death. An RTS where the enemy is your own complacency, if you've ever used a mouse, you know it was designed to play *Lemmings* with.

65: THIEF II: THE METAL AGE

LOOKING GLASS/EIDOS: PC

Of the trilogy, *Thief II* is the sceptic. Its forebear and follow-up revel in magic and ghosts, but *Thief II* instead embraces the dark rather than fears it. Looking Glass bravely made Garrett fragile, cloaking him in a rich, cohesive world in which he'll hopefully neither be seen or heard. Stealth in modern gaming is shrouded in technology – sneak suits, camouflage, heat vision – but here it's refreshingly about shadows and stillness. And his journey through the open windows of the city still resonates.

62: NINJA GAIDEN II

TEAM NINJA/MICROSOFT GAME STUDIOS: 360

Carlsberg doesn't do 3D ninja fighting games with slightly dodgy cameras. But Team Ninja does, and what do you know, it's probably the best in the world. It would be easy to say there's nothing to compare to Ryu Hayabusa in full flow, but the genius really lies in the enemies, the most devilish counterparts to player skill ever devised. It's gnashingly difficult at first but patience unlocks a fighting experience that will leave you unable to tolerate Dante, never mind Kratos. Brutal? Undoubtedly. Brilliant? Totally.

64: PUYO POP FEVER

VARIOUS: VARIOUS

Puyo Pop's sweet-toothed developers have always been wise enough to place the focus on the numbers rather than the carbohydrates. Behind sugary visuals lies a game that revels in bringing about the ultimate chain reaction, the play area riddled with hidden score opportunities until the entire screen collapses into implosions of multipliers. *Fever* takes it to unmatched heights, supercharging the combo machine and providing the only destination for players who like their snacks to have a little substance.

61: ROBOTRON 2084

VID KIDZ/WILLIAMS: COIN-OP

Robotron 2084 sliced the appeal of action games so close to the bone with its intoxicatingly pure blend of moving and shooting that you could argue every subsequent title merely represents dilution. The twin-stick shooter is now experiencing an Indian summer, but still nobody's topped *Robotron*'s magical ecology. That bestiary of things you shoot, things you can only avoid, and things that can't wait to shoot you right back remains compulsively appealing – and relevant.

60: PUZZLE BOBBLE

TAITO: VARIOUS

Few games have an aim in quite so literal a sense. Though *Puzzle Bobble* initially looks like a puzzler that's a little too influenced by others, with its frogspawn clusters of colour and simple match-three mechanic, it's the addition of precision targeting and angles that makes it shine. Controlling a harpoon that turns 180°, you line up the shot and, if your aim is true, a cascade of balls fall, their connection burst by your masterly trigger finger – or you miss, the roof inches closer, your useless shot a new cornice to be factored in. Among puzzlers, none factors skill in so seamlessly with planning.

57: DEUS EX

ION STORM/EIDOS: PC

Adored but rarely revisited, *Deus Ex* has kept surprisingly fresh. It helps that the stylised art was, to be frank, never very appealing, but that and the near-blind AI and ice-rink running animations don't compromise one of the most elegantly balanced combat equations in gaming. It's a volatile confluence of the player's broad toolbelt of abilities – large, open levels filled with objects ripe for subverting, and lethal enemies with exploitable behaviours. Conceiving a smart, slick, secret-agent ploy to navigate them all is part of the appeal. Seeing it violently backfire is the rest.

59: VIEWTIFUL JOE

CAPCOM: GC, PS2

Gaming's most affectionate tribute to cinema is rarely recognised as such. This is no interactive movie, you see. Instead, it's devoted to being a showboating movie superstar. Joe's trio of powers that speed, slow and zoom the action allow you to freely choreograph splendidly destructive scenes against a set of meticulously designed enemies, each with specific weaknesses. Sound cues tell you exactly what's going on even as the screen fills with dazzling special effects. Cheesy, visually arresting, and with the best pause soundbite ever, *Viewtiful Joe* remains in a league of its own.

56: COUNTER-STRIKE SOURCE

VALVE: PC

Although it's difficult to grasp while standing in the shadow of its vertiginous learning curve, *Counter-Strike* represents the very point at which players can exert mastery over a dynamic system. This is not a game of anarchic, from-the-hip gunplay. It's balanced to razor-sharp precision thanks to years of service by its fanbase – the variables trimmed to a golden proportion that leaves little room for happenstance, only skill. Years after its release, no online FPS has rivalled the delicacy of this balance.

58: GEARS OF WAR 2

EPIC/MICROSOFT GAME STUDIOS: 360

Does it sport a lasting greatness or one tailored for fleeting attention spans? Its influence is undeniable: even *Resident Evil*, its unknowing mentor, has now taken its lead. Epic's eye for what its mainstream audience wants is as clear and unflinching as a sniper scope, its multiplayer commitment serious, and apart from some flabby moments in the campaign, its execution is clinical. This is the shooter at its most over-the-top. Approached with tongue planted firmly in cheek, even its story is a crowd-pleaser.

55: POKÉMON YELLOW

GAME FREAK/NINTENDO: GB

It's easy to forget that *Pokémon* began as just a great game, not the phenomenon it is today. What places *Yellow*, an upgraded version of the original, above the later *Ruby*s and *Diamond*s is, simply, simplicity. Later entries expanded the original 151 monsters into unmanageable menageries of 350 or 500, while losing the tight design that made them such a joy to chase down. Gotta catch 'em all was a compulsion the first time around, and it's never been as achievable, or just plain fun, as it is here.

54: ICO

TEAM ICO/SCE: PS2

There's hardly a shortage of decent 3D platformers, but *Ico* gains its strange power by taking its sly sense of level design and shrouding it in a luxurious blanket of chic enigma – and the results, although mannered, are irresistible. From the setting, swathed in haze, dappled with moss and blessed with a rare sense of the authentically ancient, to the tender, wordless friendship blossoming at the game's heart, *Ico* manages to feel as fleeting and ambiguous as a dream, and tells a story that's been carefully reduced to the bare-boned elegance of myth.

51: R-TYPE FINAL

IREM: PS2

R-Type Final's aim was to give a classic series the funeral it deserved. It pulled it off. *R-Type Final* is one of the finest 2D shooters ever made, but it's also a sombre one, with every shot tinged with the knowledge that this really will be one of the last, each Bydo destroyed with a slight pang of regret, and its outstanding final sequence doubles as a wake. With the quality of its design and realisation and ideas beyond mere bullet hell, it revitalised a series in the act of burying it. *R-Type Final* didn't just give the *R-Type* series a good send-off: it immortalised it.

53: UNCHARTED: DRAKE'S FORTUNE

NAUGHTY DOG/SCE: PS3

From a hammy matinee serial scenario and a corny marriage of *Gears Of War* and *Tomb Raider* came something entirely more special. *Uncharted* melds a tightly designed shooter with beautifully realised exotic environments and some terrific videogame characterisation. A snappy script, everyman character design and animation, and cocky-cum-congenial voice-acting brings life to a rousing adventure that's as broadly entertaining as the matinees that inspired it.

50: METAL GEAR SOLID: TS

SILICON KNIGHTS/KONAMI: GC

Shot through with fears from before gaming existed, *MGS* turned Konami's grey attempts at early 3D into a cold, ornate, passionate tale of soldiers imprisoned by war. It wasn't a bad stealth game, either, more focused and accessible than its sequels. Silicon Knights' remake for GameCube preserves its atmosphere, the production values raised to *MGS3* standards, and makes the desire to return irresistible. It's a great second edition of one of gaming's timeless documents.

There are lots of games I really like – too many to choose from. But as this is **Edge**, I've picked a couple of my favourite European games.

The game I must name first is the first entry in the French series *Alone In The Dark*. It was one of the first games to feature full 3D polygons, which was rare in those days. Its characters and dramatic camera rendering were also impressive in comparison to the flat rendering by 2D which had been common up until then. This game's depiction of horrific scenes with full use of pictures was groundbreaking. I believe that the title contributed to the remarkable jump experienced by the general concept of visual rendering. Had it not been for this work, the evolution of visual rendering after *FFVII* might have been different.

Another game I should mention is Swedish title *Hearts Of Iron*, a simulation set in World War II. I didn't know what to expect from Swedish games but this turned out to be a well-made realtime simulation and I still get the same satisfaction playing it today.

52: FABLE II

LIONHEAD/MICROSOFT GAME STUDIOS: 360

Fable II's place is assured not by its Britishness, but because it's the least frustrating videogame of all time. Its accessibility may be mistaken for lenience, just as its combat is regularly muddled with simple-mindedness, but it takes bravery and brilliance to remove so many of the dusty fixtures of videogame design. With a quest that tugs you through to the plot and a bucolic paradise ripe for exploration, never before has so much work been put into making sure the humble player feels special.

49: REZ HD

UNITED GAME ARTISTS/SEGA: 360

Abstract yet emotional, serene but frantic, *Rez* is an elaborate study in the balancing of extremes. The simplest of shooting designs is grafted to a searing show of sound and light. By sharpening surfaces and smoothing lines, *HD* restates why, despite *Rez*'s traditional on-rail mechanics, there's simply nothing else like it. Astonishing to watch, uniquely absorbing to play, it ends, for all but the most gifted of its audience, with a beautiful stab of unresolved regret.

There are so many: *Mercenary* on C64… Any number of *Mario* games across the ages… *Tomb Raider* on PS1. Even pretending I'm Dave Grohl on *Rock Band*.

But in recent times, the one franchise that's had my heart pounding and trigger finger aching is *Gears Of War*. In an age of political correctness and caring renaissance man, I thank God I can still perch on the edge of the sofa, gripping a pad hard enough to bring on rheumatism and scream "Take that, you MOTHERFUCKER!" as my bald space marine eviscerates one more other-worldly horror.

No, it's not right. Yes, it's slightly embarrassing. But the red-blooded alpha male in me takes over; it's the *Gears* Hyde to my *Flower* Jekyll. And I love it.

I relish the overwrought B-movie sensibilities, the raw firepower, the bleak grandeur. It's an experience as engaging as the best that Hollywood has to offer. Okay, *Gears Of War* might be Vin Diesel rather than Bruce Willis, but that's fine. I've got enough high intellect in my life; I can settle for a bit of dumb from time to time.

48: FINAL FANTASY VII

SQUARE: PS1

Its cutscenes and in-game models are more incongruous than ever, but *Final Fantasy VII* still exerts an unshakeable hold on the imagination. Square's world-building was at its zenith in Midgar, steampunk clashing against a rural idyll, while Tetsuya Nomura surpassed himself with the characters that, for good or ill, would define his later output. Its materia battle design, too, is still a thing of beauty: flexible and deeply complex, a programming system that foreshadowed *FFXII*'s gambits.

45: TESIV: OBLIVION

BETHESDA SOFTWORKS: 360, PC, PS3

It may be full of clockwork people telling campfire tales and stats-buffed beasts with entry-level tactics, but by packing enough of them into verdant Cryodiil and rooting them in *The Elder Scrolls*' rich folklore, *Oblivion* works magic. Acquiescing to its quirks is required but it's the least the game deserves, even when its bugs seem to tower above the spires of Imperial City. Though as far from 'perfect' as you're ever likely to find, its oddities and beauty have earned it the most active modding community on PC.

47: EVE ONLINE

CCP GAMES: PC

The third most important industry in Iceland plays host to a virtual galaxy of a quarter of a million gamers. None of those subs-paying spacefarers has many illusions about what they've let themselves in for: one of the most complex and unforgiving games ever made. Human interaction is at the core of this evolving single-server MMOG, and whether that interaction is via text, economics or laser fire, it fuels the game. *Eve Online*'s is the one true persistent world in videogames, one so vast and encompassing that it doubles as a social, economic and political experiment.

44: JET SET RADIO FUTURE

SMILEBIT/SEGA: XBOX

Deeper, faster and harder than its predecessor, *JSRF* retains and accentuates what was important about it: the attitude. So many games have tried to recreate the skills and thrills of skating, and so many miss the trick that became *JSRF*'s philosophy: Turn It Up. The OST is peerless, and whether grinding vertically down a 200-foot dragon, leaping across Shibuya's handrails, or just cruising the wrong way down a one-way street, there's nowhere else that's so exhilarating to simply travel through.

46: DISGAEA: AOD

NIPPON ICHI/KOEI: PSP

Disgaea never felt really at home on a home console. A game so based on fiddling and excursions into tens of randomly generated levels is far better suited to PSP's portability and standby mode. There, *Afternoon Of Darkness*' diabolical mathematics melt minutes into hours of what-if play. Can I get Laharl to wipe out that group of Nekomata in a single attack? Can I get him to inflict six-digit damage? How about seven? *Disgaea* is built to arouse such fervent tinkering from devilish but strident logic that broke the rules of SRPGs. And we still find it inspiring.

43: PORTAL

VALVE: 360, PC, PS3

We'd never suggest that originality is the be-all and end-all, but it's difficult to resist the thrill of the new. And what a rush of novelty *Portal* delivers: not in its technology, not in its perspective, not in its puzzles – not in any one element – but in their combination into a deliriously thrilling, mind-breaking firstperson puzzle-platformer. And that's before Valve wraps it up in a story that's weird, deadly witty and oddly touching. Few developers could smash genres together so wantonly and produce a game of this staggering level of class. For Valve, it seems like a piece of cake.

42: FIFA 09
EA CANADA/EA: 360, PC, PS3

EA has always been able to bring the muscle of licensed teams and desirable presentation to bear on its premier football series, but until now it hasn't quite been enough to win hearts and minds dedicated to *PES*. Feel is crucial to football games – the difference between feeling a shot should go in and seeing it tipped over the bar, of having a player break through and sending the pass into space you feel he's going to reach – and, finally, *FIFA* has convincingly captured it. EA muscle's still there, of course, in bells and whistles like Adidas Live Season. *PES* has much to catch up with.

39: SUPER MONKEY BALL
AMUSEMENT VISION/SEGA: GC

Some of the most striking demonstrations of videogame skill are still those by *Super Monkey Ball* players. Seeing its sturdy physics model being used to perform incredible acrobatic feats shows just how finely honed it is. It also foreshadowed *Wii Sports*, flaunting the fine control of the GC pad, and its bright colours and loveable characters, minigames and engaging simplicity were tuned to appeal to all. The difference, though, is that *Super Monkey Ball* is hardcore. Just look at what the dedicated can do.

41: RACE DRIVER: GRID
CODEMASTERS: 360, PC, PS3

It's sometimes hard to see where car racing games can go next. *Gran Turismo* is staid – sims just incrementally better than last year's version. And then *Grid* comes along, armed with a rewind feature, spectacular smoke and burnished light, intense nip-and-tuck races and an attitude that never stubbornly insists you achieve first place. It blows cobwebs from the genre, with handling a great balance of sim twitchiness and arcade abandon, breathtaking speed, and a sense of being there like no other racer.

38: STARCRAFT
BLIZZARD/VIVENDI: PC

Of all Blizzard's games, it's *StarCraft* that has had the most interesting story since release, having become the most successful e-sport in the world, thanks to the fiercely competitive leagues of South Korea. The reason for its success is partly a coincidence of cultural circumstance, and partly down to the thrill of learning and utilising its three precisely balanced asymmetric factions amid the blisteringly fast pace of its multiplayer battles. Although initially critically overlooked, it has proven to be enormously influential and, at least on its own terms, still hasn't been bettered.

36: BURNOUT PARADISE
CRITERION/EA: 360, PC, PS3

A racing game becomes quite different when it's brought into an open world. That's why there's a race at every intersection in Paradise City – fail one and there's another only a block away. *Paradise* is all about flow, not loading and restarting, about drifting, sweeping corners and seamlessly dropping into multiplayer. Couple that with a set of challenges and cars that allow you to choose how you want to play – to shunt and bash your way through or cleanly boost – and *Paradise* becomes just that.

40: WARIOWARE, INC
NINTENDO: GBA

Breaking videogames down to their base components could surely never be made fun. The up, down, left, right of fine control, the wait, wait, wait, now! of precise timing; memory and recognition tests, logic puzzles and reaction games. But *WarioWare* is pure, barely restrained and irreverent fun. Looking back, it's yet more proof of Nintendo's experience in immediately generating appeal – almost every minigame is a masterclass in how to instantly captivate with clear goals and a captivating alchemy of sound, image and control.

37: FALLOUT 3
BETHESDA SOFTWORKS: 360, PC, PS3

It demands greater suspension of disbelief than most games, inflicting on players a litany of awkwardnesses and a patience-stretching opening that gives no clue to the freedoms that lie beyond. But once you're outside Vault 101, *Fallout 3* blossoms. With the detail and wealth of discoveries that lie in wait, you can find as much fulfilment from just meandering the open wastes as from embarking on Bethesda's missions, which boast remarkably freeform structures. Once you've surrendered to its peculiar idiom, *Fallout 3* empowers, engages and rewards to extents that few games have ever achieved.

35: CASTLEVANIA: SOTN
KONAMI: PS, 360

People argue over which *Castlevania* is 'the best'. Certainly, the series has flowered in its handheld iterations, but *Symphony Of The Night* has something more than a just a carefully plotted path through its castle. When you get to that moment when the castle turns on its head, you see that it's a work of genius. Suddenly, it's clear that every area was designed for you to run not only over its floors but over its ceilings, too. Rooms have dual purpose, and every crenellation and beam takes on new meaning – it's a transformation of fiendish beauty.

34: BIOSHOCK
2K GAMES: 360, PS3

In other games you destroy worlds. In *Bioshock*, you're an interloper in a world that's already destroyed, the crushed utopia of Andrew Ryan, tasked with not only finding out what's happened but what your own role is. Rapture's many idiosyncrasies paint a picture of paradise brought low, the excellent voice-acting sets a new industry standard, and its central revelation is a defining moment of interactive storycraft. Yes, the narrative can't quite sustain the game's length, but *Bioshock* is a game as singular as its world: long after its mechanics are surpassed, the memories will remain.

33: GEOMETRY WARS RE2
BIZARRE CREATIONS/ACTIVISION: 360

It seems the smallest of innovations – placing the next-highest score from your friends list in the corner of the screen – but it's revolutionary. Urging you to play stronger, that number also incites flurries of counter-competition. Let's not forget the brilliantly balanced designs for each game mode, though, which elegantly squeeze new play from every corner of the original formula, from the calculated precision required for Pacifism to the switches between vulnerability and invincibility in King.

32: TEAM FORTRESS 2
VALVE: PC
The hardcore MP shooter sorely needed a slap in the face. The grimacing meatheads we'd played as in the past had nothing to do with the comedy violence, petty rivalries and cartoon physics of the fights we actually enacted. *TF2*'s fresh, vivid art style gives Valve the perspective to isolate and rectify everything else the genre's been missing. The result is a sumptuous and enduring shooter with distinct classes, satisfying relationships and co-operations and many more interesting ways of interacting than just by exchanging assault rifle fire.

29: ADVANCE WARS
INTELLIGENT SYSTEMS/NINTENDO: GBA
It's impossible to imagine *Advance Wars* being improved. Every sequel since has simply tried adding to a formula that was already perfect. New units, secondary battlefields, emo storylines, multitudes of maps, amphetamined-up CO Powers – nothing has improved on the clear-cut balances of units versus CO abilities that graced the first GBA version. Winning S ranks on every Battle Map stands as one of gaming's great achievements – marshalling vast conflicts on land, sea and in the air, minimising casualties under strict time limits, is an abiding obsession.

31: BOMBERMAN
HUDSON SOFT: VARIOUS
It doesn't really matter which version of *Bomberman* you can get your hands on (apart, perhaps, from *Act Zero* on 360). So long, of course, as you have enough controllers to satisfy player demand and the option to specify the classic map, Revenge and Super Revenge off, burn, virus and scavenge on, and standard powerups. In other words, *Bomberman*'s been perfect for years. Even online can't improve it – the recent *Live* outing proves that its balance of sober bomb placement and blind panic is most certainly best experienced with all players jeering at each other in the same room.

28: GTA: SAN ANDREAS
ROCKSTAR NORTH/ROCKSTAR: PC, PS2, XBOX
How many open worlds really live up to the name? Not many, especially all those trapped in some Truman Show-esque bubble. Ask why someone prefers *San Andreas* over *Vice City* and *IV* and they'll say the same thing: just grab a bike, point it at the horizon, and after a half-hour's ride you'll find out. A titanic expression of freedom before next-gen reined it all back in, Rockstar's ode to the '90s reaches far beyond the bloodied turf and ghettos of a gangsta's paradise. A flawed epic that's arguably better because of it.

30: COMPANY OF HEROES
RELIC/THQ: PC
Windows of opportunity open but briefly in *Company Of Heroes*, so when the moment comes, it takes a bad general to look the other way. But when a lone soldier, just a tiny mass of pixels, squirms amid his battalion's scattered limbs in a distant corner of the map, that's exactly what you'll find yourself doing. Patrols get diverted, stockpiles plundered and frontlines left with just a skeleton crew. From its lofty perch above an RTS battlefield, Relic gets to the heart of WWII, turning the genre's plusses and minuses into salvation and sacrifice. If only the same could be said of countless firstperson shooters.

27: MARIO KART DS
NINTENDO: DS
You'd think it outdated. Every iteration of *Mario Kart* sticks rigidly to 17-year-old mechanics, imposing predetermined finishing positions with unabashed elastic-banding (and, in later games, unleashing the dreaded blue shell). But as much as *Mario Kart* tries to regulate and even punish player skill, everyone keeps coming back to it. Experienced players can learn shortcuts and exploit its attempts to level the playing field, while casual ones can appreciate its assistance. The first to feature online and sporting a series-best course selection, the DS version still serves unsurpassed social and solo kart racing, all in a handy handheld format.

26: MEDIEVAL II: TOTAL WAR
CREATIVE ASSEMBLY/SEGA: PC
For once, 'total' isn't just hyperbole: these games are as complete a depiction of war as there has been in a videogame – a scale of detail that extends from the swish of individual pike-points to grand diplomacy. The coming months will prove whether *Empire* can transcend it in the longer term, but right now the high water mark is *Medieval II*. Peerless in its depiction of minutiae, the game's sweep of time fixes its thrilling strategic action in the context of crusades and papal politicking – but its historical inspiration never obscures its excellence as a game.

25: FINAL FANTASY XII
SQUARE ENIX: PS2
No game has ever begun quite like *Final Fantasy XII*, in which every member of the cast is massacred. That opening is indicative of the scale in which one of the series' greatest adventures plays out. An empire will fall, says the blurb, and for once it actually does. Other series firsts include realtime battles, the MMORPG-inspired gambit system to control your team, and decent voice acting, while a bounty-hunting subgame sprawls into one of the all-time best JRPG timesinks. A masterpiece.

24: VIRTUA FIGHTER 5
AM2/SEGA: 360, COIN-OP, PS3
One of gaming's great myths is that *VF* is inaccessible to all but the initiated. It takes care of frame-counting junkies, of course, but the core of AM2's series is a beautiful balance of attack, block and counter-attack that anyone can enjoy. Each new entry refines, making that solid animation even more seamless and introducing new characters that seem like they were always there. And for those who think the series austere, you can dress yourself in a silly hat to make a beating all the more painful.

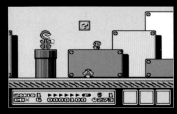

23: ZELDA: THE WIND WAKER
NINTENDO: GC
No one would pretend that *The Wind Waker* is a finished game. But other than its truncated ending, it's as sharply designed as any in the *Zelda* series, and surely the most achingly charming. The art style, so clean, charismatic and breezily fitting to the maritime setting, surely cannot age: the weighty swagger of a Moblin, Link's eyes and curlicued clouds of smoke. Remember the anticipation of setting sail towards a newly sighted island? Hyrule's high seas are always a pleasure to return to.

22: GTA VICE CITY
ROCKSTAR NORTH/ROCKSTAR: PC
Forget its comparative credentials within the *GTA* canon: *Vice City* isn't here because it introduced motorbikes, but for its distillation of a time. The details – Blondie on the radio, tinted specs and shoulder-pads – just add texture to a super-concentrated synthesis of '80s pop culture. Palpably obsessed by film, but wickedly playful in its reference to it, *Vice City* is an acerbic parody of every Mafia movie ever made, evoking a world of wiseguys, crime, coke and corruption that is as equally repulsive as it is nostalgic. Though technically surpassed, the seedy allure of its setting is yet unmatched.

21: METAL GEAR SOLID 3
KOJIMA PRODUCTIONS/KONAMI: PS2, XBOX
If *MGS2* was an exercise in confinement, *MGS3* is one in expansion. The dense and low-tech Soviet jungle broadens Snake's world, making what was right-angled organic, bringing what was distant into breathy proximity. Each area is a bubble of tactical possibilities for both gung-ho action and furtive creeping, and behind every door lies some wry detail, with every interaction a knowing response. Though hardly free of *MGS* flab and bluster, part three shines with the purest intent and most cunning imagination.

20: SUPER MARIO BROS 3
NINTENDO: NES
An early summation of Nintendo's creativity, no 2D game has so many brilliant ideas thrown at it, including a new level structure that could hold them all. Its levels mercilessly dissect and reform the platformer, working every conceivable test for players into their thoroughfares and diversions. Forget the Tanooki suit: what about a literal Frogsuit? Being a Hammer Brother? Even Nintendo could only refine 2D *Mario* after this, the one 8bit game that still shines today, no caveats required.

19: CIVILIZATION IV
FIRAXIS GAMES/2K: PC

Though the quickfire, stripped-down *Civ Rev* intelligently brought *Civilization* into sharp focus for a new audience, it's *IV* that we keep going back to. Deeper and more nuanced, *IV* carefully reconfigured a ruleset that had become punitive and over reliant on micromanagement, and committed us again into possessive obsession. Expanding cultural boundaries is as absorbing as forcing borders wider through armed conflict, making the appearance of Elvis as great a cause for celebration as creating your first tank. By stripping out the petty side to running an empire, *IV* always keeps the bigger picture of your delighted meddling with history to the fore, making it the best of the series – and the genre.

18: CALL OF DUTY 4 MODERN WARFARE
INFINITY WARD/ACTIVISION: 360, PC, PS3

The greatness of Infinity Ward's *COD* series is often attributed to its sense of spectacle and pyrotechnics. *Modern Warfare* has this, but its most profound moments are its quietest: shooting sleeping sailors, listening to whispered encouragement as you snipe an arms dealer, and the flat, bored "That's a hit" that breaks the insulated silence of a gunship. Multiplayer is noisier but just as refined, chaos and strategy balanced, the perks system endlessly tweakable and rewarding. The god of the war genre.

17: WORLD OF WARCRAFT
BLIZZARD/ACTIVISION: MAC, PC

Blizzard's take on the fantasy MMOG has, for over ten million players, almost become the principal function of their PCs. From the gentle early personal questing to the broad and compelling PvP end game, it's all wrapped up in Blizzard's careful, accessible game design. Silicon Valley wags have dubbed it 'the new golf' for its parallels as a social network – certainly, it's now embedded so firmly in gamer culture as to be a paradigm, raising the MMOG stakes with every new expansion.

16: SUPER METROID
NINTENDO: SNES

You might not think it, but *Super Metroid* is a paean to loneliness. Or is it panic? Or claustrophobia? Proof positive that you don't need 5.1 and HD for an atmosphere, Samus' back-and-forth descent deeper and deeper into Brinstar is an exercise in pressure and tension. Its other great trick, the upgrades that eventually transform Samus into a power-suited god, is always balanced against the fact that more power means travelling deeper, closer to the ultimate nightmare of the Mother Brain. Unsettling, occasionally terrifying, and still irresistible, risk and reward are rarely played off each other so well.

15: ROCK BAND 2
HARMONIX/EA: 360, PS3, WII

Three friends and beer are the accessories that catapult *Rock Band 2* to a different level of multiplayer experience. For as long as you take care of yourselves, Harmonix's eye for detail, ear for a tune and nose for how people actually play games socially take care of everything else. Apart from its better notation, it's *RB2*'s unwavering eye on the goal of making you feel like you're in a band that sets it apart, an eye that frees the song list from having to focus on heavy rock and metal, and from presenting players with features that distract from its primary attraction: playing in the band.

14: STREET FIGHTER IV
DIMPS/CAPCOM: 360, COIN-OP, PS3

To call *Street Fighter IV* the pinnacle of reimaginings is faint praise: it's a rethink of the 2D fighter from the ground up, one with the confidence to enable rather than frustrate players. By simplifying inputs, lengthening combo windows and adding an easily executed, totally flexible, Focus attack, *SFIV* opens up the depth of the genre to all-comers without ever compromising the system's depth or fidelity. Finally, fighting is about fighting your opponent rather than the joystick. Finally, *Street Fighter*'s back.

12: GTAIV
ROCKSTAR NORTH/ROCKSTAR: 360, PC, PS3

Rockstar knows that better open worlds don't just mean bigger sandboxes to smash. *GTAIV* brings us a Liberty City that is a bustling, heaving creature in its own right. More profoundly considered than in any other *GTA* before it, the city here is a breathless mix of simulation, exultation and satire that effortlessly envelops the player. Sure, you can still mount the curb to bounce peds off bonnets, or leap from a helicopter on to the Statue of Happiness's face, but Rockstar's triumph is that such actions feel incongruous in the ruins of the American Dream – a place you call home.

13: LEFT 4 DEAD
VALVE: 360, PC

It may be the only online experience outside RPGs in which personality is more important than skill. The player who's a cowardly wretch becomes an almost essential role in your own brilliantly traumatic, draining horror tale, alongside the gung-ho fool and the unflappable veteran. Survival or death drift away from their usual equation to winning or failing as you find yourself in a drama as taught and involving as any of Valve's singleplayer efforts. *L4D*'s design compels co-operation like no other online game. The results may just tell you more about your friends than you wanted to know.

11: LITTLEBIGPLANET
MEDIA MOLECULE/SCE: PS3

LBP can charm just about anyone. Children are entranced dressing its sackcloth dolls and knocking things over, while engineers can build astonishing systems of switches to form nascent CPUs. And then there are the storytellers and the spectacle makers, the Trophy whores and the fanboys – oh, and it seems to satisfy game designers, too. *LBP*'s blend of accessible game-making tools and an aesthetic that marries *Metal Gear* with Dia de los Muertos has proven as fascinating and revolutionary as it promised, and it's getting even better, as new DLC and users' imaginations expand its horizons by the day.

10: YOSHI'S ISLAND
NINTENDO: SNES

Yoshi's Island's timelessly engaging crayon-drawn storybook looks are obvious, but only half its appeal. The variety and depth in its ingenious and challenging level design is the rest. Constructed using its own robust and internally coherent clockwork physics, each evocatively themed stage is almost a puzzle as much it is a test of agility, with linear paths leading into openly rambling areas. It's all designed around Yoshi, of course. He leads a far less perilous existence than Mario, only dazed by enemies and possessing his flutter jump, a moment of hanging in the air that gives you the confidence to leap with a squeak and a strain into the unknown. His ability to throw eggs broadens your opportunities for interaction as you run, bounce and target your way through, your egg stock flowing along behind. And then there's the overall collection quest, which requires painstaking exploration to score the magic 100 for each level. Yoshi subtly modifies the *Mario* formula from movement and reaction to create a sparkling 2D platformer that's all his own.

9: HALO 3
BUNGIE/MICROSOFT GAME STUDIOS: 360

Perhaps the best argument for sequels, *Halo 3* isn't just a superb standalone game, but the culmination of Bungie's decade of redefining and refining the console shooter. Its underrated campaign features fascinatingly AI-driven battles, which, alongside the option to fight alongside three other players, allow dynamically emergent chaos to blossom. Online is where *Halo*'s now-perfect balance of weapons, vehicles and character movement really shines, though, a peerless matchmaking system and ever-changing gametypes offering a skill level and variant to suit any player. For other games, this would be enough, but for *Halo 3* it's the start. Its integration of Theatre mode (which can be used to take screenshots or videos) and Forge (a level editor that can be played collaboratively), and ease of sharing content still hasn't been matched. We haven't even mentioned the campaign's scoring metagame, the special weekend playlists, or the ongoing DLC. In terms of concept, content and coherence, *Halo 3* remains an imposing presence in videogames.

8: SUPER MARIO GALAXY
NINTENDO: WII

"Let's play!" says the rabbit to Mario when he reaches his first planetoid. But what else were you going to do? Woven from networks of plump patchwork globes and shining metal superstructures, breathtaking flights through showers of star bits and shifts from jaunty 8bit riffs to lavish symphonics, *Super Mario Galaxy*'s levels are intoxicating in their imagination and variety. But though change is a constant, Mario's galaxy is never restless or lacks self-assurance – the ground keeps shifting under his feet so that the level of challenge, surprise and delight in play never subsides. Even technology refuses to get in the way – when do you have to think about the camera, the clarity of the graphics, or the precision of the physics? They're so finessed as to never intrude; in a world that changes the rules of gravity and pacing every few minutes, you never feel anything less than in control, eyes fixed on the next sparkling reward. Having taken the three dimensions of *SM64* and stretched them as far as they will go, just where can Mario go next?

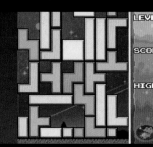

7: TETRIS
ALEXEY PAJITNOV/NINTENDO: VARIOUS

Its appeal is universal. It's been said many times before that *Tetris* taps into everyone's impulse to impose order on chaos, and that base psychological response is surely at the heart of its appeal. Bending the random nature of the blocks to your will is intensely satisfying, but it's a feeling that's sublimely countered by the fear that it's all about to go wrong. And when it does, you only chastise yourself. Don't forget, however, that all the while, *Tetris*' score system is subtly prompting risk-taking, impelling you to build perilous block-wide chasms ripe for pulling off Tetrises. For all that *Tetris* seems to tell you that you're the one playing and the one that is, or should be, in control, all the while the game is playing you. Its skill at levering human compulsions reveals *Tetris*' true nature and genius, its abstract four-square blocks showing videogames' potential to sway behaviour and drive emotion. As with many such perfect games, attempts to bolster the core design fail to add much to it, but as a definitive version, our money's on the breezily presented and portable *Tetris DS*.

6: SUPER MARIO WORLD

NINTENDO: SNES

Super Mario World is a joke. Well, not just one, but actually hundreds of jokes, stuffed with cameos, remakes and reimaginings of 2D lore, all layered over a ravishingly pure platform adventure that dared to play with your assumptions about the form. Why should an exit be the exit? Why should the bottom of the screen always mean death? And why should you just drop like a stone when you've soared into the sky? But then, Mario set those assumptions in the first place, so there's no one else more appropriate to set about questioning them. On the surface it's simply a refinement of the 2D platformer, but in the hands it's a sugar rush of new possibilities and new worlds waiting for you to explore each of their corners. Which other game would build a secret world, then another super secret world hidden right in the middle of it, then spell out in coins what a Super Player you are for completing it? In substance, *Super Mario World* is merely the best 2D platform game ever made: in reality, it's more play, more of the time, than anything else.

5: ZELDA: A LINK TO THE PAST

NINTENDO: SNES

It takes a special kind of confidence for a game to only reveal its central conceit several hours into its course. That's exactly how *A Link To The Past* presents its dual world setup, first giving you, transformed into a pink rabbit, a taste of a mysterious somewhere, and then showing how it's a mirror of the world you've just come from. Except it isn't, quite. *LTTP* also shows great confidence in allowing you to figure out for yourself the ways in which the two worlds differ. And, as you do, Hyrule opens up into a canvas of enormous and captivating possibility. Ripe with puzzles and secrets that are never condescendingly spelt out for you, the map is a resource to pore over, every ridgeline and cliff face worth testing, every rock worth lifting. It's hard to imagine how *LTTP* could be recreated quite as well in three dimensions, because its taut design is a document of the value in the unwavering gaze of two. Knowing that every detail is laid out before you, *LTTP*'s designers made its intricate and multi-layered dungeons the apex of 2D level design. Much of this self-belief is down to it having confidence in you, a bond of enduring respect that lends *LTTP* a maturity that only now is beginning to fit its years.

4: RESIDENT EVIL 4

CAPCOM: WII

In the common mob, Capcom found something infinitely more terrifying than shambling monsters: hate, and the idea of casting the player as 'un forastero' – an outsider. The opening of *Resident Evil 4*, a short series of straggled encounters and traps leading to a face-off against an entire village, sets a relentless pace that never lets up. From here it's all up for the player and down for Leon as gaming's greatest rollercoaster picks up speed. The genius isn't in the wicked imaginations behind the countless bizarre monsters and pantomime villains, though, but in the restraint with which they're used: each given a short section that perfectly exploits their characteristics, and then discarded. The structure is a masterpiece of variation, always combining and recombining enemies, your weapons and position, and one-off elements of the gameworld so no two fights play out in the same way. Add to this the greatest lineup of bosses ever to roll off the Capcom production line, a mix of environments that runs from rural atavism to baroque vanity projects and the inevitable secret lab (complete with the series' most terrifying enemy, the Regenerator), and a script smart enough to play up the schlock factor. Then imagine all of this in a beautiful Frankenstein's monster where you can't see the stitches. Irresistible.

INDUSTRY PICK
MARK HEALEY
CO-FOUNDER, MEDIA MOLECULE
SUPER MARIO 64
NINTENDO: N64

I chose my favourite game not only because of its inherent quality, but also because of the people I was with when I first played it.

Trenched in for the weekend, with a stash of supplies, a huge empty room with nothing but the latest offering from Nintendo, and a huge TV to play it on, we fired it up.

"Ooooh, that's nice: look, you can squash his face! Heheheheheh."

"Go on, then – press start."

"Cool! Someone's baked us a cake – let's go get it."

"Woah."

"Hey, check it out! It's like having a real little remote-control man. Wahey!"

Lots of laughter, loads of "woah"s and many "Give the controller to me, you muppet" exclamations later, we had a stack of fond memories, all filed under 'Super Mario 64'.

3: HALF-LIFE 2

VALVE: 360, PC, PS3

Gordon Freeman is a floating gun. Sometimes he's just a crowbar. He exists only in the reactions of others, his repertoire of self-expression locked within a reticule. And yet, through Freeman, you're rooted in a world with a conviction that almost no other game can claim. Beyond the character chit-chat, the story of this world is riddled through the environments: from the draconian sterility of City 17 to the lonely roads of the coast, there are tales of desolation, atrocity and loss, never demanding your attention but pervading your unconscious. And yet for all the high-minded accolades that are lavished upon its world-building, this is a game that revels in halving zombies with saw-blades. It's easy to reflect on Valve's achievements in quiet moments, but *Half-Life 2*'s combat, though mechanically aged, is no less brilliantly orchestrated. That first rooftop flight; that protracted feud with a Combine chopper; that sudden, shattering encounter with a pack of Hunters as they effortlessly outflank you – adrenaline shunts into you with every spent shell. In a genre that avariciously cannibalises itself, it's remarkable that *Half-Life 2*'s strengths either remain unsurpassed or entirely its own – but with so many to choose from, perhaps other games just don't know where to start.

2: SUPER MARIO 64

NINTENDO: N64

Before Mario existed in 3D, there was a faceless, shapeless block. Shigeru Miyamoto insisted that before there was a game, before gaming's most famous character was recognisable, he had to be fun to control. *Super Mario 64* didn't, as is often claimed, translate Mario from 2D to 3D. It built a new world around that block, invented a structure – the stars which gradually unlocked new areas to explore, the playpark hub world – that fitted it perfectly, and enlisted the industry's most brilliantly surreal minds to make it feel real. Why shouldn't you jump into a painting to explore it, or a clock face, or a toy house? Why should a world stay the same size, or a level be the same every time you enter it? There's no reason, of course, and there's no rhyme to how it all slots together – from the carpet that travels on a rainbow to the castle's secret slide. *Super Mario 64*'s greatest achievement is how effortless it feels in the hands, how a child can spend hours running around the first level, and an adult can do exactly the same. It's that rarest of combinations: intoxicatingly deep and imaginative, as simple as cause and reaction, and consistently surprising until the very last star. Over a decade and countless imitators later, that first venture into 3D is still breathtaking.

Seeing Hyrule as an adult remains shocking. Hyrule town is a mess of burned houses, grey stone and hideous ghouls. The castle is suspended over a lake of fire, the bones of those foolhardy enough to defend it scattered on the ground

1: ZELDA: OCARINA OF TIME

NINTENDO: N64

Over a decade after release, *The Legend Of Zelda: Ocarina Of Time* has achieved a distinction reserved for a true classic. It's been forgotten. Writing about it garners nothing but grandiose adverbs and scattered memories of Hyrule Field. It's 'unquestionably' and (even better) 'indefinably' great.

Deserved or not, opaque hyperbole doesn't help explain why *Ocarina* works so well now, particularly in terms of it being a big-budget adventure in a technology-driven industry. To be blunt, if you want sunsets look at *Far Cry 2*; if you want advanced animations then play with *Assassin's Creed*. Visually and procedurally, *Ocarina* can't compete.

They're not small considerations – the drop in resolution alone from current standards to an N64 is huge – and yet here it is. There's a difference between dazzle and brilliance. Sophistication – it's the most important concept in videogame design, the balance and blending of function, fun and feedback into a coherent environment.

Ocarina understands how people play games, the curiosity that weighs up cause and effect, the importance of the player's own impulses in creating entertainment. Link's inventory is made for experimentation, almost every item having subtleties to be discovered. The hookshot has a simple function: to be shot at targets and used to pull Link towards them. But it can also be used in combat, its effect

surprisingly variable. Hit a bat and it dies; hit a lizard and it freezes; hit the glutinous body of a Yum-Yum and the hook sinks, freezing the enemy as Link is pulled in. Link can't swing his sword or hammer underwater, but the hookshot's spring-loaded action means it can still be fired as a makeshift harpoon.

Implicit in the latter example is another of *Ocarina*'s rare qualities, one that dovetails with the inventory. It's a type of logic that's recherché, but utterly resonant: the hookshot finds purchase in wood, but bounces off stone; hitting hollow walls with your sword produces a wobblier thwack; when Link is on fire, swinging or rolling puts out the flames more quickly; Link can't wield the adult shield as a child, but he can hide under it like a turtle; iron boots increase your weight but slow you down; cutting a Deku Baba at the stalk gets you a Deku stick (a tool to light fires and hit enemies with), while cutting it in the bud gets you Deku nuts (ammo for your slingshot and basic flashbangs). In some cases you could say there's no logic, simply superficial association, such as with the tunics: blue allows Link to breathe underwater, red to survive extreme

temperatures. That's fair in isolation, but in the context of *Ocarina*'s internal logic of palettes and themed properties there's no dissonance. *Ocarina* plays with appearance and effect like this: placing a bomb under one of the many Gossip Stones around Hyrule makes it prepare for lift off, then blast into the sky like a rocket. It may not be realistic, but as visual association and as play it's a delight to discover.

This inventory is the core of *Ocarina*, and the world and challenges are the fruit.

THE NARRATIVE IS LINEAR BUT THE STRUCTURE IS BRANCHING, EVENTUALLY ALLOWING YOU FREE ACCESS TO THE MANY DIVERSIONS AND SIDEQUESTS

The narrative is linear but the structure is branching, beginning with few choices as to where to go and what to do, eventually allowing you free access to the many diversions and sidequests in its world, and then narrowing your focus as the final battle draws nearer. This is combined with the fact that there are two worlds – you're a child to begin with, then an adult in a nightmare future, and soon have the capability to change between the two at will.

They rub off on each other. One of the challenges you face as a child is destroying the dodongo dragons infesting a cave on Death

CLINT HOCKING
X-COM: UFO DEFENSE
MICROPROSE: AMIGA, CD32, PC, PS

As much as I would love to talk about why *Fallout 2* or *System Shock 2* moved and inspired me and changed the way I thought about games, both of those games have already been given a new life and a new audience by similarly minded developers. So instead I'll talk about a game that has not (yet) been tapped for a modern update (though I hear rumours).

X-Com: UFO Defense [known in Europe as *UFO: Enemy Unkown*] has been lauded as the best PC game ever made, and while that's tough to validate, there is no question that the game was powerful on many fronts.

The scope of the game is stunning – talk about an open world where you can go anywhere and do anything... In *X-Com*, you can not only go anywhere on Earth – you even go to Mars! You not only fight on the ground in the streets of Rio de Janeiro or in the open wilderness of the South African Veldt, you fight in the air – engaging UFOs with interceptors over the Alps. You construct and manage your own bases, manage political relationships with all the countries of the world – protecting them in exchange for funding, while all the time conducting research and experiments on captured alien life forms and technology to upgrade your structures, vehicles and soldiers. Go anywhere, do anything indeed.

The game has politics, strategy, management, tactics – and it has a heart. *X-Com* is the first game in which I ever built real relationships with characters through the actions of game mechanics and dynamics. Recruited soldiers would live or die based on my decisions in combat, and those that lived would get better and better... I would grow attached to them, give them nicknames, make sure they had back-up and the best gear. And when they died, I would mourn.

Having a promising rookie battle his way up to a psionically-trained colonel in flying powered armour is the height of accomplishment. Having him singlehandedly hold a chokepoint in your high command while Chrysalids, Mutons and Floaters overrun his position is sheer terror. Having him give his life to save your base is the very meaning of sacrifice – it is the beating heart of a game that has still not been outdone in many respects.

Personally, there is no question that the investment I had in my soldiers in *X-Com* was central to the vision of the buddy characters in *Far Cry 2*. If the difficulties we faced there are any indication of what the Gollop brothers faced, then their accomplishment cannot be overstated – nor can the complexity of the challenges that lie ahead for anyone who might be reimagining this game for a modern audience.

HORSE WHISPERER

Rescuing Epona from the wicked stablemaster Ingo isn't just a great moment because of the races you have to go through to do it, the song you have to learn as a child to tame her as an adult, or the escape over the walls into Hyrule field. It's a great moment because the horse is an outstanding mechanic: practical, an enabler, and most of all a simple joy to ride. Epona remains the absolutely convincing adaptation of what riding should feel like in a videogame – *Shadow Of The Colossus* took almost its entire concept, if not execution, from this one detail – and still makes the dashes and leaps across Hyrule Field exhilarating.

The Shadow Temple is introduced like no other dungeon: 'Here is gathered Hyrule's bloody history of greed and hatred'. And you get its compass, guide to its treasure chests, near its beginnning

Mountain, the home of the Gorons. After your success you return as an adult, but find the Goron Village desolate. A single Goron remains, rolling endlessly around the abandoned village. Trying to stop him with your hands or projectiles doesn't work, but laying a cunning trap with a bomb does. Startled by your approach, he shouts: "Hear my name and tremble! I am Link! Hero of the Gorons!" You have to laugh.

But it's a serious piece of design. Quite apart from the thematic coherence of the whole there are the threads that cross different branches of *Ocarina*, and one of its most simple ideas – what about making a dungeon a story, with a wider significance in the game's world? If *Ocarina* was about running from dungeon to dungeon, it might drag, but it's a master of sleight-of-hand narrative. Heading to a temple, you'll be sidetracked before you get close, the Gorons are enslaved by Ganon or your former home is overrun with monsters. Put as baldly as that, it seems like a crude diversionary tactic, but they're story-led missions that establish Hyrule's coherence as a place, as a world, and free up the dungeons' pure puzzling for conceptual flourishes.

What about, for example, an ice dungeon that is actually about ice, that leads to a water dungeon about water? Returning to the Zora kingdom as an adult you find it frozen, with stretches of ice to slip around on and get used to the effect it has on Link's momentum. Afterwards there's a series of jumps across revolving icebergs, tipping like seesaws as you land, to get to a cave. Inside, everything is constructed from ice, and the game is to play with its properties. Blue icicles wait to be shattered; ice statues turn transparent, detectable only by their steaming breath, before reappearing to freeze you; a huge revolving blade covers a rink you have to scramble on for silver rupees, before the standard block puzzle is turned into a sliding maze. It's play rather than work, the monsters kept to a minimum, and of course there are prizes at the end: iron boots, a blue tunic (for walking and breathing underwater) and the means to warp to Lake Hylia and the Water Temple. This is typical of the organic logic with which you're guided around Hyrule.

Then the Water Temple. Thought of as the most mind-bending dungeon in the series, it's an advanced test of spatial awareness and memory. The theme might be water, but the inspiration is deep-sea diving: watching Link sink to the bottom of the giant branching cave that forms its centrepiece, legs uselessly searching for purchase as bubbles rise, it's all too obvious. "The fact of the matter is, I love diving in the sea," **Eiji Aonuma**, the game's director, has said, adding: "I thought I should put plenty of diving puzzles in it." The enemy in the Water Temple is your own sense of direction; the puzzles aren't particularly hard, but finding them, realising that they're even there, is another story. It makes you sink through water, swim on its surface, raise and lower its level, dodge whirlpools, swim in rapids and climb waterfalls. Part of its effectiveness is the sound distortion

CHANGING ROOMS

Within certain environments the standard thirdperson view of Link's back changes to a fixed perspective in a manner that naturally fuses with challenges. The top floor of the Fire Temple is a narrow stone maze, complete with obligatory Indiana Jones balls of doom rolling around. The camera zooms up and out, high enough to show the tops of the walls that form the maze's paths. Two rooms later, Link finds himself at one end of the maze again – on top of the walls, which he now has to navigate by hurdling the deceptively long gaps. You're here in the standard thirdperson, yet you've already seen the route while negotiating the maze with the perfect measuring tool – perspective. It's entirely possible to gauge without this touch, but anyone who falls once or twice and has to re-negotiate the maze can't fail to notice the little helping hand.

underwater, accompanied always by the muffled clump of iron boots and sluggish movement. In any other game, it would be a stretch too far to tie in the enemies: here, the sub-boss is yourself, a Dark Link that mimics your movesets, and the final boss is simply a mass of water. The implications are obvious, but never overbearing.

The final coda to the Water Temple is the restoration of Hyrule Lake. As you leave, the parched riverbed fills up with crystal-clear water, the overcast sky clears, and the sun appears. What *Ocarina* does here is so much more than the current fashion of surface lushness. When Lake Hylia is restored, it's a great toy to play around in, but also lets you swim to a new island and a fishing minigame, or fire an arrow into the newly rising sun to

YOU'LL SPEND MORE TIME STANDING STILL THAN IN ANY OTHER GREAT GAME, LOOKING INTO CORNERS, WATCHING A ROUTE, WAITING FOR A CLUE AS TO WHAT'S NEXT

obtain flaming arrows (another playful flourish in *Ocarina*'s internal logic). This is how *Ocarina* begins at the east end of the map and takes you to the west during a single quest, maintains internal consistency – your next trip after the Water Temple, incidentally, is to the desert – and gives extraordinary significance to your achievements.

There's another reason why these achievements matter, and in the current climate a surprising one. *Ocarina* is really hard. It's a difficulty far removed from the current meaning, though, rarely about your ability to fight, and never about manual dexterity or confusion over where to go. The difficulty is in puzzles that test physical and perceptual skills in a 3D space. You'll spend more time standing still than in any other great game, looking into corners, watching a route you'll have to run through, waiting for a clue as to what's

going to happen. It's the reason that the 'discovery' chime brings such a rush.

These puzzles are inextricable from the internal design of the temples. The Forest Temple, the first adult dungeon, is not a conceptual challenge in the physical sense of water, but rather concentrates on thematic coherence. Composed of two main floors and two sub-levels, it literally twists itself into new shapes as Link gradually progresses, two corridors spinning 90° when triggered. These triggers have to be hit with arrows and the second, encased in ice, deserves particular mention: you can see the switch, you know an arrow triggers it, but that arrows can't penetrate ice. Four platforms revolve around a torch in the centre of the room: stand on one, fire your arrow through the flames at the

right moment, and the ice melts. It's simple put like that, but it's the forerunner for the later puzzle design. Link has shot switches, burned things with fire, and obtained fire from torches before this point, but the combination has to occur to the mind before the physical attempt is made.

There's a subtle, but absolutely crucial, distinction to be made here: although you're doing a lot of similar things in *Ocarina*, very rarely are you doing exactly the same thing. The puzzles encourage creative use of the tools, so while the solution might ultimately be 'hookshot to that point', the real challenge is often working out exactly how. This is where *Ocarina* is pre-eminent: its faith in your spatial reasoning. Even now, no thirdperson game has used 3D space and the possibilities for player manipulation in a manner that deserves

comparison. It makes you consider Link's position when triggering an action, and look upwards and downwards constantly as well as straight ahead.

If *Ocarina*'s puzzles demand a mental leap of faith or a clever eye, however, the reward is the rare semiotic richness and thematic coherence in their design. When you first enter the Forest Temple (reaching it via the Forest of Illusion, a network of dead ends you have to negotiate by sound alone) four ghosts see you, and take off. When exploring the temple these ghostly sisters appear in paintings, disappearing with a mocking chuckle when you get too close. When you gain a bow, however, you can destroy their images (if they don't see you first) and draw the ghosts into the open. In other words, a narrative element assumes mechanical importance partway through the dungeon – form becomes function. Another ghost features in a huge painting soon afterwards – too easy, you think, as the arrow hits home.

The game might not look like a spring chicken, but Link's animation is surprisingly fluid. Miyamoto was apparently upset Nintendo couldn't fit a horse in the mo-cap studio for Epona

Games can be played with time. A windmill you visit as an adult is home to an angry man who says, "It's all that ocarina kid's fault! Next time he comes around here, I'm gonna mess him up!" But he'll still teach you a song, which you can then use in the past to mess him up

> Oh, no! A storm again!!
> You played the Ocarina again,
> didn't you!!
> Grrrrrrrrrrrrrr!!

LINK UP PLAY

Perhaps the real reason Link's so empowering is that controlling him is peerless, reconciling two opposites – player freedom and developer control – in a manner as functional as it is graceful. Automatic controls take over where repeated player input would be unnecessary, such as jumping at an edge, while the N64 pad's face buttons are mapped on to the screen, the icons replicating their colour and placement, with a visual representation of the player's chosen item or, in the case of the A button, a single word to indicate a context-sensitive action. Instant access to a selection of your inventory, and all of the clambering, opening and fighting moves needed: the balance is perfect.

Of course it is. Five blocks fall from the ceiling, each rendered on all six sides with sections of the painting, and a timer starts as you try to recreate it. A giant-sized puzzle that adds another layer to the dungeon's theme, trapping the ethereal by symbolically fixing it in place. All of this dungeon's puzzles are linked to illusion: a chequer-board floor with a falling chequer-board ceiling, a skeleton that walks on air, a room whose doors are opened by revolving its floor, a corridor with walls drenched in blood.

The Forest Temple's boss is Ganondorf – except it's Phantom Ganon, another symbol, another echo. It's typical that the strategy needed for defeating this enemy has been prefigured: it attacks from multiple paintings at once and you have to quickly shoot in firstperson, Link's body being wracked with electricity every time you miss. After it's defeated, the real Ganondorf speaks from somewhere, complimenting you on defeating a poor copy of him, mocking. He banishes the puppet to 'the gap between dimensions' and after its death rattle you are finally left alone, the insistent beeping of your remaining

heart the only constant at the illusion's conclusion. You've killed four sisters, condemned a spirit to limbo, and Ganondorf is watching, waiting for you. You pick up your heart container and run to the light, away from it all. Some Hero of Time. Some Link.

It's a triumph, but a peculiarly serious one – Link's childhood friend Saria is bound to the Temple as the Forest Sage, and gone forever from Hyrule. The world of *Ocarina* is multifaceted, and like all great works is a magpie, grabbing plot details and visual cues from hugely varied influences: the Sword In The Stone, Peter Pan, A Christmas Carol (the gold skulltulas), the Pied Piper and even something like Maurice Ravel's Bolero (the Bolero of Fire theme's percussion is borrowed wholesale). These are the colours and flavours of Hyrule, but the meat is the mythology it all revolves around, three figures, three powers, and a perfectly geometric symbol. Link is gaming's greatest adventurer: he doesn't have Nathan Drake's halftuck or the Prince's wall running, but then nor do his ironic quips come to the fore when faced with a new challenge. More importantly, he's not defined by a single ability. Link never speaks, his only sounds the grunts of exertion and cries of pain you cause while exploring, the game concentrating personality in those he talks to.

The creation is brilliant: a character with a backstory and a presence in the world, but one foot firmly planted outside of its repeated goings-on. At the very beginning of the game, Navi the fairy is sent to wake him up. She enters the sleeping Link's room and her little "Hello!" speaks of a hundred lie-ins, a hundred wishes for just five minutes more. The world can wait; Link's knackered. "Hey, c'mon!" she insists, and Link, the Hero of Time, finally crawls from his pit. "Can Hyrule's destiny really depend on such a lazy boy?" she wonders. It couldn't be any other way. The

THE OCARINA

The titular ocarina is a mechanic par excellence. The base function is as an all-purpose key: one item to serve as a deus ex machina in the place of multiple contrived ones. The genius, though, is how deeply the ocarina is rooted in the world as a digressive and subversive toy. Play the right song in front of a cow to get milk, teach a scarecrow a tune as a child then call him to your aid as an adult – but make sure you don't choose the forgetful one of the pair – then use it as a Hylian mobile phone to call Saria and ask where you're going next. Only a supremely confident game would create a day and night cycle that alters what can be done in the world, then give you a song to change it at a whim, or tunes to simply teleport. And then that golden touch, letting the player freestyle and change between tones and semitones: of no practical value within the game but still being played on YouTube today.

little tricks – making Link look a little bored with exposition, or run towards the interesting bits during cutscenes – further help the player's identification, but there's one part of his characterisation that, in terms of confluence with the player and the game's narrative, can't be ignored.

Link's role in *Zelda*'s triumvirate is as the bearer of the Triforce of Courage, and this makes clear a surprising aspect of *Ocarina*. It's about failure and persistence. You fail to save the Deku Tree, and are blamed for its death. You open the Sacred Realm for Ganondorf as a child, and let him decimate Hyrule. You can't

much, no other game has that brutal twist between adult and child, no other game is set in a world that you've already failed to save.

This isn't the whole story. It never could be. The problem with looking at *Ocarina*'s woods is that you miss the trees, the innumerable tiny touches that fit no pattern but make its world so detailed, so rich, so much fun to be in. The triumphant jingle that grants the same importance to capturing a bug as it does to finding a legendary item; the Hyrule Field theme beginning with the notes of the Sun's Song, distorted to sound like birdsong. Diving hundreds of feet in Zora's cavern; causing a

NO OTHER GAME HAS THAT BRUTAL TWIST BETWEEN ADULT AND CHILD, AND NO OTHER GAME IS SET IN A WORLD THAT YOU'VE ALREADY FAILED TO SAVE

stop him capturing Princess Zelda. Your friends become sages, necessary to stand a chance against Ganondorf, but removing them from the game's world permanently. When you finally enter Hyrule Castle and confront Ganondorf, a world rests on your shoulders. Link's destiny is irresistible, because no other game makes you feel so responsible for so

This is Z-targeting. Navi, your fairy helper, flies to enemies and allows you to 'fix' the camera to their position – this letterboxes the screen and changes Link's movement and stance, allowing full access to his offensive and defensive repertoire

storm inside a windmill; finding a message in a bottle; winning a cow for your house; scaring people with masks; scoring big at the bombchu alley; buying magic beans; landing a lunker; chasing chickens; racing horses. Walking on nothing but air for the first time. Diving into battle against something massive, with a plan and a Master Sword.

The coherence and pacing of Link's world are no happy accident. They're the result of some of rare craftsmanship. *Ocarina*'s structure is deep and intricate, in harmony with an inventory that knows what its players most want things for is to use them on other things. How unusual is it to play a game that refuses to condescend to its players, and turns that complicity into a bravura performance? How unusual to have such faith in players, trusting them to experiment and explore, and then build your narrative and world around that? *Ocarina Of Time* is here in the list not because Nintendo had the power and wisdom to make a great game, but because it had the courage to make a unique one.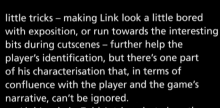

9/10
"KILLZONE 2 UNLEASHES THE POWER
OF THE PS3. NOTHING ON ANY CONSOLE
COMES CLOSE."
VIDEOGAMER.COM

9/10
"THE MOST IMPRESSIVE LOOKING
GAME EVER"
OFFICIAL PLAYSTATION MAGAZINE

Only on PLAYSTATION® 3

PLAYSTATION 3

MASTER OF THE ARTS

TRIP HAWKINS TELLS US WHAT IT WAS LIKE TO LEAD EA TO THE PROMISED LAND – AND THE 3DO MULTIPLAYER TO ITS DOOM

We were right, you know, way back in issue zero: '3DO is the videogame future'. It just wasn't a future that the console would live to see. If there's a message to be taken from **Trip Hawkins**' remarkable career, it's that all failure is relative. Even in its death, 3DO was a triumph of technology – the project as a whole pre-empting innovation within the industry that continues to be felt to this day.

"I find it amusing that I am better known for failing with 3DO than for being the founder of

Panasonic FZ-1 REAL 3DO Interactive Multiplayer

Electronic Arts," Hawkins says when we ask him if there are any final words he'd like to add to the 3DO story. "It says something about our culture; morbid fascination; recognition that our society needs to fail in order to find the path to advancement. Out of 3DO came processor technology that is now in the Sony and Nintendo consoles, and insight about digital video that led to the DVD format. Key executives at Google came from 3DO. And here I am at Digital Chocolate bringing some of the same kind of thinking to the iPhone. And that is why we are here talking about it now."

3DO became the whipping boy of the videogame media – a fact that becomes apparent when looking back through the early issues of **Edge**, wherein the tone swings with vicious speed from early adulation to barely mediated contempt. But time has granted a more objective view – the scorn with which Hawkins' enterprise was later dismissed only reflects the promise it originally held.

"I think one of the things you often see in the technology business is ideas that are ahead of their time," says Hawkins. "There were ideas embodied in 3DO that are now very common in the marketplace. What plagued 3DO is the fact that we were pushing the envelope on 3D

graphics and the amount of performance required to do it, the amount of memory required to do it, and the fact that you needed an optical disc drive back when CD-ROM drives were still fairly expensive." Hawkins chuckles as the list of 3DO's ambition grows: "*And* it was a little bit too difficult to do digital video with that generation of technology, *and* we were trying to use it as a set-top box, too – you know, there were a lot of interesting things that we were pioneering and integrating together. In any human endeavour, the pioneers end up choking on trail dust and getting arrows in their backs."

But not always, as Hawkins himself has proven. Familiar though it has now become, EA is a company that was assuredly radical in its conception. Its success has shaped the industry and become the measure of ventures that came after it, becoming the largest thirdparty publisher in the world prior to the recent merger of Activision and Vivendi. But all success is relative. As mighty as EA became under Hawkins' guidance, it too bears scars of his risky futurism – and though his farsighted schemes ultimately paid off, many of his ideas foundered in a market ill-prepared for change, only to be later adopted by the industry at large.

Photography:
Winni Wintermeyer

Pinball Construction Set, MULE, The Seven Cities Of Gold and *Archon* were among EA's earliest games, contracted while Hawkins still worked from home

"While at Apple, I refined the three foundational ideas behind EA, all of which used Hollywood as a reference point," says Hawkins. "One, the software artist; two, creating the equivalent of a recording studio for games; and three, direct distribution to retailers. Idea number two led to what became known later as EA's Artist Work Station, which gave software artists more powerful tools while also making it easier to support more platforms in the market – in other words, it made it much easier to get the

of Nintendo, Game Over, recounts a board meeting in which, under heavy criticism from financial advisors about the direction he had led EA, Hawkins took off his shoe and beat the table in order to get attention. Having emphatically gained the ear of the board, Hawkins recanted his position on consoles and, in his words, "ate a lot of humble pie". Within two years, Hawkins had redeemed himself but, typically, at great risk. The first buy of Nintendo cartridges cost four million dollars, more than the value of EA's entire PC software inventory. But while Hawkins' approach to Nintendo was bold enough, EA's most brilliant gambit was to reverse-engineer the Mega Drive hardware and use this to broker a favourable agreement licence with Sega.

"EA never did any more than dabble with the NES, but we bet the farm on the Sega Mega Drive and our risky strategy ended up paying off and transformed EA as a company. As one illustration, the company's stock value had been stagnant for a number of years, but after we demonstrated growth from Sega, our market capitalisation in a two-year period rose from $60 million to $2 billion."

Hawkins had secured EA's future, at least for this generation of hardware. Immediately, he began to formulate how EA would conquer the

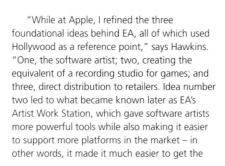

"I WORRIED THAT IF NINTENDO MONOPOLISED THE INDUSTRY, THE PUBLIC WOULD GET ONLY ONE TYPE OF GAME AND ONLY ONE COMPANY WOULD SURVIVE"

Atari 800 and Apple II versions of a game out of the same primary studio initiative.

"The irony of these foundational ideas is that the public never really cared that much about the artists behind the games," Hawkins says. "And the direct sales gambit was a disaster – it took us three years to really make it work. In hindsight we would have been in much better financial shape if we had used distributors the first two years and then made the transition."

Of the remaining ideas that shaped the birth of EA, only the Artist Work Station has persisted in robust health to this day. But while the increasing costs eventually drove the industry towards sequels and branded licences to reduce risk, EA's efforts to foster independent talent had already produced standout titles like *Pinball Construction Set*, *Archon*, *MULE* and *The Seven Cities Of Gold*, establishing the company as a major force in the personal computer revolution.

Though Hawkins ensured EA's early rise in the PC market, by 1989, his disregard for consoles had almost brought about the company's doom. "Atari caused the console market to implode in 1983 and the videogame was written off by the press as a hula-hoop. When Nintendo tried to bring it back in 1985, virtually everyone in the western game industry did not believe they would succeed."

Accounts differ as to how easily Hawkins came to the realisation that EA would have to enter the console market. David Sheff's history

next. In December 1990, Hawkins passed on day-to-day management to Larry Probst and rumours quickly surfaced in The New York Times that he had a secret project under construction deep in the California woods.

"Sega, Nintendo, and any other hardware licensors would have eyes in the back of their head about EA from that moment forward, to prevent a repeat occurrence," says Hawkins. "I wanted the industry to have a good, open gaming platform and worried that if Nintendo monopolised the industry the public would get only one type of game and only one company would survive. In talking with other industry players like Microsoft, IBM, Philips and even Sony, I got the feeling that nobody was going

TRICK UP THE SLEEVE

In an attempt to clearly align videogames with the creativity of other media, Hawkins developed another idea for EA: to use the bold design and shape of record covers as a packaging format for games. "This again derived directly from the big idea of the software artist and wanting to have packaging that represented both the creativity of the product and of the creator," says Hawkins. "But the other thing that I had on my mind in 1980 was that game packaging was amateurish or expensive. I knew that record albums were both satisfying and low-cost." Indeed, the covers for Interplay's *Wasteland* and Free Fall Associates' *Archon* would be little out of place among a selection of striking album cover designs. But the idea proved to be sadly shortlived, as Hawkins explains: "To compete for sales we had to shift away from the album eventually and spend more of the space on the packaging to explain what was in the game."

Early print adverts for EA pictured its stable of software artists in the cool repose of rockstars

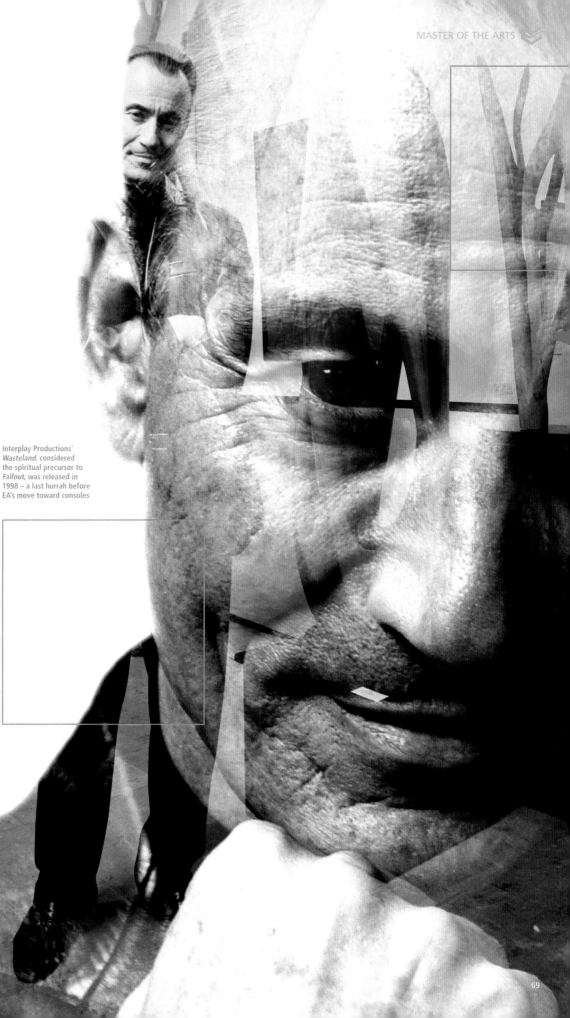

Interplay Productions'
Wasteland, considered
the spiritual precursor to
Fallout, was released in
1998 – a last hurrah before
EA's move toward consoles

to do anything about it. For example, nobody in the PC hardware and systems software market had any interest in gaming or, for that matter, in multimedia, optical disc drives, 3D graphics, joysticks or social features."

3DO was formed out of a perceived strategic necessity, but its timing proved disastrous. The thrilling, far-sighted technologies it brought together were perhaps spurned by the big industry players for a good reason.

"A lot of people struggled with the idea of the 'Multiplayer' – that more than one type of media content could be used on the same platform," says Hawkins. "Sega and Nintendo went to great lengths to point out that it would be silly to have a product that was any more

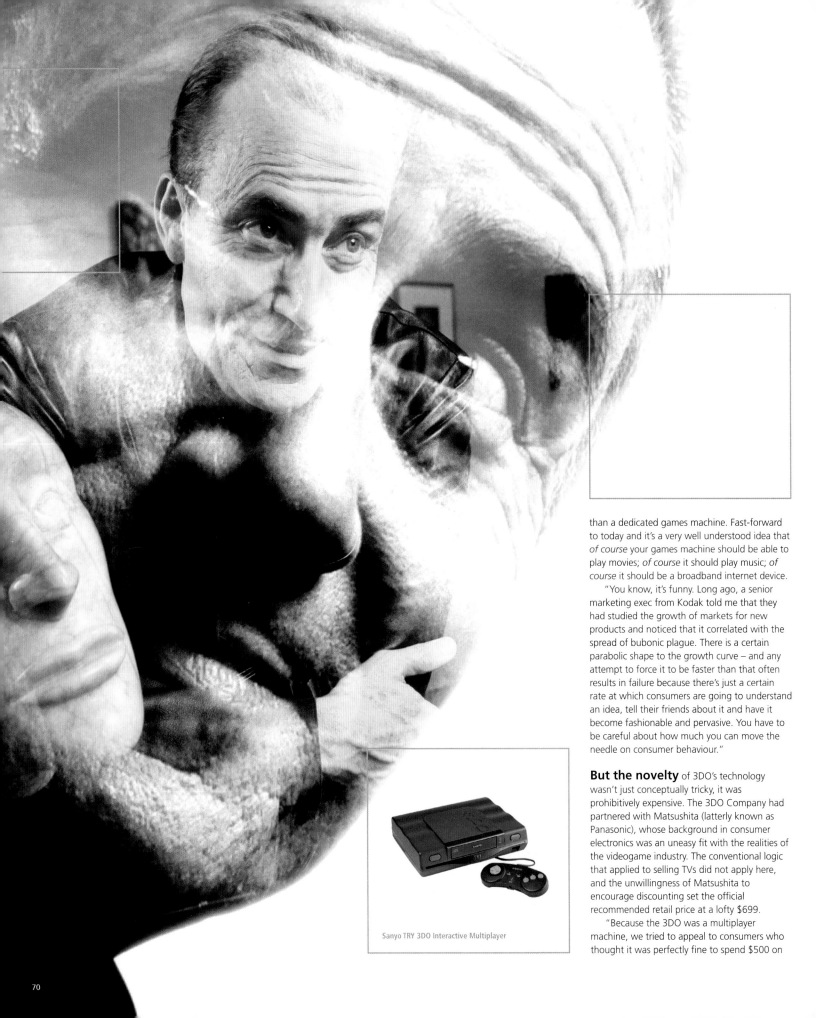

than a dedicated games machine. Fast-forward to today and it's a very well understood idea that *of course* your games machine should be able to play movies; *of course* it should play music; *of course* it should be a broadband internet device.

"You know, it's funny. Long ago, a senior marketing exec from Kodak told me that they had studied the growth of markets for new products and noticed that it correlated with the spread of bubonic plague. There is a certain parabolic shape to the growth curve – and any attempt to force it to be faster than that often results in failure because there's just a certain rate at which consumers are going to understand an idea, tell their friends about it and have it become fashionable and pervasive. You have to be careful about how much you can move the needle on consumer behaviour."

But the novelty of 3DO's technology wasn't just conceptually tricky, it was prohibitively expensive. The 3DO Company had partnered with Matsushita (latterly known as Panasonic), whose background in consumer electronics was an uneasy fit with the realities of the videogame industry. The conventional logic that applied to selling TVs did not apply here, and the unwillingness of Matsushita to encourage discounting set the official recommended retail price at a lofty $699.

"Because the 3DO was a multiplayer machine, we tried to appeal to consumers who thought it was perfectly fine to spend $500 on

Sanyo TRY 3DO Interactive Multiplayer

Goldstar 3DO Interactive Multiplayer

a nice colour television and even $1,000 on a nice stereo system. We thought, sure, there's a perception that a game system is only worth about $200, but maybe with more functionality and more features and more power we can establish a higher price point. But clearly that was not the case at the time."

In the event of its US launch, most retailers opted to sell it at $599, but this also proved too high, leading to slightly tepid Christmas sales of around 50,000 units. Such sales seem miniscule

million machines as fast as it could in order to get the volume up to the point where the software industry felt comfortable. This was all a hard thing to communicate to a company like Matsushita. They were like: 'Hey, if we ship a new colour TV, it's OK if we have a small unit volume the first year. We wouldn't want to sell it at a discount because that would undermine our dealers'. But the reason you can get away with that is that a TV is backwards compatible: it already runs all the old shows."

Despite further reductions in the price, 3DO was underperforming. In attempting to create an open standard, 3DO neglected the selling power of exclusive games, and strong launch titles such as *Crash 'N Burn* didn't quite manage to persuade customers of their killer app status. Hawkins had also presumed that his connections with EA would lead to unerring software support for his venture, but promising titles such as *Road Rash* shipped woefully late.

The final axe-blow came in the form of Sony's US launch of PlayStation, however. Its 1994 release in Japan had seen Sony set a fairly high pricepoint of ¥39,800 (then equivalent to $400, rising to $480 by mid-1995), and speculation in the industry was rife about what

Panasonic FZ-10 REAL 3DO Interactive Multiplayer

UPON ITS AMERICAN LAUNCH IN 1995, PLAYSTATION'S LOW PRICE TORPEDOED 3DO, BUT SONY TOOK HEFTY LOSSES ON EVERY CONSOLE SOLD OVER CHRISTMAS

today, but from the perspective of a consumer electronics company in the early '90s, such figures weren't so obviously a disaster.

"Matsushita's previous big consumer electronics hit had been VHS video," explains Hawkins. "When the VCR was first introduced in 1970, the entire industry unit volume for that year was 10,000 units. We have very different standards today about first-year volumes on electronic products – but what changed that was the game industry. In order to attract thirdparty developers you have to have this critical mass of installed base, and the consumers aren't going to buy the hardware unless there are enough games for it. Nintendo had realised it had to hit the market hard and sell half a million or a

kind of figure would be deployed in the American market. The announcement came at E3 in the May of 1995 on a stage shared by Sony's US head Steve Race, Nintendo's Howard Lincoln and Hawkins himself.

"Everybody anticipated that Sony was debating between $399 and $499," recalls Hawkins. "The logic suggested that it would be the former. But even that was a stretch because it was such an expensive product to build. Lo and behold they announce that they will launch at $299. Right after that little number comes out of the mouth of Steve Race, Howard Lincoln glibly says: 'Well, I hope your shareholders like that'. He knew that they would lose a lot of money at that price. But Sony was saying to

everybody: 'We're here to stay, and we're going to be really aggressive – so deal with it. 3DO may have a hundred million dollars, but we're going to put a couple of billion into this and if we have to lose a hundred bucks on the first two million machines, we don't care'."

When it launched in September that year, PlayStation's low price torpedoed the hapless 3DO, and though Sony took hefty losses on every console sold over the Christmas period, it was able to declare a sweeping victory. But the magnitude of Sony's coup only really became apparent in January of the following year.

"The RAM and the disc drive really drove up the cost of both the 3DO and PlayStation," explains Hawkins. "But if you're Sony, you're a

Panasonic M2 Interactive Mediaplayer (model 1)

SOMETHING WIKI THIS WAY COMES

We ask Hawkins about the recent fiasco concerning edits of EA's Wikipedia entry – the effect of which seemed to obscure his role in its foundation, as well as remove reference to controversies such as the 'EA Spouse' debacle. It's not the first time Hawkins' role has suffered thanks to incorrect information from EA's own press department: a release from 2005 refers to Bing Gordon as a founder, when, by Hawkins' account, he was the seventh employee, and puts the date of incorporation as 1981 – a year earlier than the true date. "I would prefer to have a good and healthy relationship with EA," Hawkins responds carefully. "I would like it if EA's shepherds, none of whom were there at the foundation, would honour the true history of the company. Quite frankly, it is hard for them to do that without my help, because for such a long period of time it was in fact just me, so nobody else would know."

Twisted: The Game Show for 3DO was Hawkins' own baby. Its effervescent tone and obnoxious presenter set the format for the likes of *Buzz*

"3DO assumed that EA would be the killer app supplier," says Hawkins. "But EA wasn't a captive studio. *Road Rash* was fabulous, but a year late"

but how can we trump them with the next round of technology?'"

Hawkins' answer was M2, or would have been had it ever come to fruition. Throughout Hawkins' recollection of events, this is the only point at which he seems anything other than magnanimous in his defeat: rather, he is rueful at the missed opportunity to lock horns with Sony for round two, and bitter at the ungraciousness shown him by a sceptical media.

"Frankly, they had no right to be sceptical," says Hawkins. "The M2, in hindsight, could have been a successful machine – a PlayStation 2 that came out three or four years before the PlayStation 2. Just because 3DO became a popular topic of ridicule doesn't mean the press said anything particularly intelligent about the M2. We made some really interesting moves where we got very close to putting together a stronger coalition of companies to support the M2 and take on PlayStation. At one point I had a verbal deal with Philips and Sega to join forces with Matsushita. That grouping of companies could have given Sony a run for it."

But it was not to be. The technology was strong but, as Hawkins tells it, the business relationships between Sega and Matsushita ultimately proved unworkable.

"In hindsight, it turns out that social gaming has been my primary motivator in my entire life," Hawkins says when we ask what he sees as the high points of 3DO. "I only realised this myself a few years ago, actually. In terms of 3DO you can see my thinking reflected in the daisychaining of up to 16 controllers, multiplayer sports games such as *FIFA* and *Madden* and my pet project and invention, *Twisted: The Game Show*, which was years ahead of its time."

"AT ONE POINT I HAD A VERBAL DEAL WITH PHILIPS AND SEGA TO JOIN FORCES WITH MATSUSHITA. THAT GROUPING COULD HAVE GIVEN SONY A RUN FOR IT"

big manufacturer of disc drives. They pushed the cost of a CD-ROM drive down from $200 to $50. Then in January 1995 the semiconductor industry had a huge amount of capacity come online – more than they knew what to do with. On a single day in January 1995 the price of 1MB of RAM dropped from $20 to $8."

The incredible growth of the PC industry in the '80s and '90s had pushed demand for computer memory to an all-time high, compelling semiconductor companies to commit billions of dollars to new fabrication facilities. Whether or not Sony had been prescient of this sudden explosion in memory production, it was clear that it had got the timing very, very right and 3DO had got it in the eye, attempting to enter the market at the apex of the technology's cost.

"Sony foresaw how quickly it'd be able to bring down the cost of the disc drives and how fast the price of memory would just drop through the floor," says Hawkins. "By this time 3DO, as a viable platform, you could pretty much consider dead in the water."

It wasn't, however, the end for The 3DO Company, or for Hawkins.

"At the time you're just thinking, 'I've been working my butt off for this for years, I'm not going to give up on it yet'. And you look in the trick bag for more tricks – but eventually you start to think strategically and you say: 'OK, so we've lost this round,

"Matsushita wanted to kick Sega out of the deal and then Sega obviously got all mad, and Philips backed off," he says. "I spent a year putting that coalition together, but in the end they just couldn't get along."

Nonetheless, the process of getting M2 off the ground led to developments about which Hawkins has a right to be enduringly proud. He points to 3DO and its near-successor as the origin of the research and development initiative that led to Matsushita's lucrative involvement in the rise of DVD. Similarly, IBM's entry into videogaming was largely a result of deals brokered to produce a specific processor for the M2 – technology that ultimately made its way into both Sony and Nintendo consoles.

It's true, even if Hawkins does say so himself: a fourplayer trivia game, *Twisted* managed to out-buzz *You Don't Know Jack* by a couple of years and *Buzz* itself by 12. And he still has his sights set on the horizon, occasionally looking back down the curve, hoping that others clamber up it after him. Now CEO of mobile publisher Digital Chocolate, Hawkins champions what he calls 'omnimedia', which he sees as step one of becoming 'the EA for iPhone'.

"Omnimedia is short-form digital media that is simple, convenient and social. Think texting, ringtones, YouTube, Miniclip, Facebook, Wii, *Guitar Hero* and mobile games and how those ideas are now blossoming on platforms like the

Crash 'N Burn by Crystal Dynamics was one of 3DO's few standout launch titles. Hawkins admits that ignoring exclusives was a shortsighted move

Return Fire is remembered as one of 3DO's finer games, but it didn't stay exclusive long and was ported to PlayStation, PC and Sega Saturn

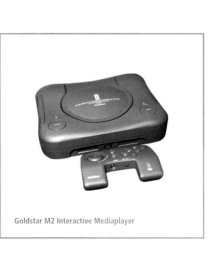

Goldstar M2 Interactive Mediaplayer

iPhone. For the first time in history we have interactive digital media that is for everyone and driven by social benefit. Even hardcore gamers bought the Wii and *Guitar Hero* and have become social players. The iPod Touch is rocking Nintendo's world. Our game, *Crazy Penguin Catapult*, was the number one Apple app download at Christmas – it was downloaded by four million people in just a few weeks. Stop and think about that for a moment."

Hawkins has been around the block – more than once – and when he tells you to stop and think, it's worth doing so. Is his omnimedia mission going to result in his farthest-reaching successes to date? Games are changing, ⬇ so it may not be wise to bet against it.

Panasonic M2 Interactive Mediaplayer (model 2)

EMPIRE
TOTAL WAR™

Actual in-game screenshot

DOMINATE THE 18TH CENTURY ON LAND AND SEA

There can be only one master of the 18th Century world. Through political manoeuvring and military might, on land and sea, you must crush those who dare stand in your way. Out of the smoke of battlefields, out of the flames of naval bombardments, a new empire will be born...

OUT NOW

Special Forces
Collector's Edition
(Contains additional content)

GAME
game.co.uk

amazon.co.uk

▶ PLAY.COM

SEGA®
www.sega.co.uk

Games for Windows

ROGUE LEADERS

IN THESE EXCLUSIVE EXTRACTS FROM HIS BOOK, ROB SMITH TELLS THE STORY OF LUCASARTS AS IT ENTERED A NEW ERA

CREATING A JEDI KNIGHT

In videogame development it's oft noted that there are "lies, lies, and release dates". The moving targets of new PC graphics technology standards, coupled with the intrinsic difficulty of evolving a game design process into a true 3D era, resulted in the hugely anticipated *Star Wars: Jedi Knight – Dark Forces II* being delayed until 1997.

The PC games enthusiast press had latched on to every morsel of information about what this *Dark Forces* sequel promised to deliver, generating incredible hype among the community through numerous magazine cover stories. But the wait was worth it, with the retail release becoming one of the most critically

Movie-like scenes were created to add cinematic styling to the *Jedi Knight* story

acclaimed games of the year. At this point in time, the concept of licensing another game developer's technology to use as the foundation for building your own game had yet to catch on. The Quake engine, which would later be significantly

THE TWIST TO THE STORY WAS HOW THE PLAYER COULD MANIPULATE THE GAME WORLD DOWN A DARK OR LIGHT PATH

Concept sketches of boss characters in *Star Wars: Dark Forces II – Jedi Knight* (above and right) by LucasArts artist Peter Chan, January 1996

licensed, was not yet complete during *Jedi Knight*'s initial development. And at any rate, the ambition level for this game's features pushed it beyond what a thirdparty technology would have been able to supply. No other game had Jedi, the Force and Force powers; *Jedi Knight* gave PC gamers all those new toys to play with, and it supported the singleplayer experience with a supremely engaging online multiplayer element.

Pushing the storyline set up in the original *Dark Forces*, *Jedi Knight* used about an hour of live-action video cutscenes to show your interactions with other characters in plot-advancing moments. *Jedi Knight* also helped revolutionise narrative techniques that wove the story into the all-out action of a firstperson shooter. How? By introducing moral decisions that actively impacted the player's abilities in the game world – decisions that also affected how the finale would play out.

As the game title implies, Kyle Katarn becomes a Jedi, learning the powers that

go with that exalted position. The incredible twist to this story was in how the player could manipulate the game world down a dark or light path. Killing civilians would direct the character down the dark path. But the player could choose to learn new Force powers from either side of this eternal battle, such as Force Healing (light side) or Force Lightning (dark side). While the game allowed you significant flexibility in the powers chosen throughout most of its compelling course, a key plot point in the later stages made you pick a path, and that decision directed you toward one of

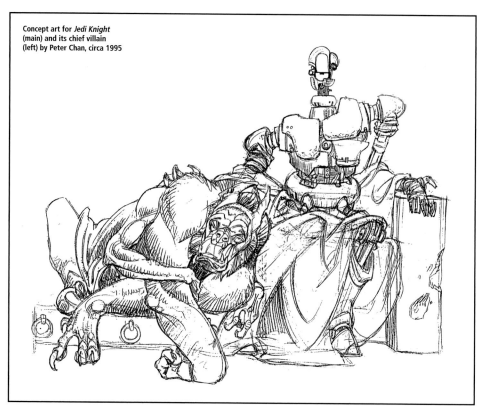

Concept art for *Jedi Knight* (main) and its chief villain (left) by Peter Chan, circa 1995

two distinct endings. The technical complexity of modern games made this form of multiple-path or multiple-ending design mechanism (which LucasArts had helped pioneer) more difficult to execute, and thus increasingly uncommon.

In addition, the elevation of Kyle Katarn to Jedi status meant that the hero would now be able to wield a lightsaber. *Jedi Knight*'s developers introduced an effective gameplay mechanic that would allow the player to view the character from the third person, rather than the

JEDI KNIGHT ALSO MADE THE LEAP ONLINE, WITH GAMERS FIGHTING EACH OTHER WITH FORCE POWERS

familiar firstperson perspective used when moving and shooting with traditional weapons. This vantage point enabled players to see the sweeps, thrusts and parries of the lightsaber. Deflecting enemy shots and using abilities such as Force Push to move objects around the environment put the power of the Jedi in the hands of gamers. Firstperson action games were built around instilling the

feeling of terrific power – of being a one-man army – and *Jedi Knight* delivered the ultimate example of that. It was simply irresistible. Also illustrating LucasArts' flexibility with the canon of the Star Wars movies, this Jedi could use the Emperor-like Force Lightning powers and even become invisible. If a power made sense in the game, and it made the experience more fun, then it was able to pass muster and give gamers the experience they truly wanted.

Through a partnership with Microsoft to use its Internet Gaming Zone software so gamers could meet and set up online matches, *Jedi Knight* also made the leap online, with gamers flinging each other across maps with Force powers, slashing with lightsabers, and flexing every Jedi power at their disposal. The combination of engaging, expertly paced singleplayer action and a new online multiplayer mode helped propel *Jedi Knight* to the vaunted status as the most critically acclaimed game produced thus far by LucasArts.

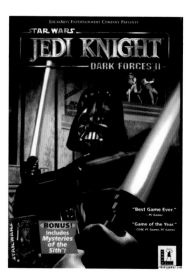

The boxart for *Star Wars: Dark Forces II – Jedi Knight*, complete with 'game of the year' and 'best game ever' plaudits from an enthusiastic gaming press

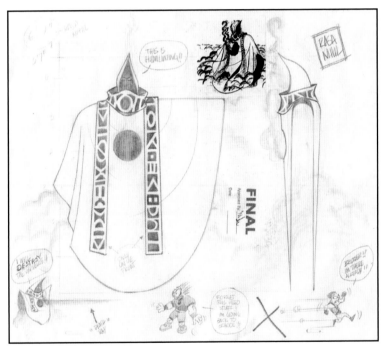

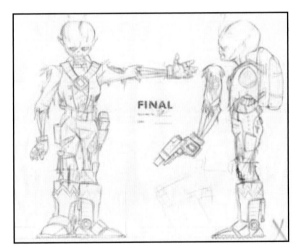

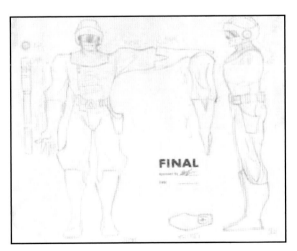

JUSTICE UNLIMITED

From 1997 to 1998, LucasArts worked on a game concept meant to challenge Blizzard's popular *Diablo* action-RPG. The entire concept was essentially "*Diablo*, except with superheroes," recalls LucasArts designer **John Stafford**. Lots of concept art and story was generated for the game, but no work was completed on a game engine, and the idea was shelved.

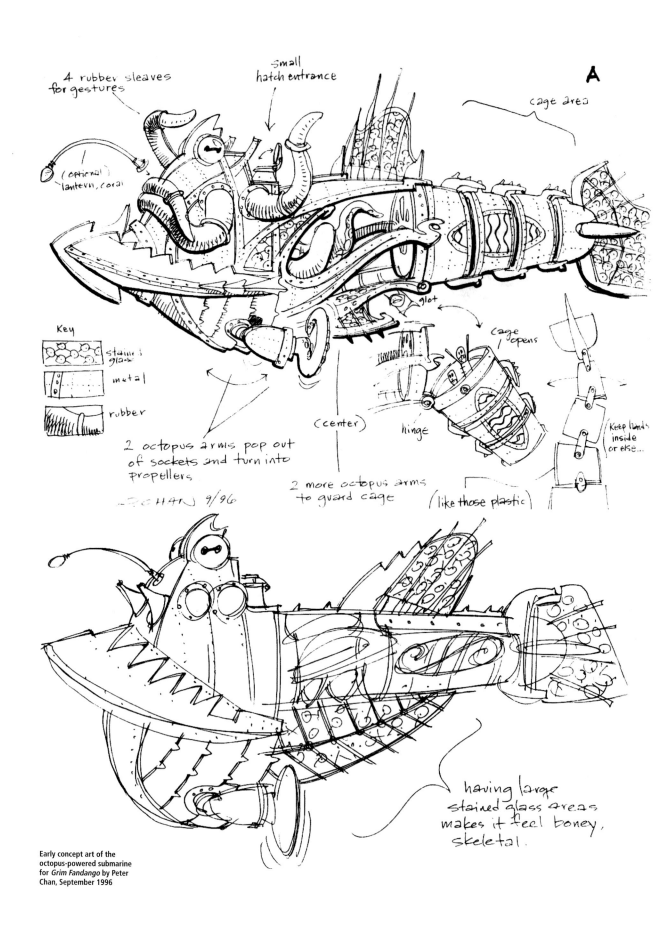

4 rubber sleeves
for gestures

small
hatch entrance

A

cage area

(optional)
lantern, coral

Key

stained
glass

metal

rubber

2 octopus arms pop out
of sockets and turn into
propellers

—CHAN 9/96

(center)

slot

cage
opens

hinge

Keep hands
inside
or else...

2 more octopus arms
to guard cage

(like those plastic)

having large
stained glass areas
makes it feel boney,
skeletal.

**Early concept art of the
octopus-powered submarine
for *Grim Fandango* by Peter
Chan, September 1996**

MEXICAN DAY OF THE DEAD?

Whereas **Tim Schafer** had to rework the initial design for *Full Throttle* so it would be greenlit, "*Grim Fandango* was a breeze," the game's designer says. That may come as something of a surprise for a concept inspired by the Mexican holiday Día de los Muertos (Day of the Dead) – hardly mainstream in the US – but such was the reward for having delivered a critical darling with his previous title.

However, the days of 2D adventure game development were over. *Grim Fandango* (1998) required a true 3D engine, and so was born GrimE. While using some elements of the SCUMM scripting system, this new engine enabled lead character Manny Calavera, travel agent at the Department of Death, to move throughout each scene in full 3D. The challenge of composing new

Lead character Manny Calavera and Slottis with their souped-up car, ready to "soar like eagles… on pogo sticks!" (top). Manny and the clown set about making unusual balloon animals (above)

technology for an original (and highly creative) setting established *Grim Fandango* as a significant risk for LucasArts. "Somehow, Tim pulled it off," recalls public relations manager **Tom Sarris**, who had to communicate this unusual concept to the enthusiast press.

With the proliferation of 3D graphics cards transforming PC gaming in the '90s, Tim Schafer's *Grim Fandango* took the adventure genre into the third dimension

CONCERNS AROSE ABOUT SHOWING SMOKING. "OUR ANSWER WAS: 'WELL, WHY? THE CHARACTERS ARE DEAD!'"

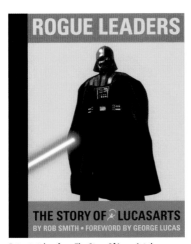

Extracts taken from The Story Of LucasArts by Rob Smith, published in the UK by Titan Books

Dealing with such a specific cultural event brought its own potential problems, as did some issues endemic to the game's film noir story. According to Sarris, concerns arose about showing certain characters smoking. "Our answer was: 'Well, why? The characters are already dead!'" he recalls.

Grim Fandango's quirky setting and creative style, along with Schafer's reputation within the games press, generated generally positive reviews. Unfortunately, that goodwill didn't translate effectively at retail, where the game failed to produce the sales that its budget and its positive reputation warranted. Internally, *Grim Fandango* also impacted projects in early development at the same time. Another **Hal Barwood**

[project leader on *Indiana Jones And The Fate Of Atlantis*] game design had made it on to the development roster, but it, too, was eventually cancelled. This project was set in the Star Wars universe and was called *The New Emperor*. It takes place after the end of the original trilogy, when the Emperor had been overthrown. Rumours around the galaxy that a new Emperor is to be named cannot be confirmed, so C-3PO is sent as a spy to find out what is happening. That's right, C-3PO. The premise was that in a disorganised Empire, the innocent-looking protocol droid would be the perfect spy to slip around each location.

Bluescreen video technology would have brought the world to life with real actors creating the key roles, and the story would continue the Star Wars lore beyond the silver screen. Unfortunately, *Emperor*'s cancellation came when, as Barwood recalls, "Tim [Schafer] was busy going over budget and over schedule on *Grim Fandango*. [LucasArts president Jack Sorensen] saw another one coming and cancelled it."

David Braben

FROM HERE TO 2016

HOW WILL GAMES CHANGE OVER THE NEXT 100 ISSUES OF **EDGE**?

Videogames continue to evolve at a dizzying rate. When, in the 100th issue of this magazine in August 2001, we asked 100 people for their future forecasts, nobody predicted *World Of WarCraft*, *LittleBigPlanet* or the Wii Remote, or that games would integrate with Facebook.

So it was with some trepidation that we invited four game developers with reputations for innovation in various fields to discuss where current trends could take videogames over the course of the next eight years. Take it away, **David Braben** of Frontier Developments,

Lionhead's **Peter Molyneux**, Relentless Software's **David Amor** and **David Smith** from Media Molecule.

Games have been following recent internet trends in embracing user-generated content, but where do you think it will take us by 2016?
David Smith: Any developer or publisher you talk to, you sense that behind closed doors they're making a *LittleBigPlanet* clone, or they're taking the UGC aspect and making a game based on it. So there's going to be a whole rash of those coming out. Most will be rubbish because they

don't get the core concept. I don't think all games will be using UGC by 2016 – it won't become the defining factor of what games are. But perhaps for 20 per cent of games, UGC will be a defining characteristic.

Is user-generated content going to put you out of a job?
Peter Molyneux: I'm going to be very negative about UGC. We've had user-generated content for years; anyone can be the author of a book or pick up a video camera and make a film, but they don't because it's such a rarefied talent. I do

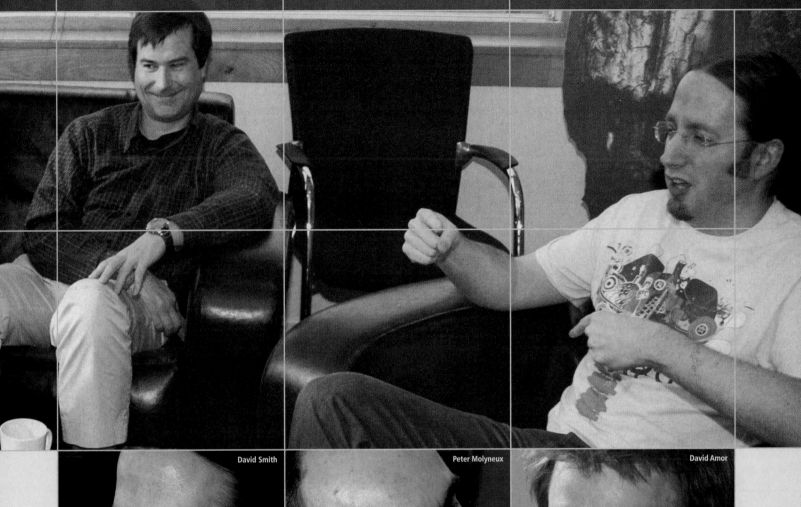

David Smith

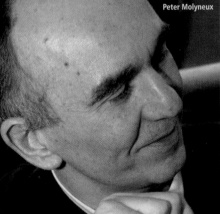
Peter Molyneux

David Amor

think there's an opening for what I'd call private user-generated content, though – such as me making a level for my son.
David Braben: Woody Allen said we'll be a nation of bad poets, and I think that's spot on. We're already starting to see that a bit with *LittleBigPlanet*: a lot of games created that you wouldn't necessarily want to play mixed in with a few gems.
David Amor: I can see a different kind of UGC where the game is hosted by people, rather than created by people. So rather than a singing game hosted by Ant and Dec, it's hosted by somebody on the internet.

DB: Another part is the joy of the creation itself, irrespective of whether the result is something that you're going to make millions from.
DS: If you look at a two-year-old playing around, they're creating. And that's something games can tap in to and prolong – that craving to learn.

The flipside to UGC is crafted storytelling and design. By 2016, will we be any closer to that completely immersive narrative experience?
DB: It's like climbing a mountain – as you get to the summit, you realise there's a

whole other bit you couldn't see. We'll keep getting to false summits, but even now we've made huge progress in storytelling compared to eight years ago. We will still be criticising games in 2016, but what I hope is that the story will be a lot more flexible – it won't be a rigid thing. We'll start to branch out as a medium of our own, not mimicking film.
PM: We're starting to realise our uniqueness, and that we've got the ability to do things that no other medium has had before. I think by 2016 we're going to have a truly amazing story, which will be cited as the equivalent of The

Godfather on film. The uniqueness and adaptability of the content, the fact you feel you *are* the hero character more than you are empathising with the hero – these are all things you can see evolving. I look at *Grand Theft Auto* and the Niko Bellic character, and I realise that we're really getting a handle on how to characterise somebody.
DS: There have been objections to *GTAIV*, that having the character imposed upon you can be quite annoying. In the early *GTA* games I enjoyed the fact that you could drive around listening to the music and forget the missions.

one where you determine the outcome, or will you follow a path?
PM: I think, as David [Smith] says, there will absolutely be both.

But which would be the breakthrough?
DB: That's a silly question, frankly. It's not like there was one film that completely changed the world. Different films changed different elements of the tapestry of the time, and a whole richness flowed from that. Because of all the things they did, the industry turned from madcap zany entertainment, such as Harold Lloyd and Buster Keaton, to storytelling epics

social experience. Do you see that pushing out into further new areas?
DA: Well, shoot me now if there are still seven or however many subgenres of social games – singing games, dancing games, quiz games – by 2016. That will show a sad lack of creativity. I think most of the games are still to be found. Who imagined *Wii Fit* two years ago? Next year's *Wii Fit* is yet to be thought of, and there's probably 20 more to come. Gaming is now accessible to more people – that's probably one of the biggest changes in the past 100 issues – but the largest set of people still aren't being particularly well catered for. There's some social games on Facebook, some on cheap consoles, but there are still more core games being made.
DB: One of the things that we've seen in the last year and extrapolating to 2016 we're going to see way more of is what the *Wii Fit* did – a new way of communicating with your computer, and vice versa. I think Nintendo has actually opened up something. The industry had got very obsessed with graphical beauty, which we've largely cracked. Graphics will get better, but I think it's no longer a driver.
PM: That's for sure. It's interesting how we talk less about exploiting the hardware and more about exploiting the user and what they hold on to, and do. From *Guitar Hero* to *Wii Fit* to *Wii Sports* – that's the new generation right there.
DA: I think *Rock Band* is an interesting case. It seems like people are willing to spend £150 on a game, and I'm not sure that's an anomaly, for the right experience. Not just for a game disc, of course.

"YOU'RE GOING TO SEE NEW FORMS OF CHARACTERS THAT WE'VE NEVER SEEN BEFORE, TOTALLY ADAPTING TO WHAT YOU'RE LIKE AS AN INDIVIDUAL"

DB: For me *GTA* is very grounded in what previous *GTAs* have done. The story is very much planned out, you can't make it very different – whereas things like *Fable II* and *Fallout 3* actually change the world. It's what we're trying to do with *The Outsider*, and it's a hugely difficult challenge. But we're starting to achieve it as an industry, and I think that's wonderful.
DA: There's an assumption that a completely open world might be a more entertaining game. But we were discussing recently the merits of *Fable II* and *Fallout 3*, and *Fable II* was deemed more enjoyable because it took you down a path. I think people still want a story that has strong narrative that leads you through.
DS: I don't think we're going to see games all converge on one point. I think there are also many different types of games we haven't yet discovered.

So will 2016's world-changing game be

such as Citizen Kane and The Third Man, and other films from the '30s. We'll only really see which game it was looking back with hindsight, at the time it won't necessarily be all that apparent.
PM: If you look at early storytelling in film, it was much less character-driven and much more plot-driven: Harold Lloyd falling off a skyscraper or trying to move a piano. Part of the revolution that Niko Bellic started to unveil – and what we're attempting with *Fable* – is to say the characters, especially who you are as a character, matter as much as the plot. Moving forward to 2016, you're going to see new forms of characters that we've never seen before, and those characters totally adapting to what you're like as an individual.

You're operating in a new area, where games like *Guitar Hero*, *SingStar* and *Buzz* have opened up gaming as a

What kind of technological breakthroughs might we see in 100 issues' time? Speech recognition?
DB: I think it's possible. The issue is the social circumstances. The layers of technology we need to make it enjoyable and not feel dweeby is a challenge. But as to whether it's by 2016, and how good it is… You could argue we've got speech recognition already, but it's only used in very limited circumstances. Partly because of boring techie things like vocabulary sizes, but also because people don't really want to be seen shouting "Left!" at the television.

It's an AI problem, isn't it? You can already have a word processor that can understand the words you've said, but it doesn't *understand* the words.
DB: It's got to be able to chip in in a way that doesn't sound cringing. And in-game,

it's got to add to the game's richness and experience. Speech has to be a two-way street, otherwise it doesn't really work.
DS: I think everyone would love to see viable VR, because it's totally failed to appear. That would be fantastic.

Will it be there in 2016?
DS: No! I'd love to see it, but my bold prediction is it will continue to not be there. The goggles and things are hideous, so you'd need to find a nicer way. There's also the interface. We've seen VR systems with silly joypads – that's not virtual reality.
DB: One thing we've hardly touched as an industry is artificial intelligence, and that is a real block to story. We've found it very, very hard to let go of the scripted character and let the characters find their way.
DS: That's a long way off! AI and VR are both chimeras the industry has been pursuing, but it's always felt like we've been on the cusp of generating these things. The Victorians thought that if they put enough little cogs in a little box they'd make something intelligent.
DB: I strongly, strongly disagree, because I don't think AI will come along like a train arriving at a station. I think we'll look around and say: "Wow, it's here".
DS: What do you actually mean by AI then?

DB: My point is if you decouple all the baggage it's got – call it 'approximated intelligence' instead – we're seeing much, much better behaviour of 'bad guys', for want of a better term. And good guys. Good guys are actually much harder to do from an AI point of view. Bad guys just have to run at you and shoot.
DS: But improvements in the bad guys are never to do with intelligence. It's all to do with animations and telegraphing what they're doing.
DB: We've reached the end of that road!
PM: In fact you're both right. What's important is the player believing something has intelligence. Whether it has intelligence – true AI – or whether it's a combination of an empathetic AI or a scripted AI, or a hybrid of what academia have been doing for a long time – the important thing is the belief that something is intelligent.
DS: And if you ask a man in the street what makes something look intelligent, he'll say it's because he walks so realistically.

What will games look like in 2016? Are there significant chokes that are still holding us back?
DB: This relates to the intelligence point. The more you start breaking things off

from rigid scripts – which we have to do – the more performance it takes. And that is still a big bottleneck, even on today's brutally powerful machines. My guess is it will always be a bottleneck, but having said that, you will appreciate the difference. A lot of beauty and subtlety depends on how many layers you can put on. Animations can still be motion captured, but it takes a lot of grunt to do them and hold them in memory, so memory is also a major issue.
DS: More horsepower also means you can be less aware of the restrictions. If you're not keen on being at the cutting edge of the visuals, you can focus more on artistic quality. You don't need to care that you're doing something that's grotesquely inefficient, so you can have smaller 'art-house' studios. That can only be good.
DA: We're still hand-animating our characters in our games, and we've now hit a problem where if we want to make downloadable content, it's quite expensive to build up as rich a set of contestant animations as we have in-game. We need to find more clever ways of delivering animation and characters, because they're becoming just too expensive. Luckily, the popularity of games is increasing at a rate that compensates for the expense, but

VISIONS OF THE FUTURE (2001)
IN ISSUE 100 WE ASKED 100 PEOPLE: WHAT WILL GAMING BE LIKE IN 2009? WHO GOT IT RIGHT? AND WHO GOT IT WRONG?

DEFINITELY ON TO SOMETHING

"There will be massively multiplayer worlds that have more people in them than some countries, and generate more revenue in intra-game trading than a small African state." **Ian Baverstock, Kuju**

"Broadband will be the delivery medium of choice, with gaming increasingly based on an episodic, pay-per-view system. I can certainly envision a time when there's a choice of downloading a TV show, or a new movie, or the latest chapter in a videogame."
Steve Jarratt, launch editor, Edge

"A result of new alternative distribution schemes made possible by broadband, I think we'll see the birth of an independent game development movement." **Warren Spector, Ion Storm**

POSSIBLY ON SOMETHING ELSE

"Microsoft will buy out Sega for its expertise, then release the 32Xbox – a peripheral that attaches to the current Genesis." **Steven Kent, author of The First Quarter**

"I will have achieved my goal of making a psychoactive experience, and my latest 'ware will have been declared a class-A numerical construct, illegal in 23 countries." **Jeff Minter, Llamasoft**

"In the future, all graphics will be replaced by a detailed description, whispered into the player's ear by an organic accessory shaped like a church mouse." **Charlie Brooker, TV bloke**

"I think the big breakthrough will be virtual reality." **Peter Snow, Tomorrow's World**

that's not a safe journey to be on.

DB: As an industry, we've been able to grow team sizes and it's been funded by the fact that games sell a lot more these days. But there are only so many people in the world.

PM: So how many generations of games machines are we going to have between now and 2016?

DB: One, I would think.

PM: There's certainly not going to be more than one. And where will the generational leap be? I don't see a quadrupling of anything in particular; it's almost certainly going to be more about cost and about usability than graphical power. The trouble is, subtlety is incredibly expensive. We're experimenting with some new animation fidelity, and it's just enormously expensive. But if we don't concentrate on the graphics then we will go down more of an iconic style, and we need something of both.

DB: We've done a lot of work that we know is prodigiously expensive, that's the trouble. Obviously, we will use whatever we are given as best we can. As an industry we're actually very good, I think, at pushing performance. People have done very well getting what they can out of the Wii, for instance.

PM: That's right, and what's interesting is that the Wii is starting to make us realise – and this is a pretty harsh thing to say – that as an industry we haven't been as successful as we perhaps should have been.

DA: So would you work on another hardware generation?

PM: Oh, it's a nightmare, isn't it? I feel exhausted at the mere thought of it.

Could the hardware cycle finally die off as games go online, or become more of a service?

PM: There's a very interesting argument about how much local processing is done versus how much is done remotely.

But what if the videogame publisher becomes more of a gatekeeper, almost in the way that Sky is, and you have a variety of gaming boxes that access that same experience?

DB: Do we not have something like that now – we just haven't recognised it? The PC today is really just becoming a window on the web world. And there are many other machines that can look through that window, so the spec of the PC is now much less important.

DS: There are good technical reasons why it's very useful having local processing,

because you'll have a laggy experience if all the computation is done remotely. But certainly, I think that's a really exciting idea, especially if you look at MMOs, where, in a sense, it's already being done. There's interesting mileage there – certainly from the point of view of improving the quality of the experience without you having to replace your hardware. It's a big ask for Sony or Microsoft to expect consumers to buy this new big lump of technology. But with a subscription base, it's more palatable to pay £10 a month to subscribe to a service.

DB: In our televisions now there's an awful lot of local processing. It's become so invisible that a Freeview tuner can now be built in to your telly or set-top box. That's no different to a games machine metaphorically – a big lump of electronics that needs power and has to meet various standards. So we may see games machines disappearing. We'd probably have to establish more of a standard for that to happen, but certainly it wouldn't surprise me at all if we were to have web-browsing TVs by 2016.

Looking at other internet trends – what some would call Games 3.0 – such as integrating games into Facebook and exporting your videos to YouTube, will there be a seamless integration by 2016?

DS: It won't be seamless, but by 2016 there will be many more niches where games can connect with the internet.

What if every significant thing in a game had a kind of internet 'node'? Should a car in _Burnout_ have an internet address so that your friends can see whether it's in the garage, or if you're driving around, or if it's in another game you've driven it into, or to find it on something like YouTube?

DB: But apart from you, who would really care?

Nobody will care in the round, but what if it means you can go to YouTube and see the 100 best players doing a _Burnout_ lap of a track that only got uploaded yesterday via UGC?

DB: Well, the big block to that is who owns the portal? If you can get [some of] the value of _LittleBigPlanet_ without actually owning it, then are people going to be happy with that? Are we going to see that content being viewed on rival consoles or desktops? I'd love to see more co-operation, but there are quite a few obstacles.

DS: There are obstacles, but there's definitely quite a strong will to do it somehow. It ties back to the point about social gaming. At the moment it's seen as a unique genre or niche, and over the next eight years it will become less well-defined, as all games find ways to leverage the value of social gaming – even the most hardcore game you play on your PC in your bedroom.

DA: We found when we introduced an online mode to *Buzz* it was played in a completely different way, and now the versions are kind of pulling apart. I used to think that all there was to the online component in this generation was the ability to play against each other, but there has turned out to be many more aspects to online. Some of them will be false starts. I remember reading with excitement about a spectator mode in one of Bizarre Creations' games, but to echo [Braben's] earlier point, nobody wanted to see other people race around. So there's a thousand things we can do, and it will be interesting to see which ones stick.

Peter, with *Fable II* you did away with player death. How hard is it question these design shibboleths that have existed for the past 30 years, and what others could change by 2016?

PM: Well, there is this move towards this greater accessibility. My ideal is to have a game that is ultimately accessible by anyone, no matter what age they are, but that's also so incredibly deep that core enthusiasts would get a reward out of it. It comes back to games adapting to what we're doing. What is absolutely for sure is that games are becoming less about that repetitive experience that's been going on for years, and more about enjoying the moment you're having. Things like dying or failing are being redefined, as are a lot of the mechanics. Just look at the graphical user interface around the screen, and what's happened since **Edge** 100. We used to slap health bars in the top corner just because we always had. And that has really changed significantly in the past eight years.

DA: People are more likely to try out simple, accessible ideas now. The idea of putting maths in a game, like with *Brain Training* – people would have resisted doing something that simple. A rhythm action game attached to a guitar – five years ago if that was pitched to me I just wouldn't have bothered.

PM: Another thing that is changing is

So we're looking at having a new model of ownership?

DB: I think we're moving to a licence-based model that will be account-based and that you can migrate across machines and to future generations.

PM: For sure there are going to be different ways of making money out of computer games. That's already happened in the last eight years – who would have predicted that *World Of WarCraft* would have made so much money? All the talk of online experiences and local versus cloud processing plays to this idea that walking into a shop is going to be about buying a gift. People will do that, absolutely. But whether if I'm thinking I want to play something tonight I'll walk into a shop or press a button, I'm not sure.

DS: The music industry is well ahead of us with this, so we'll be stealing all their ideas.

Finally, can everyone predict one change to come by 2016?

DS: I think there'll be some really exciting games that will teach you significant, interesting and valuable things, whether that's cooking or guitar playing. And you'll see those in a game shop.

> ## "I THINK THERE'S GOING TO BE A NEW FRANCHISE THAT WILL REDEFINE THE WAY WE PLAY GAMES. IT WILL REDEFINE EVERYTHING, JUST LIKE WII"

the saving and loading process. You can't save and load in an MMO.

DRM seems to cause more problems than it solves, and second-hand sales impact on new sales – will we still be buying games in the shops in 2016?

DB: Well, we've got to embrace the retailers and make their life better. On the whole rental and pre-owned issue, it has to be like film – we need two separate SKUs, something for rental and something for buying, and the user gets to build a collection with the buyable one, and DRM does not mean you can't play it in ten years time. It's already the case with *WarCraft* and other online games that you can't sell your subscription – it's not a problem, it just says so on the box. If you drop the price correspondingly to the current price of preowned, the user doesn't see a change, and they get to keep the disc forever.

DB: We'll see the PC platform change into a much more agnostic platform, where we'll see games like *WarCraft* playable not just on what we call a PC today, but also on little notebooks and things that don't have necessarily the same processor. The graphical experiences will be better than today's *WarCraft*, but it will be on an agnostic platform – which might well include your TV.

DA: I'll say pay-to-play. Play once, play once a month, and so on.

PM: I think there's going to be a new franchise, and that franchise will redefine the way we play computer games, how much we play computer games, and where we get that experience from. That's what everyone will be talking about. I can almost feel it coming. It will probably arrive in the next three years – certainly in the next eight – and it will redefine everything, just like Wii redefined everything.

AGES

The man most famous for his involvement with a certain hedgehog talks us through his career at the gaming world's true blue-sky company, Sega

 s one of Japan's most famous and successful gaming exports, Sega's foundation in Hawaii is surprising. Started in 1940 to provide coin-op amusements for American military bases, Standard Games morphed into Service Games and moved to Tokyo in 1951. In 1952, Service Games became Sega. Over the next three decades Sega grew into one of Japan's pre-eminent videogame companies, and chalked up several firsts – among them the first Laserdisc game, *Astron Belt*, and the first 3D game, *Subroc-3D* (a contraction of 'Submarine Rocket', the game used two-dimensional sprites and a special eyepiece that alternately covered each eye to create the effect). It was in the early 1980s, however, that Sega's real legacy began to take shape – both in arcades and in the home – and a young, enthusiastic programmer named **Yuji Naka** joined its staff. We meet him to find out why, to be this good, you need ages.

So, did you always want to be a videogame programmer?
[Laughs] As a child I was interested in vehicles, like cars or trains. I can't be specific but somehow that led to an interest in music, which led me to become interested in composition, and that led me to computers. From there, it was a short step to programming.

How did you come to join Sega?
At the time I joined Sega there were actually other companies that were quite prominent in the games industry that I was interested in, such as Namco, but Sega was the only company that accepted people without graduate degrees. I'd left education after high school, I didn't want to go that route. And also in Japan, culturally speaking, you have the east and west which are very different, and I'm from Osaka in the west, and I wanted to try Tokyo – Sega were there, and I was interested in that.

At that time, 1984, Sega's home system was the SG-1000 console. What do you remember about that hardware?
It's very memorable personally, because the first program I coded from scratch for Sega hardware was on the SG-1000. We made a game called *Girl's Garden* as a kind of freshman training assignment, and my boss requested we try to program something that was targeted towards girls. Then it turned out pretty well and he wanted to put it on the market, so various parts of it were tuned in a rush to make it a decent product! This became my first work, so it's a good memory for me.

In those early days you were often credited as YU2, and worked on converting some of Yu Suzuki's games to Sega's Master System. Why was that, and what did you learn from him?
Well, the name YU2 has dual meaning: I am next

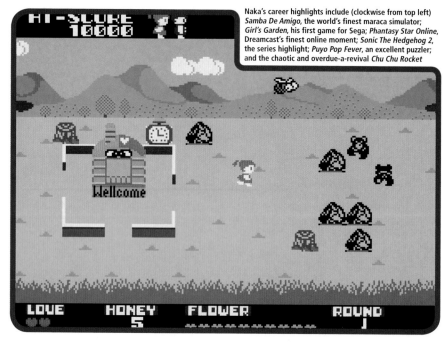

to Yu-san, for one, and then there's Yuji, my own name. I used this name in credits a few times, because back then Sega didn't allow their personnel's real names in the work. Mr Yu Suzuki didn't have a lot of experience of making traditional games at that time, but I respected him for being able to adopt what he liked in real life into a game. Back then, 3D wasn't common like it is now, and I still remember how he taught me the concept of 3D technology and how to control the screen.

When you were working with the Master System hardware, Nintendo's Famicom was beginning its domination of the Japanese home videogame market and would eventually control over 95 per cent of it – what was it like competing with Nintendo?
I joined Sega in 1984 and the Famicom came out in 1983, so when I joined there wasn't a sense that we were really way behind Nintendo. But, eventually, when that became apparent… [laughs] we felt kind of… erm, kansei… I'm finding it a bit hard to translate, but it's like

that's the justification for allowing him to attack enemies when he was on the ground. And as for the blue and white, of course that was the Sega identity!

You must have spent a lot of time with the *Mario* games. What did you think of them?
Well, *Mario* was already on the market, so obviously I played it a lot and studied it, but the important idea about *Sonic* was trying to create something that was completely different

Now, my idea with *Sonic* was that as you get better you can learn where things are and clear the stage quicker. So when I was programming it I thought about how to push that speed factor, and I think it was more about trying to make it feel different from *Mario* in the hands, and having a more fluid movement than in *Mario*, which can occasionally feel a little jagged and stop-start.

"Where did I get the idea for Nights? When I created Sonic I covered the ground, and then I wanted to make a game that covered the sky"

knowing the situation but having a more feisty quality at the same time, where you refuse to accept being beaten. We wouldn't be beaten by Nintendo! So we kept pushing out the boat and trying, and when the Mega Drive and *Sonic* came out, and then there was recognition in America and Europe, that was a really, really big point for us at Sega.

So, you are now Yuji Naka circa April 1990. Sega has asked you to make a mascot to stand toe-to-toe with Mario. What do you do?
Ha! Well, when Sonic was developed I already had it in mind that it would be great to have a character who could not only jump, but was able to run through the game without stopping, to smash through the enemies on the ground… That's kind of where the hedgehog part comes in, that ability to roll up into a spiked ball –

from *Mario*. So the way the idea was developed was away from the *Mario* paradigm which was already well-known and copied. Having said that, I want to make it clear I think the *Mario* games are really well made and great games, and I have nothing but the greatest respect for Mr Miyamoto's achievements with the character.

How much of that differentiation was technology-driven, in terms of making *Sonic* a Mega Drive showcase and emphasising the machine's abilities?
Well, I mean, *Sonic* has developed from the initial concept, but rather than it be more about trying to communicate the power of the Mega Drive, it was trying to do something that *Mario* didn't. For example, when you play *Mario*, however good you are it always takes, let's say, 30 seconds to go through a level.

Following the success of the Mega Drive hardware, Sega released the Mega-CD and 32X add-ons, which had only modest success. Were you in favour of those?
The Mega Drive was still selling well in the west, so I enjoyed witnessing its development in that way. The only fact I regret is that I didn't have a chance to produce a game for that part of its life myself, since the project for Sega Saturn had already begun at Sega Japan.

Why do you feel that the Saturn hardware wasn't a great success? And how did *Nights* come about for it?
When Sega released Saturn, I wanted to create

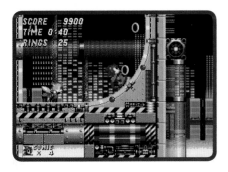

a new character game and so *Nights* was the result. You mean where did I get the idea for *Nights*? It's simple, really. When I created *Sonic* I felt I'd covered the ground, and then I wanted to create an action adventure that covered the sky. However, nowadays I think that the sales of Saturn could have been different if I had developed *Sonic* at the Saturn launch timing. As for the first part, the new technology for Saturn made the price slightly high. I guess that might have also affected the sales.

The experience with Saturn presumably led to Dreamcast's forward-thinking technology and focus on network play, and it had an extremely successful US launch. Yet just over two years after its release, production was discontinued. What are your memories of that time?
I think Dreamcast was a very fine piece of hardware. However, the problem was that it was way ahead of its time and the market couldn't catch up – that's a characteristic of Sega even these days! It would have been better if the videogame market had evolved more

Photography: **David Levene**

rapidly. What is especially memorable is that upon producing Dreamcast, meetings called Dream Team Meetings were held repeatedly with all kinds of creators and executives until late at night to discuss the various specifications, and it was exciting to challenge myself to make a network game.

Presumably you're talking about *Phantasy Star Online*?

There was *Chu Chu Rocket* first! At the time these two games were released the net structure wasn't really… [laughs] *Chu Chu Rocket* was released as a test to see what it was capable of. *Phantasy Star* was the big attempt, but around that time in 2000 not everyone had internet access – back then it was quite a minority.

And then, after Dreamcast, Sega stopped developing consumer hardware.

I was really against Sega ceasing to develop hardware, mainly because at that time *Phantasy Star Online* was just about to come out! Okawa-san [Isao Okawa], who was the head of Sega, said that the networked approach to gaming was something we should pursue and so that game was developed with that concept fully in mind. But, yeah, until the very final moments I was really against Sega leaving the hardware business. In a way I feel that, had that decision not been made, Sega would have gone bankrupt, so maybe it was a good business decision. But at the same time, I also feel like, what the hell – we should have given it a go, and we should have taken that risk. But that is just my personal opinion, because I really enjoyed the hardware side of things at Sega.

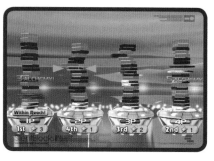

Why did you enjoy that part of the company's activities so much?

At Sega, when they were developing the hardware, they were open and keen about listening to a lot of our, the creators', opinions. They really took us seriously, so any hardware developed had some sides that reflected that. It was great that the hardware development department was located within the same office, so we could exchange opinions with each other whenever.

Were you ever tempted to focus more on the company's arcade interests?

I was always interested in arcade games, so I made three arcade titles while I was at Sega: *Samba De Amigo*, *Samba De Amigo Ver 2000* and *Puyo Pop Fever*. I really enjoyed creating those games, and I would like to produce some more in the future.

After that you left to form Prope, but you're still working with Sega as an investment partner. How did it all happen?

Rather than viewing it as my departure from Sega… In the past I've witnessed many creators leaving a company due to conflict, and so I formed Prope because I wanted to make an environment where I can create new games while keeping good relations with Sega. When you stay in one company for a very long time, responsibilities other than game creation pile up on you and it gets too hard to concentrate on games any more. That's the negative side of today's games industry. It is no good for the company, for a start, and I find it a pity if good creators can no longer create

good games. It's a fact that there isn't much time left for me as a creator, and I'm now in an environment with Sega's full support, so I feel very lucky to be able to create new games at Prope.

***Let's Tap* is certainly an innovative first title, but do you see it more as another aspect of the work you've always done?**

It is such an honour to be called innovative as a creator, and I felt great to be able to bring forth something new out of Prope's first product, which was a combination of all of our staff's thoughts. Because of the complex nature of games I have always wanted to design simple interfaces – I suppose it's kind of a philosophy I have. For example, my favourite mode in Visualizer is the gem game. At first with *Let's Tap*, I launched a teaser site with the tagline 'The game even a penguin can play', and I do

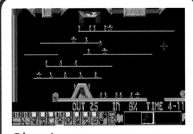

Oh no!
Naka's favourite non-Sega game? "*Lemmings*. I consider the system of the game, and the structure around it, really quite superior. I like the fact that each one of the lemmings can be designated their own roles, and their little different movements that go with that have such character. And in a way, their basic characteristics are based on real lemmings, so from a character design point of view as well as everything else, I find *Lemmings* quite fascinating."

"It's a fact that there isn't much time left for me as a creator, and I'm now in an environment with Sega's full support, so I feel very lucky"

believe that the gem game has really turned out to be a game playable by a penguin! By just hitting the box mindlessly you can get excited, so it can be enjoyed in a different way from traditional games.

Who have you worked with at Sega that you particularly admire?

I wouldn't say that we developed together, but it has to be the late Mr Isao Okawa, Sega's CEO,

who insisted that we create network games as the era of the internet would be with us very soon. Because Mr Okawa told us to create games that utilised the internet, Dreamcast had its internet functions, and I was able to develop *Phantasy Star Online*, which I feel very grateful for. He had amazing foresight and was a wonderful person. It might be hard for me, but I would like to be someone like Mr Okawa as I get older. [Isao Okawa (1926-2001) was the founder of CSK Technology Holdings and chairman of Sega Enterprises from 1984 until his death. In that time he supplied tens of millions of dollars to fund Dreamcast production, forgave debts that Sega owed him, and gifted his $695 million of stock in Sega and CSK to Sega Corporation.]

After two-and-a-half decades of working for and with the company, what does the name 'Sega' mean to you, and what do you hope it means to gamers?

Sega is my favourite company by a huge margin. Without Sega I wouldn't be a creator as I am now, and I am so grateful for the many good experiences I've had and disciplines they've taught me. I want to work on Sega's projects as much as possible. Sega always tends to look to the future – maybe too much – but I hope it will always be that way with Sega, always in the lead! As for players… think that Sega is the one which can offer you something different. Sega is the one company from which you should expect something different.

Let's Tap (8/10, E199) has been confirmed for a European release in the summer. Along with *Let's Catch* on WiiWare, it marks an auspicious debut for Prope. Naka says his next project will be a "character game" in the Sonic mould

THE UNTOLD ATARI STORY

FORGOTTEN MAN TED DABNEY PLAYED A KEY PART IN THE MAKING OF A GAMING LEGEND. THIS, FOR THE FIRST TIME, IS HIS ACCOUNT

Atari co-founder Ted Dabney outside his family home, 1968

In June 2008, Paramount Pictures announced that it had greenlit a full-length feature about the story of **Nolan Bushnell**, the co-founder of the pioneering videogame company, Atari. The movie, which went by the working title Atari, would star Leonardo DiCaprio and would be produced by the actor's company, Appian Way. The script had reportedly been read and approved by Bushnell himself.

But although press releases for the movie announced that Atari had been founded by Bushnell and **Ted Dabney**, the latter man had never been consulted. Nobody at Paramount, Appian Way, or even the screenwriters, contacted Dabney for his side of the story.

Whether or not the movie about Bushnell is eventually made, Dabney's role in the origination of the videogame industry slides further into obscurity each year. Because Dabney was a silent partner who had never spoken with the press, the early stories about Atari have always been told by others. Now, after 35 years of just being a

footnote, Ted Dabney has finally decided to talk about the founding of Atari from his point of view.

Unlike Bushnell, who hailed from Utah, Dabney was a native of Silicon Valley. He grew up in San Mateo, a suburb south of San Francisco, and attended San Mateo high school. Shortly after graduating from the high school in 1955, he joined the Marine Corps and attended the Navy's electronics school on Treasure Island and the Radio Relay School in San Diego. Although Dabney felt that neither school taught him much, he admits that he did at least walk away knowing the jargon of the electronics industry.

After his military discharge in late 1959, Dabney returned to San Francisco searching for jobs. Thanks to his knowledge of the technical terminology that he learned in military school, he was hired by the Bank of America's research lab, where he worked on the prototype of IRMA, an electronic cheque scanner. Dabney wasn't particularly happy with the position, and when a colleague left to work at Hewlett Packard in nearby Menlo Park, Dabney expressed an interest in following him. However, the colleague wasn't at Hewlett Packard long, and soon jumped to the Military Products group at Ampex in Redwood City. The co-worker suggested to Dabney that he apply to both Hewlett Packard and Ampex. Dabney followed his friend's advice and, after passing Hewlett Packard's technical tests, he was hired as a test technician on a production line. Ampex offered him an engineering position six weeks later. Dabney took the job although he had never considered himself an engineer, and he figured that Ampex would learn this within three months. Still, he figured that even three months of engineering experience under his belt couldn't hurt, so he accepted the job.

Dabney's self-assessment was wrong. He wound up working for Curt Wallace in Ampex's Military Products group for six years. According to Dabney, Wallace was "very strong technically and an excellent manager". When Wallace took over Ampex's Videofile project in Sunnyvale, Dabney transferred with him.

The Videofile system was groundbreaking technology used for the storage and retrieval of data and video. It could store 250,000 document pages on a 14-inch rhodium-plated disk. If a document needed to be viewed, in less than a minute the Videofile computer could automatically locate the individual document, and then either display it on a TV screen, or direct it to a printer. When Dabney joined the project, the market for such a retrieval system was $23 million, but Ampex expected it to grow to $1.5 billion within ten years.

Another of the engineers assigned to the Videofile system was 25-year-old Nolan Bushnell. Six years Dabney's

concept around for several months. Dabney finally modified a TV set to simulate how a white spot could be moved into various positions on a screen, using address programming so that the TV's raster sync signal and video sync signal were generated separately. Both signals were generated with 256bit counters. The raster sync counter was preset to 254 and the video sync counter was preset using switches from a control panel that could go from 242 to 256. A blip on the screen was generated in the middle of the horizontal and vertical video sync counters. The difference between the raster sync count and the video sync count caused the blip to move.

The work Dabney and Bushnell did to get the blip moving on the screen was done, contrary to legend, in Dabney's daughter's bedroom. He relocated his daughter Terri from her bedroom, which was the smallest in the house, to the master bedroom. Then he expanded her former room and made it the largest.

Once they got an object moving around a television screen, they approached Larry Bryan. Dabney and Bushnell weren't quite sure where they were going to go with the moving blip, but they were confident that whatever they did with it, they would need a programmer. Bryan was pretty excited about the idea and as the three discussed the project, they formed an agreement whereby each of them would contribute $100 to start the venture. Bushnell and Dabney put in their money right away, but Bryan never got around to it.

Actually, Bryan never got around to doing much of anything as far as the project was concerned, while Dabney and Bushnell soon came to the conclusion that the high costs and low speeds of the computers available

at the time made the project unfeasible. They decided to abandon the idea of time-sharing a computer for entertainment purposes.

But Bushnell wouldn't give up the idea of using a television set for interactive entertainment even though, at the time, he knew little about TV circuit design and function. When he had a question about why a television picture would roll up and down when the vertical hold knob was fiddled with, it was Dabney who he consulted. Not only was Dabney able to explain how it worked, he also told Bushnell that the horizontal hold knob could do the same thing. He then went on to explain that the process could also be done digitally. Although Bushnell didn't have any video engineering experience, he was a quick learner. He realised right away that if Dabney could digitally control the horizontal and vertical controls, then in theory, they would also be able to control the movement of onscreen images. And if they could do that without the need for an expensive computer, there were no limits to where they could go with it.

After Dabney successfully tested the concept at his home, Bushnell was further convinced that they had a great idea on their hands. According to Dabney, Bushnell was an excellent student. He immediately grasped what Dabney taught him and he designed his first TTL (transistor-transistor logic) circuit design based on what he and Dabney had built in Dabney's home. Dabney recalls that one of the toughest things they had to do was generate a rotating spaceship with a diode matrix. After Bushnell began creating a functioning breadboard (a reusable solderless device used for experimenting with circuit designs) of Dabney's design, he and Dabney agreed on a new partnership. This one didn't include Larry Bryan since he had never contributed his $100 from the first agreement. They then went to **Irv Roth**, one of the senior engineers that Dabney had worked with at Military Products, to see if he could help them. Roth told them that he "had tried that sort of thing and it didn't work

THE WORK DABNEY AND BUSHNELL DID WAS CONDUCTED, CONTRARY TO LEGEND, IN DABNEY'S DAUGHTER'S BEDROOM

junior, the two shared an office together, and they became good friends, along with two other Ampex employees. One was a programmer named Larry Bryan. The other was a young engineer named Al Alcorn, who worked at Ampex during his summer breaks from the University of California-Berkley.

Bushnell told Dabney that he had worked his way through college (where, he confided, he had not done well in class) as a carnival barker. This background, along with his vivid and creative imagination, gave him an appreciation for arcade games, and his dream was to open a pizza parlour filled with animated scenery and talking bears. At that time he thought that if the restaurant had arcade videogames, the customers would at least have something to keep them busy until their food was ready. Additionally, he thought that a pizza parlour filled with arcade games might also attract kids who didn't normally visit arcades, and would thus be another venue for gaming products that he would manufacture. As Bushnell developed the concept, he felt that it would be a nice touch for the restaurant to have Disneyland-like robotic animals that could play music and give the impression of a fun amusement park.

Both men agree that it had been Bushnell who came up with the idea of using computers and TV receivers to provide arcade games. As computers were getting more common, Bushnell thought he could use one to move images on several TV screens at one time, an early form of computer timesharing. The two men threw this

Ted Dabney (left), Nolan Bushnell (second left) and Al Alcorn (far right) line up to promote *Pong*

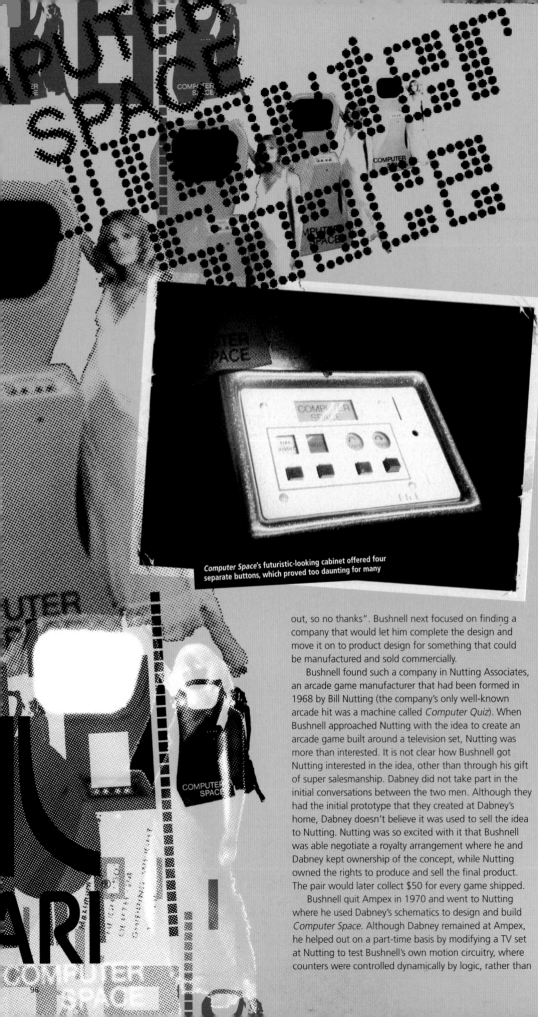

statically with switches. Unknown to Dabney, Bushnell applied for a patent for this method in November, 1972, and it was issued as No. 3,793,483 on February 19, 1974. Dabney was not included in the patent. As the project took shape, a cabinet was needed to house the circuit board, the power supply and the TV monitor. Dabney used some of the initial $200 to buy material to design and build one, and worked on the cabinet at night at Nutting while maintaining his day job at Ampex. However, this task soon became a full-time job so Dabney quit Ampex and officially went to work for Nutting. Dabney's design was only used to house the prototype. Before the game went into production, Bushnell came up with a futuristic-looking fibreglass cabinet that was used for the final product.

According to Bushnell, Nutting manufactured 2,300 copies of *Computer Space*, which was released in August 1971. Despite reports suggesting that Nutting sold only 750 units to distributors, Bushnell has since claimed that all were sold. The number of units that actually made it into arcade locations is not known.

Dabney and Bushnell kept working for Nutting but wanted to continue receiving royalties for the games that they designed. Nutting didn't like that idea, because he felt that since he was paying them a salary to design games, both the concept and the completed product should belong to him. According to Dabney, Nutting was careful when it came to paying out money, even to those who deserved it. Nutting had one great salesman, who by sheer tenaciousness kept the company alive selling *Computer Quiz* machines, even though the game was very outdated. "*Computer Space* took off very well but when Nutting saw how much money he was paying his salesman, he fired him. Nobody ever told Bill that the salesman should always be the highest-paid person on your payroll," recalls Dabney.

In order to separate the products they designed for Nutting and those they designed for themselves, Dabney and Bushnell each kicked in $250 from their *Computer Space* royalties and started their own company. They called it the Syzygy Game Company, a name that had actually been suggested by Larry Bryan, even though he had no part in it.

To make sure that Nutting didn't stray from the licensing relationship that he had with Dabney and Bushnell on *Computer Space*, a tag stating 'Syzygy Engineered' was put on the front of each production *Computer Space* cabinet.

In the end, *Computer Space* didn't prove as successful as its designer hoped it would. An argument could be made that most arcade gamers didn't want to try out this new technology after playing pinball for generations, but some people did try it and were scared away for a different reason: the game was complex to play. Bushnell felt that if a more simplistic game was offered on a TV screen, the public would clamour for it.

Bushnell told Nutting about his idea for a simple game and Nutting was enthused by it. However, before Bushnell actually began designing it, he demanded that Nutting give him a bigger share of the profits since he felt he was the brains behind the game. He wanted 33 per cent of Nutting Associates. Nutting countered with five per cent as long as Bushnell agreed to remain with the company as an engineer. Bushnell decided to go elsewhere.

Dabney and Bushnell began contacting other arcade companies with their intent to design games for them. One of the companies that Bushnell visited was

Computer Space's futuristic-looking cabinet offered four separate buttons, which proved too daunting for many

out, so no thanks". Bushnell next focused on finding a company that would let him complete the design and move it on to product design for something that could be manufactured and sold commercially.

Bushnell found such a company in Nutting Associates, an arcade game manufacturer that had been formed in 1968 by Bill Nutting (the company's only well-known arcade hit was a machine called *Computer Quiz*). When Bushnell approached Nutting with the idea to create an arcade game built around a television set, Nutting was more than interested. It is not clear how Bushnell got Nutting interested in the idea, other than through his gift of super salesmanship. Dabney did not take part in the initial conversations between the two men. Although they had the initial prototype that they created at Dabney's home, Dabney doesn't believe it was used to sell the idea to Nutting. Nutting was so excited with it that Bushnell was able negotiate a royalty arrangement where he and Dabney kept ownership of the concept, while Nutting owned the rights to produce and sell the final product. The pair would later collect $50 for every game shipped.

Bushnell quit Ampex in 1970 and went to Nutting where he used Dabney's schematics to design and build *Computer Space*. Although Dabney remained at Ampex, he helped out on a part-time basis by modifying a TV set at Nutting to test Bushnell's own motion circuitry, where counters were controlled dynamically by logic, rather than

Bally in Chicago. Bally was interested in the idea but told them that they couldn't do business together as long as the men were employed by Nutting, as this would cause a conflict of interest. They were told that they would have a deal if they left Nutting.

Since the two men were getting pretty good royalties from *Computer Space*, they figured they could afford to quit Nutting, which they did. They then leased an office at 2695 Scott Blvd in Santa Clara, California, and hired the Syzygy Game Company's first employee, 17-year-old Cynthia Villanuavo. The company's first receptionist had previously been a babysitter for Bushnell's children. Since there weren't any additional funds, Dabney and Bushnell didn't include themselves on the payroll.

Once they were untethered from Nutting, Bushnell returned to Bally where he secured a contract that awarded them $4,000 a month for six months to design a new videogame and a new pinball machine.

Aside from the basic idea of concentrating on a simple design, Bushnell wasn't sure what kind of videogame he would deliver to Bally. "There was some talk early on of a driving game but it wasn't in the plan," says Dabney, who worked on the pinball machine.

Once Dabney and Bushnell had this infusion of cash, they were able to hire Syzygy's second employee.

Al Alcorn had since graduated from the University of California at Berkley. However, by then Ampex's Videofile project was having problems and the company elected not to rehire him. Bushnell lured Alcorn, whom Dabney fondly recalls as a "real Teddy Bear", to Syzygy by telling him that they had a contract with General Electric to design a videogame.

Much has been made of the story that Bushnell got the idea for a simple ball and paddle game after

However, he never explained to the audience (and no one bothered to ask) how a product that had not yet been released (and which would eventually sell over 330,000 units) could be deemed a failure.

Al Alcorn became Syzygy's first engineer but he had no experience designing videogames. Bushnell claimed that the Odyssey didn't impress him, yet he still had Alcorn design a similar ball and paddle game as an exercise using their new digital motion circuitry. Although the project was only meant to get Alcorn's feet wet, Bushnell and Dabney were so impressed with the finished product, which they called *Pong*, that they decided to offer it to Bally.

Believing that they had a sure-fire hit on their hands, the duo decided it was time to incorporate Syzygy. To their surprise, they learned that a roofing company had already registered the name. Desperate for a new name, Bushnell borrowed three favourite Japanese terms from Go, their favorite boardgame. The names were discussed at great length, but in the end the name Atari was liked the most. Atari was incorporated on June 28, 1972.

Pong was offered to Bally as per the contract, but the pinball company didn't know what to do with it, and rejected it. The same deal was offered to Bill Nutting but he also turned it down and later sued Atari, saying that *Pong* really belonged to him. He lost before Atari could even plead its case.

Bushnell visited Bally several times but failed to get it enthused by *Pong*. Finally, Dabney and Bushnell decided to test the waters themselves. Alcorn hand-built a tabletop *Pong* unit that was tested at Andy Capps, a Sunnyvale, California bar. The game was so successful

A *Computer Space* motherboard, as restored by Legacy Engineering's Atari expert, Curt Vendel

THEY DECIDED TO BUILD MORE PONG UNITS FOR TEST MARKETING. EACH OF THE TEN MACHINES AVERAGED $400 PER WEEK

witnessing a 1972 demonstration of Ralph Baer's Odyssey, the world's first videogame console. Although Bushnell had denied it for years, the fact is that Magnavox and Sanders Associates hosted an open house at the Airport Marina in Burlingame, California, on May 24, 1972, to introduce its Odyssey game console. The fact is that one of the games displayed on the unit was a form of video ping-pong. And the fact is that Bushnell, thinking he designed the only TV game, attended the open house in order to see the Odyssey. It has always been maintained that Bushnell attended the open house as a representative of Nutting. While Dabney's best guess is that this was the case, he is also certain that they had already left Nutting by May 24, 1972. The attendees who represented Nutting specified this in the guest book. On the other hand, Bushnell's signature appears on a different page and doesn't state what company he represented.

Whether he went as an agent for Nutting or Syzygy, the fact is that Bushnell did attend, and signed the guest book. And the fact is that the courts sided with Magnavox and Sanders. Despite this, Bushnell continued to claim for the following three decades that the ball and paddle game that he saw at the demonstration didn't inspire him to produce his own. Eventually he began to change his story, however. During a keynote address at the Classic Gaming Expo in 2003, he finally admitted that he had indeed seen the Odyssey. However, he claimed that when he saw it, the console was already a failure.

that Dabney and Bushnell decided to build an additional 12 units, from which ten were sent out to local bars, restaurants and pizza parlours for test marketing. The response was overwhelming. Each of the ten machines averaged $400 per week. Dabney and Bushnell tried Bally again and sent them one of the hand-built *Pong* units. However, because they didn't think Bally would believe the amount of money that they were generating weekly from each machine, they cut the gross report to Bally to a third of what the games actually earned. Bally still thought they padded the numbers but never gave a definitive answer as to whether it wanted *Pong* or not.

Another Atari legend pertains to a phone call that Alcorn received from the manager of Andy Capps complaining that the *Pong* unit in his bar had malfunctioned. Alcorn rushed to the bar only to find that the coin box that was used to catch quarters inside the machine had overflowed. Over the years, many critics have questioned whether this episode ever really happened. Dabney not only attests to the authenticity of the story, he claims it occurred many times. "Neither Nolan or Al had enough money to stuff those coin boxes with as many quarters as we were getting," he recalls. "We had ten machines out on location and they were averaging about $400 per week. The coin box could hold about $550 so, yes, we had several failures caused by too many quarters."

Dabney and Bushnell knew that they had to do

something but they weren't sure just what. Since they couldn't get anyone to license *Pong*, the three realised that they would have to build the machine themselves. The problem was that the cost of going into production was higher than they could afford. Dabney told Bushnell and Alcorn: "Either we go into production or we go home. I don't want to go home." Bushnell argued that they couldn't afford to produce the units themselves. Dabney responded by saying that they should make the decision to go into production, and then they could figure out how they would make it happen. "We felt we would be idiots to give up on such a promising prospect, so we decided to produce it ourselves," recalls Dabney. "Nolan was very worried about our legal commitment to Bally, and wasn't sure how to handle it. I told him to get on the phone to Bally and acknowledge their reluctance about *Pong* and that we could create another game for them but only if they formally reject *Pong*. We got a letter from them rejecting *Pong* and I told Nolan to put it in a really safe place. Our obligation to Bally was cancelled since our agreement with them didn't give them the option to reject our game." And since, in their eyes, Bally rejected the contract, it also released them from the work that Dabney had been doing on the pinball machine.

After they decided to build 50 upright units, each got on the phone to line up the parts they needed. Bushnell and Alcorn worked on getting the circuit boards and components while Dabney went after the TV sets and cabinets. He found a Hitachi distributor in San Francisco who sold him 50 sets for $3,000, which he paid with his own money. He then called PS Hurlbut Inc about the cabinets. Dabney had dealt with the company before while he was at Nutting. He had also given the cabinet company a drawing when he was shopping for cabinets for Atari's first 12 demonstration machines, although he had gone with another supplier to save money. Dabney ordered 50 cabinets, and when he told Hurlbut that he might not be able to pay for them, he was told that he could pick up the cabinets two weeks later. Meanwhile,

Bushnell and Alcorn were able to secure the parts that they needed, and they were in business.

Dabney and Alcorn did most of the work building the units. The Scott Blvd location that they leased contained 1,300 square feet that they could work in. By the time they completed putting together the 50 cabinets, they didn't have much elbow room left. Dabney explains how they doubled their space: "It just so happened that the guy next door slipped out unknown to the building's manager. I decided to bust through the wall and take over the 1,300 square feet of space. This gave us 2,600 square feet. The manager said we couldn't do that but Nolan told him that we already did it and all he had to do was tell us the amount of the rent."

While Dabney and Alcorn were assembling the machines, Bushnell was walking around like a "tom turkey". Dabney told him to quit strutting because it was his job to sell the machines, and recalls him adopting "a real hang dog" look as he headed to his office. Bushnell returned about an hour later looking very perplexed. He said that he had made three phone calls and had orders for 300 units. He said 50 went to one distributor, 100 to another, and 150 to a third.

Bushnell designed *Computer Space's* cabinet, which made an appearance in Soylent Green

Determining the price that they charged for each unit was another area in which the group had no experience. They wanted each machine to sell for under $1,000 but they didn't know by how much. Dabney looked out at the parking lot of their office complex one day and noticed a car that had the number '937' on its licence plate. They charged $937 per unit.

So although they eventually could bill the three distributors for close to $150,000, they still didn't have the money in hand. And between the three of them, they couldn't afford to produce 150 units. Bushnell did a very bold thing. He got Bob Portal, the distributor who wanted the 150 units, to give them a purchase order for his machines. This had never been done in the arcade industry before and it was on something that Portal had never even seen. However, he did know about *Computer Space* so he trusted them. Dabney and Bushnell felt that they could take the purchase order to a bank and borrow the money that they needed. Dabney contacted his personal Wells-Fargo branch and was told that he and Bushnell had to visit the bank. On the way over, Bushnell said that he should do the talking because he could paint a very rosy picture. Dabney disagreed and said that they should also explain any negatives that might arise. Bushnell told the loan officer what he wanted to say and the bank rejected their request. Dabney went back later by himself and managed to change the loan officer's mind. In the end, they got the money.

After that, the orders just kept rolling in at a preposterous rate. In their sixth month of production they had billed over $1,000,000.

Bushnell figured out tricks on how to make money for the company. During the early '70s, logic ICs were very hard to acquire. Bushnell found that suppliers offered 'two per cent ten days' terms, which meant that they could get a two per cent discount on what they owed if they paid within ten days. Most companies liked to take as long as possible to pay for their supplies, some taking as long as three months. This worked favourably for Atari in two ways. First, it received the discount. But it was also treated favourably by the vendors. Since suppliers liked to get paid as soon as possible, once they learned that Atari paid its bills within ten

days, they made sure that Atari received priority when supplies were being shipped.

The *Pong* board used approximately 55 logic ICs and a few transistors. Among the most costly items were the 70 decoupling capacitors which cost around 8¢ each. Being the consummate showman, Bushnell wanted to demonstrate to Dabney and Alcorn how he could save money. He got on the phone and an hour later he told them that he got the price of the decoupling capacitors down to 3½¢ each. Not long afterwards, Alcorn was assembling PC boards when he ran out of the decoupling capacitors. He asked Dabney how that could happen because they had very good suppliers who always delivered them their parts as soon as they were ordered. Dabney looked into it and discovered that the supplier who Bushnell had contacted for the capacitors wouldn't ship them at 3½¢ each. Dabney had to run out to a nearby electronics store on Bascome Avenue that sold bulk capacitors where he bought what they needed at 15¢ each.

Although they were on a crusade to save money, they never sacrificed quality for frugality. Dabney recalls: "National Semiconductor had great gates, but their counters ran too hot. They wouldn't sell us gates unless we bought the counters too. So we bought counters and gates from National Semiconductor but we didn't use their counters. Instead we bought superior counters from AMD, but they couldn't sell us gates because they didn't make them."

Dabney admits that it was Bushnell's job to make all of the decisions, despite the fact that they owned the company equally. Bushnell was the president and Dabney was the senior vice-president. Dabney's job was to do the book-keeping, a task at which he admits he wasn't very good. But the two worked well together. Unfortunately, that wouldn't continue.

The beginning of the end of their partnership occurred as they were looking at the 10,000-square-feet Amphenol-Cardre building in Los Gatos which could house their constantly growing business. They both liked the place, but Bushnell felt that it would be hard to justify moving so far out. Dabney reminded him that they owned the company and didn't have to justify anything to anybody. Bushnell suddenly became very quiet. When they got back to their office, Bushnell looked out at the parking lot that was filled with the cars of their employees. He said: "All of these guys depend on us, don't they?"

Dabney replied: "Yes. And their landlords and grocery stores do too."

"What's it going to be like to be very, very rich?" asked Bushnell.

Dabney told him: "Everything would be the same. The only thing that would change is the number of zeros."

As the money came in, Dabney noticed a change in Bushnell. "Nolan became his money," he recalls sadly. "Nolan was a neat guy when he still owed money for his car and education. Once he got rich, he became his money. He hired a PR firm to promote himself, not the company. He hung around with people that worshipped him. He truly believed the measure of a man was how much money he had. I was really appalled by that shallow evaluation and told him so. Money has never been a big thing with me. I believe that anything over a full belly is just gravy."

That was it. The idea had been building up in Dabney for a long time. He didn't like the man Bushnell was becoming. He didn't like the direction that Bushnell was taking the company. He didn't like the fact that Bushnell did everything without ever discussing it with Dabney. He finally decided that there was no reason for him to put up with it any longer. So he told Bushnell that he wanted out. Bushnell came up with a number that Dabney agreed to – $250,000 – and that was it. Nolan Bushnell owned all of Atari.

Atari wasn't doing well around 1974 after Dabney left. According to Dabney, "It was going down pretty fast and the money was getting tight. Bushnell had hired a president who was on an ego trip and couldn't take care of business." He also brought in a VP of engineering – not Al Alcorn – who found it difficult to make decisions, and then made a salesman the VP of marketing, even though the salesman had no idea about marketing. Dabney finally took Bushnell out for pizza several months later to tell him what he thought of his staff. "He seemed shocked that I knew so much about what was going on. It was just from observation. After this little encounter, he got rid of these 'bad actors' and brought in Joe Keenan as president. That's when Atari started to turn around and things got much better." But as things turned around for Atari, the relationship between Dabney and Bushnell began to deteriorate.

A few years later, the two men were at Bushnell's house drinking wine. Dabney had introduced Bushnell to Gamay Beaujolais, a wine he liked very much. When he happened upon a really good deal on an older vintage in Paris, Bushnell bought several cases. Unfortunately he hadn't known that Beaujolais had a very short shelf-life,

less than good enough was unacceptable. Bushnell ignored him, believing that Dabney was not qualified to make such a judgment.

However, Bushnell respected Dabney's input when it came to engineering. Dabney fixed the pizza order problem by designing and building a number callout system called Notalog. He then started his own videogame company that designed an Isaac Asimov quiz game for Pizza Time Theater. Both products did very well until Pizza Time Theater went bankrupt, at which time Bushnell couldn't pay Dabney what he was owed. Not being paid by Pizza Time Theater was a massive blow to him, but being misled by Bushnell hurt him even more. Dabney terminated his friendship with Bushnell for good. He never saw, or spoke to, him again.

Following Atari, Dabney decided that he wanted to learn more about semiconductors, and he figured the best way to do that was to work for a semiconductor manufacturer. He got a job as an applications engineer at Raytheon Semiconductor in Mountain View, California, where he learned much about semiconductor technology during his tenure of several years. He then went to Teledyne Semiconductor where he was part of a group that had developed a chipset that executed every known multimeter function from voltage and current to temperature and frequency. He got hold of a Japanese microcontroller (essentially a functional computer system on a chip) and wrote a complete multimeter program in assembly language using TelCom's chipset. Later, the management bought the operation from Teledyne and renamed it TelCom Semiconductor. After a short time,

Bushnell believed *Pong*'s simplicity, from control to instructions, would be crucial. He was right

DABNEY LOOKED OUT AT THE PARKING LOT AND SAW A CAR WITH '937' ON ITS LICENCE PLATE. SO THEY CHARGED $937 PER UNIT

so he invited Dabney to his place to try and drink it up before it went bad. When both men were pretty plastered, Bushnell said: "Dabney, do you remember when you said to me that 'The only thing that changes is the number of zeros'?"

"Yes", replied Dabney.

"Dabney, you know what I really don't like about you?"

"What?"

Bushnell repeated: "Dabney, you know what I really don't like about you?"

"What?"

"What I really don't like about you is that you had no right to know that!"

Shortly after Bushnell opened the first Pizza Time Theater, he asked Dabney to work with him at the restaurant. "He did warn me that he may do to me again what he did to me at Atari," says Dabney, who replied: "Been there! Done that! I'd rather be your friend than your partner."

Bushnell then asked Dabney to check out the restaurant to see what he thought about it. Dabney discovered the restaurant was dirty, the pizza wasn't very good and the place was so noisy that he couldn't hear the announcement that his pizza was ready. Dabney shared his findings with Bushnell who said he would take care of the cleanliness. He wanted to keep the noise, so he asked Dabney to figure out a system to let customers know when their pizza was ready. As far as the quality of the pizza was concerned, Bushnell seemed to think that mediocre was good enough. Dabney told him that that was a very dangerous standard to set, because anything

feeling that the new owners weren't up to scratch and also feeling pretty burnt out himself, Dabney decided that it was a good time to call it quits.

After retiring, Dabney and his wife Carolyn bought a small grocery store in Crescent Mills, California, which they successfully ran for ten years. They sold the business in late 2006 and moved to the state of Washington where they live a comfortable life on 40 acres in the middle of Okenogan National Forest. Although Dabney left the world of writing assembly language programs for chipsets years ago, he keeps himself entertained by writing Visual Basic applications for his own use.

Since leaving the videogame industry, the industry he helped create over 30 years ago, Dabney hasn't looked back. He has no interest in videogames, and hasn't kept tabs on Atari, which has famously gone through a number of manifestations since he sold his half to Bushnell. As for Bushnell, even after all the years that have passed, Dabney only feels contempt for his former partner. He believes Bushnell feels the same. "I'm sure he has no desire to even acknowledge that I ever existed," says Dabney. "Sharing the spotlight is not his style. He wouldn't give me any credit even while I was still there."

While Dabney happily lives in relative seclusion and obscurity, perhaps one day he, like Ralph Baer – who on February 13, 2006, received a National Medal of Technology from President Bush for his 'groundbreaking and pioneering creation, development and commercialisation of interactive videogames' – gets his day of recognition for all that he contributed to the beginnings of the arcade videogame industry.

E0 "3DO is the videogame future." **Edge's optimistic beginnings**

E1 "How did you make the helicopters shiny?" **The foundations are laid for Edge's trademark style of informed, incisive and investigative interviews**

E2 "One thing is certain: in 1994 some of us will be feeding our 3DO, Mega Drive and SNES systems with broadcast signals rather than carts." **Edge's old mission statement: 'The future of interactive entertainment'**

E3 "It's inevitable that people are going to compare any one-on-one beat 'em up to *Street Fighter II*, but after they play *Rise Of The Robots* they will see it's nothing like *Street Fighter*." **Sean Griffiths, lead programmer of *Rise Of The Robots*, was right**

E5 "Sony is hedging its bets by developing software for both the PS-X and Saturn, so whichever system eventually takes off, Sony is sure to be backing the winner." **Things were a little hazy in the early Edge days**

E6 "*Night Trap* does have an intense atmosphere and has converted quite well, but it's just that it's, well, *Night Trap*." **Sega's Mega CD enfant terrible gets a 3DO port and a 5/10 review in Edge**

E7 "If only you could talk to these creatures, then perhaps you could try and make friends with them, form alliances… Now, that would be interesting." **In his 7/10 review, Edge's reviewer just wants to sit down with the creatures of *Doom* and perhaps work things through**

E8 "Sources close to Konami have hinted that *Contra* for the Mega Drive will be better than the SNES version but have less variety." **Look, this was hot Edge news back in the day**

E13 "You wonder just how much Nintendo actually had to do with [*Donkey Kong Country*]. There is still no sense of humour and I don't think it will entertain children like *Aladdin* did." **Shiny Entertainment's David Perry – who just happened to work on *Aladdin*, of course**

E17 "On the Saturn, [*Virtua Fighter*] will make many people stop, run off to look at their bank balance and then fork out for Sega's new machine." **Edge's reviewer is suitably impressed by the debut of Sega's 32bit console hardware**

E18 "Many people who have seen… these so-called next generation machines have already said that they just can't see what the difference is…" **Gumpei Yokoi – whose next console, Virtual Boy, will offer some extremely visible differences**

E19 "No matter how great Saturn is, or PlayStation is, or Ultra 64 is, we will outsell them by an enormous amount with 32X." **Every so often, Sega US chief Tom Kalinske, we remember why your company's hardware business imploded**

SOUNDBYTES
THE PROCLAMATIONS, PREDICTIONS AND POINTS OF VIEW THAT WENT INTO MAKING 200 ISSUES OF **EDGE**

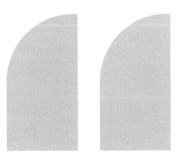

E4 "I was so convinced that it was going to make me my first million, I rang up the local post office and warned them that they had better get more postmen on the job to cope with all the extra mail I was going to receive." **Peter Molyneux received just two orders for his first game, and reckons one of those was from his mum**

E9 "If it's not realtime, it's not a game." **Akira Sato, director of SCE Japan, talks our language**

E10 "I think that about five years from now, a standalone CD system will be so much more powerful than a PC for playing games. It will be so inexpensive that the idea of playing games on a PC – well, nobody would care about doing that any more." **Trip Hawkins sees the future, but fails to consider quite how deeply the whole PC/user interface goes**

E11 "It's our mission to foster new programmers. Once people have bought the PS-X, they will stick with it until they become bored with it, or it becomes obsolete: software is the single most important factor." **A Sony insider says all the right things prior to PlayStation's launch**

E12 "Ah… nice graphics." **The entirety of Shigeru Miyamoto's opinion of Donkey Kong Country**

E14 "The machine must carry out one million operations every 1/30th of a second. For the record, one processing step on the Saturn takes 35 nanoseconds, or 35 thousand-millionths of a second." **The Saturn iteration of *Virtua Fighter* knows how to press Edge's buttons**

E15 "We're hoping to sell one copy of *Ridge Racer* for every PlayStation sold. Well, if it's at all possible." **Namco's Youchi Haraguchi aims for the stars**

E16 "Sega's president, the feared Hayao Nakayama, was among the first to be informed. His reaction was typical. He immediately marched down to his consumer R&D division and proceeded to ridicule the sum of his team's achievements over the previous year." **Edge reports what happened when Sega found out about Sony's PlayStation**

E20 "The 'she's represent a very interesting opportunity for all of us. It turns out that I think I've actually figured it out." **Nolan Bushnell is on a casual gaming mission**

E21 "Historically Nintendo is the only company that has sold more than ten million units of hardware. The claim that Sony or Sega would be able to sell as much hardware as Nintendo sounds uncertain." **Shigeru Miyamoto is really a software man, remember, not hardware**

E22 "M2 and its revolutionary design and groundbreaking features provides us with an excellent vehicle to deliver our software… and meet our goals to stay on the leading edge of this fast-paced industry." **Interplay's executive VP Dick Lehrberg still believes in the 3DO dream**

E23 "I think that we will do a first-class job of marketing [Virtual Boy], and ultimately the consumers are going to make the decision." **Unfortunately for NOA chief Howard Lincoln, the decision is: "Um, yeah, I don't think so"**

E24 "Initially Nintendo will not be inviting third parties to produce [N64] games… Sony… pushed thirdparties to begin [producing] games before the [console] release… This is just absurd." **NCL PR manager Hiroshi Imanishi, who's still not convinced that Sony has a clue about this gaming stuff**

E28 "[There was] the feeling that Sega – more than Nintendo, which came across as very safe, very Disney – had a bit of a 'fuck you' attitude." **John Hackney, VP of McCann Erickson Europe, the company charged with promoting the Saturn launch, before ultimately seeing consumers reflect Sega's stance**

E29 "The question is, are we going to go around stuffing tissue paper in the bras of our games? I for one am not going to do that." *Balance Of Power* creator **Chris Crawford thinks that sex in videogames needs underwiring**

E33 "Does xenophobia count as good clean family fun then, Nolan?" **Another Edge scribe questions the motivation behind Nolan Bushnell's attempts to wrestle videogame superiority from Japan**

E34 "There's this notion that you can sort of rip off the Japanese companies and – no, really, I mean, that's sort of the 3DO model." **Bill Gates attempts to sum up Trip Hawkins' failure in the East**

E35 "I don't see what left, left, A, C, A, down has got to do with kneeing someone in the balls." **Andrew Graham, a lead programmer at Codemasters, had better not try a spinning piledriver**

E36 "We're trying to set up [Segasoft] as an independent software publisher. It really should be publishing on any platform." **It's 1996, and Sega's Tom Kalinske seems to be getting a proper handle on it now**

E38 "The consumer will ultimately prove that 32bit wasn't different enough, wasn't better enough and wasn't cheap enough to be a big product category all by itself." **You have to admire Trip Hawkins' never-say-die attitude**

E39 "This buxom brunette has been making game players and developers drool at her hard-hitting, in-your-face babe antics. Does life really get any better than this?" **Lara Croft in the eyes of a (lonely?) Edge writer**

1993–2009

E25 "My biggest concern about the industry is that we're surrounding gameplay elements with a lot of fluff. And that scares me." **EA Canada's Bruce McMillan, who gave the world** *FIFA*, **lays it on the line**

E26 "In terms of consumer spend we're fighting for the same £300 that could be spent on a mountain bike, a stereo or a couple of pairs of designer trainers. That's where the real battle is." **Sony's Phil Harrison on PlayStation's other competitors**

E27 "I personally could never really care enough about Princess Zelda to spend 40 hours battling through the forest in order to rescue her." **Digital Pictures founder Tom Zito no longer has a videogame company**

E30 "Imagine yourself in a hot game. Derek has just made a move on your girlfriend… Things are really cooking." **Chris Crawford takes the theme to the next base**

E31 "This [PlayStation projections on to walls] will let us put our subliminal messages in clubs – if people are in a club off their faces looking at PlayStation graphics, they'll associate them with all that's good in life." **The words of Geoff Glendenning, marketing manager of SCEE, were in no way ever officially endorsed by Sony**

E32 "Edge has only one grievance with the game so far – Fred Flintstone as the lead character. So what if the film made millions of dollars? Fred is just a reactionary swine with one joke." **An Edge staffer cuts directly to the heart of one of popular culture's great debates**

E37 "We're spoiled by having the most ignorant consumers in the world – parents who are buying things for their kids – so many people in the business believe that all you have to do is bullshit a parent who doesn't know crap about games into buying your box, and then you move on to another money spinner." **Perhaps Eugene Jarvis should have released** *Robotron 2084* **on Commodore's Amiga as** *That Shooting Game*

E40 "We opened a Photorama booth in an area of Tokyo called Iraksho. What we didn't realise was that one has to pay their respects to the local… uh… call them what you will. I hesitate to think of a name. In this particular case, we didn't realise that this particular party was so sensitive to the issue. He sent some emissaries to tell us of his displeasure." **David Rosen, co-chairman of Sega, disrespects the Yakuza. Is this how Sega got the licence?**

E41 "No, it is fucking not." **DMA boss David Jones is asked if** *Lemmings* **is his favourite game**

E42 "Come on, son, give it loads… No, not like that, like this… And try and look hard, if you can…" **Edge's photographer attempts to coax perturbed** *Street Fighter III* **producer Noritaka Funamizu to put on his war face for the camera**

E43 "Entertainment is not a necessity. When it is not interesting we can leave it and ignore it. What happened to Atari can happen any time in Japan." **You wonder what Nintendo's Hiroshi Yamauchi thinks about the current economic climate**

E44 "Shigeru Miyamoto, naturally, because he makes such great action games. I really think he's a god as far as game development goes." **Masato Maegawa, president and CEO of Treasure, hails the king**

E45 "If you've got a shit game, then it doesn't matter how big the licence is, it won't sell." **Activision's** *Transformers* **may beg to differ with Gremlin man Steve McKevitt**

E46 "We wanted to incorporate the Godfather character into a space adventure and eventually it became a space adventure without the Godfather at all… This was why Conrad was originally called Michael, after Michael Corleone." **Denis Mercier, of Delphine Software, on the origins of platform adventure** *Flashback*

E47 "The quality of the engine and detail of the environments are already well ahead of the pack… The game isn't due out until November…" **Edge previews** *Daikatana* **in 1997. If only Ion Storm's game was so far ahead of the pack when it finally made it to market in mid-2000**

E48 "You can get a lot accomplished if you live at work. It's not for me." **John Romero on how id cramped his style**

E49 "It inflicts great pain and suffering on the programmers using it, without returning any significant advantages… It is a gigantic pain in the ass." **John Carmack summarises Microsoft's Direct3D API**

E50 "Pentium 1000 is announced, EA purchases Microsoft, Lionhead finishes its first game (joke!)." **Peter Molyneux offers his predictions for E100. Well,** *Black & White* **arrived in E96 – perhaps it would have benefited from four months of polishing. (Joke)**

E51 "Sega was number one in the market with the Mega Drive, and it will be again in the future – there is no doubt about that" **Jo Bladen, Sega's UK marketing director, stocks up on the hubris, pre-Saturn**

E52 "Gumpei Yokoi leaves behind an unforgettable legacy of innovation that touched the lives of millions the world over." **Edge pays tribute to Gumpei Yokoi (1941-1997)**

E53 "New genre alert!" **Edge breaks out an exclamation mark for its cover to hail rhythm-action**

E54 "We are currently working on a system where Mario and Luigi can both co-exist, and they are both controllable by the player." **It's taking Shigeru Miyamoto a while to realise this particular idea**

E55 "*Space Invaders* has a story. All these guys are landing on your planet – shoot them. I mean, that's a good story – that's a solid story." **A young Tim Schafer says that, actually, story is a pretty important component within games**

E56 "A game is a far more emotional experience than, say, a dishwasher, and perhaps the time has come for scores to be removed altogether." **Edge presents its most compelling argument to date in support of killing review scores**

E57 "We now believe some people perceive it contains a reference to drugs." **Sony responds to criticisms of its** *Cool Borders 2* **'powder' ad campaign, and reasserts that it would never dream of fostering such connotations**

E58 "Sandra Bullock meets Marky Mark in a Trappist monastery." **Edge's pitch for the Tomb Raider movie envisions a casting combination that could surely only result in timeless, classic cinema**

E59 "If Katana arrives, we are confident that our polygons will be more entertaining than their polygons." **SCEE president Chris Deering dismisses Sega's Dreamcast before it's even been named**

E60 "A rejuvenated Mac games market is there for the taking." **And, despite Edge's optimism, it remains stubbornly untaken**

E61 "I want a Ferrari for every toe I have." **Lara Croft designer Toby Gard has his mind on the money**

E62 "Everyone should support [third parties], every platform company: there shouldn't be a profit centre making money from developers – which you could accuse some people of, not mentioning any names…" **Argonaut chief Jez San isn't a fan of Nintendo's publishing model**

E63 "Bigger than Godzilla? Better than *GoldenEye*?" **Edge's coverlines talk up the genre-defining** *Turok 2: Seeds Of Evil*

E64 "That's it. You played it for 30 tortuous hours and then one of the main characters popped her clogs and it was bad." **Peter Molyneux sums up** *FFVII's* **emotional appeal**

E65 "Lionhead's triumvirate of technical gurus, Alex Evans, Jean Claude French bloke and Scawen scary name, have delivered a superior 3D engine." **Why Edge's production editor was taken outside and beaten with a length of iron pipe**

E66 "The game single-handedly restores faith in both the creative might of Nintendo and in the power of the videogame as an entertainment medium." *The Legend Of Zelda: Ocarina Of Time* **scoops up Edge's third 10/10 review to date**

E67 "Edge reviews being biased towards the firstperson shooter, and downgrading 'younger' character games." **Jez San reveals his biggest disappointment of 1998, the year Argonaut's** *Croc* **topped the charts**

E68 "Let's respect the competition and admit that some companies did a very good job recently and we just haven't. They are the mistakes of the past. We won't be making them again." **Sega of Europe CEO and Arsenal follower JF Cecillion talks a good game, at least**

E69 "They probably know what they're after as much as I do. And I haven't got a fucking clue." **Ex-Zzap! editor Gary Penn ponders whether gamers really know what they want to play**

E70 "I think the rudder on this ship had holes in it. We've patched them up and I think our games are going to speak for themselves." **A candid, if optimistic, assessment by Ion Storm's vice president of marketing, Mike Breslin**

E71 "Share options." **Glenn Corpes tells us what he misses most about working at Bullfrog**

E72 "You could have… a pink blob. And if it's made very clear that the pink blob is a pregnant woman, and the next collection of pixels is you with a gun…" **Gary Penn considers the future of** *Grand Theft Auto*

E73 "I dunno, it just feels good. When they explode in the air and there are body parts flying around – it's like fireworks." **Id level designer Brandon James explains why the railgun is his favourite weapon**

E74 "[Miyamoto's] a very simple guy – his reward for Mario is that he doesn't have to wear neckties." **Henk Rogers doesn't value a free and airy neckline enough**

E75 "It really fucks me off, actually." **Emily Newton Dunn addresses the issue of being a woman in an industry whose most prominent female is Lara Croft**

E76 "It's really hard to see Dreamcast as anything other than a Milky Way: a snack to consume between PlayStations without ruining appetites." **Gary Penn makes a meal out of the console war**

E77 "I am interested in making firstperson-viewpoint games. Rare's *GoldenEye* game is already a good game with a firstperson viewpoint. I'm almost of the opinion that my style of making small characters on the screen appear and go here and there, it may be old-fashioned by now." **We're glad that Shigeru Miyamoto had a cold shower after saying this**

E78 "Should we try and use the whole rebellious attitude of the game to sell it into the lifestyle press and let goateed media types in Soho and Covent Garden persuade you that it's unbelievably bloody cool and if you don't own it you might as well kill yourself because you're obviously fat, spotty and unattractive?" **PR man Brian Baglow experiences a fleeting crisis of conscience during the promotion of *GTA2***

E79 "Phone games will start out as poker, simple boardgames and quizzes. More complex titles will follow. In the most advanced games the user's phone will ring." **Take that, Apple's iPhone. Edge cracks out the blue-sky thinking for the future of mobile games**

E80 "I once kidnapped a baby kangaroo from Windsor Safari Park." **Peter Molyneux's penchant for moral choices and furry friends takes shape**

E81 "We had all been working 100-hour weeks. I was trying to get some new info related to a bug to a member of staff. I knocked on the office door. No response. So I opened the door. The person I was looking for was in – so was his wife. They were making love on the Persian rug." **Game designer Harvey Smith on the perils of overworking coders**

E82 "I think as far as *Shadowman* was concerned with journalists… well, it takes at least two to three hours to get into it. That posed certain problems with the reviews…" **Such as them not really enjoying the first few hours very much, Guy Millar?**

E83 "It's interesting that some people are trying to say that [broadband] is here. We're producing the best you can get. Do consumers look at that and say, 'Yeah, I understand that they've got a problem with broadband infrastructures' or do they just say 'That product's crap'?" **SCEE MD Ray Maguire suggests that Dreamcast's 'six billion players' tagline could be a little on the misleading side**

E84 "It is the first time sensors are to be used in a home videogame. Imagine a baseball title, a boxing game or even a game like *Phantasy Star Online*. You could use a sword controller!" **Sega's Yuji Naka anticipates the world of waggling and waving heralded by *Samba Di Amigo***

E85 "Watch out for the next-generation *Tomb Raider*. It will offer something different." **Unfortunately for Core's Adrian Smith, 'different' meant *Angel Of Darkness***

E86 "They won't let me on the carpet over there [gestures to neighbouring Sony stand], but from what everyone tells me it's pretty boring." **Sega America president Peter Moore doesn't want to play with Sony's stupid ball anyway**

E87 "The latest in a long, long line of small technological marvels which we struggle to come to terms with before it becomes obsolete." **Ken Fee, lead artist at DMA Design, gives an insightful reading of Dreamcast's tea-leaves**

> I was looking at PC hardware and I thought, 'Good Lord, we could make one monstrous son-of-a-bitch console with these things

E88 "It came to me on a plane, of all places. I was looking at PC hardware coming out at the end of the year and I started thinking, 'Good Lord, we could make just one monstrous son-of-a-bitch game console with one of these things'." **Xbox evangelist Seamus Blackley explains the conception of the big black beast**

E89 "It is 100 per cent gameplay, sober and very advanced." **Yuji Naka on Sega's achievement with *Virtua Fighter***

E90 "The first time I probably created something using a PC was when I created the Mario character for *Donkey Kong*. I programmed the Mario character, burned it on to a ROM, and handed it to our programmer." **Shigeru Miyamoto can't wait to get stuff off of those nasty PCs**

E91 "Piracy is a reality that's been with the industry since… well, forever, really [and security measures] end up adding fuel to the piracy lobby. The cracked version doesn't have a code number you have to type in." **Peter Molyneux in a sensible mood**

E92 "Some bloke called Jeff Minter from the stall opposite had apparently been asked what he thought of it and said it wasn't bad." **Sandy White remembers word-of-mouth shifting a few copies of *Ant Attack* at a computer show at the Barbican**

E93 "It would appear that plot isn't the game's strong point." **Edge gets a first look at *Devil May Cry***

E94 "Launch difficulties produce really funny Sega adverts." **Seamus Blackley on what Microsoft learned from PlayStation 2**

E95 "Assuming such things were possible, to spend some time inside Jeff Minter's mind would almost certainly be a unique experience." **Edge's review of *Tempest 3000* begins with some rumination**

E96 "I can't really say anything about SCUMM. If I do, George Lucas will come to my house and bust the place up with a baseball bat." **Ex-LucasArts employee Ron Gilbert stays frosty, but with a somewhat parental smile**

E97 "The Times did an article on *Way Of The Exploding Fist*, saying how games were growing up and mature games like *Exploding Fist* proved it. Not exactly what I had in mind at the time…" **Greg Barnett, the game's creator, harks back to simpler days**

E98 "It can't hurt to name your game what the game is about." **A young CliffyB. We can't wait for *Quasi-Ironic Meatman Blastathon III***

E99 "For audiences this is going to be really amazing, because you have this really strong girl dripping wet in a little dress fighting for her life." **Believe it or not, Milla Jovovich told us about her role in the Resident Evil movie with a completely straight face**

E100 "When I try to look inside arcades and game shops in Akihabara, other people tend to recognise me, and that's kind of embarrassing." **We've been there, too, Shigeru Miyamoto. Awful, isn't it?**

E101 "The world is at war, and **Edge** exists only as a 100-foot-tall videogame review robot dispensing verbal justice from the skies with acerbic, cliché-free missiles." **RedEye's futureshock moment**

E102 "Superficial resemblances to *Zelda*'s N64 outings aside, *Dark Cloud* is a potentially more intriguing proposition." **Sony must've paid us particularly handsomely that week**

E103 "Link's new cel-shaded appearance generated mixed reactions from the press. The Americans didn't like it. Everyone else did." **Edge reports back from Space World 2001 and the first appearance of *The Wind Waker***

E104 "I probably tweaked the stats up a bit, because I like them. You've got to. You don't want your favourite guy out there looking like a monkey." **Especially not one that's 12 pixels high. Norwich fan Jon Hare lets slip which team to plump for in *Sensible Soccer***

E105 "Ken Kutaragi wanted the platform to show our wish to expand. I thought about this for quite some time and my solution to this was the Earth… I focused on the colours blue and black. Blue represents the Earth, meaning water or life, and the black segment represents the rest of the universe." **We hope you appreciate the hard work that Teiyu Goto put into designing PlayStation 2**

E106 "Come – you've got to see how we create worlds." **Pre-release, CCP's Hilmar Petursson's excitement would have been put down as hyperbole if it wasn't about *Eve Online***

E107 "I walked into the Origin offices full of piss and vinegar. I was going to show these computer game guys what interactivity and roleplaying were all about. I was assigned to work with Richard Garriott on *Ultima VI* and Chris Roberts on *Bad Blood* and *Wing Commander*. It took me about a day and a half to realise I knew nothing." **Warren Spector knows that the day you stop learning is the day to find a new career**

E108 "The biggest surprise was certainly a retired WWII soldier who sent us a postcard with these comments regarding the *Tekken* series: 'According to my own experience, it is impossible that bodies can be projected into the air like this'. We were all astonished." **Katsuhiro Harada, *Tekken* series designer, on fan feedback**

E109 "I would not say there are any new features in this sequel." ***Crazy Taxi 3* producer Kenji Kanno causes a few heart palpitations for Sega PR**

> **I know when something's appropriate and when it isn't. We've never offended anyone. Um, apart from that one man**

E110 "The Rattle and Pram award for Outstanding Industry Petulance: THQ, who issued a legally worded warning to all magazines that, in theory at least, barred publishers from using any screenshots of any THQ product if the attached copy was going to portray it in a negative light. Presumably **Edge**'s reviews of *Nightcaster* and *Red Faction* would have to be illustrated with courtroom-style artist's impressions." **RedEye makes his own contribution to 2002's awards issue**

E111 "We have an eject button. We wanted it to be under a glass plate so the player would have to break it in order to access the button. This was obviously too risky as it could wound the player and be costly for users to replace the plate. Yes, we had some crazy ideas… we want the experience to be extreme." **Atsushi Inaba's ejector-seat proposal for *Steel Battalion*'s controller didn't get off the ground, either**

E112 "We looked very briefly at trying to make money off it, but it turned out at the time you couldn't copyright software and you couldn't patent software. We thought about it for a week, then decided, nah, there wasn't any hope, so we gave away the sources freely." **Steve Russell on *Spacewar* (though, to be fair, it should also be noted that the hardware it ran on in 1962 cost $120,000)**

E113 "No, female characters only. I mean, this is obvious. There would be no meaning in adding male characters." **Tomonobu Itagaki knows his target audience for *Dead Or Alive Xtreme Beach Volleyball***

E114 "The Ministry of Defence is looking to exploit synthetic environments for a variety of purposes. One of these purposes is to experiment with new weapons and tactics, which is where *Half-Life* comes in." **Despite the interest in videogames from QinetiQ's Chris Morris, the British army has yet to deploy Snarks in the field**

E115 "The profitable part of the online business is very likely several years away. Entering the business because it's the hot topic of the day makes neither a profitable business nor satisfied customers." **Satoru Iwata outlines the place that online has in Nintendo's strategy**

E116 "Nintendo had the ability to continue its exclusive relationship with Rare, but in looking at the company's recent track record it became clear that its value to the future of Nintendo would be limited." **NOA's executive vice president of sales and marketing, Peter McDougall, merely adds insult to injury**

E117 "I recently saw a crow fly into a powerline and watched as it fell dead into the road. I took it home with me and gave it a place on the property. The bugs are still working on it and in the end it will probably take me a good nine months to go from full bird to perfect skeletal mount. I look forward to posing it in a very natural motion like a single frame of animation that embodies the natural movement of the life from which it came." **We decide not to follow up with a question about the contents of Lorne Lanning's walk-in freezer**

E118 "How often do you walk down the street and see two strangers being incredibly rude to each other and using foul language? Not very often. How often do you see that on the telephone? Not very often. How often do you see that on the internet? A lot. One step of anonymity gets removed once you start using voice; it's much more intimate." **Xbox chief J Allard possibly overestimates the sedative effect voice comms will have on 12-year-old tongues**

E119 "I'm a mature adult. I know when something's appropriate and when something isn't. Ten years on, and we've never offended anyone. Um, apart from that one man, about epilepsy." **Mr Biffo protests too much, shortly before his departure from Digitiser**

E120 "[Rez] was *Panzer Dragoon* with its trance trousers on, wasn't it?" **Jeff Minter isn't happy when we compare *Unity* with *Rez***

E121 "If you're going to imagine yourself as a kickass babe in a chainmail bra, it ain't gonna be an ugly one with a flat chest, is it?" **The Creative Assembly producer Luci Black looks for gender stereotyping's silver lining**

E122 "Games used to be rotten; frustrating things with three lives and no savepoints. Nostalgia can do a lot but it can't make you play *Tir Na Nog* again." **Edge prises off the rose-tinted retro specs**

E123 "People die of disease and accident. Death comes suddenly and there is no notion of good or bad attached to it. It leaves not a dramatic feeling but a great emptiness… these are feelings I wanted to arouse in the players with Aerith's death relatively early in the game. Feelings of reality and not Hollywood." **FFIV director Yoshinori Kitase recalls the reasoning behind Aerith's abrupt and untimely end**

E124 "My boss promised/threatened to put his 'plonker on the table' if ever we got a 100 per cent review. Well, shortly after that rash statement, *Xenon 2* scored 100 per cent. We ran into the boss's office, interrupted his meeting and slammed the magazine down in front of him. Luckily for us he wasn't a man of his word – either that or he did get it out and we didn't notice." **PR guru Alison Beasley shines a light on the inner workings of the game industry**

E125 "It's ironic that a film so successful in adapting videogame tropes to the cinematic form is rewarded with a videogame tie-in that's so singularly unable to reciprocate." **Edge's reviewer opts for the blue pill when faced with *Enter The Matrix***

E126 "The worst submission I saw was a two-page document from an inexperienced developer for a game combining 'the scale and realism of *Operation Flashpoint* with the attitude of *GTAIII*'. The player character was a heavily armed eskimo in a quest for a sacred seal. Any takers?" **Dean Trotman, acquisitions manager for Codemasters, recalls the one that got away**

E127 "One of the programmers points out that *Killzone* has three weapon slots as opposed to *Halo's* two. There's an uncomfortable pause. It's the kind of silence you get when someone cracks a bad joke at a funeral." **Edge learns that the H-word is not welcome in Guerrilla's offices**

E128 "**Edge** has had it with colons, and the simpering subtitles that trail after them. No more Bland Franchise Follow-up: The Verbing Of The Noun." **Edge's Tenth Commandment, issued on its tenth birthday, unfortunately falls on deaf ears**

E129 "ERSE? It's OK, **Edge** can take a joke. They're those things that other mags use to fill up space, right? Here, let's try one. '*Grand Theft Auto* is shit! NOT! It's wicked! We cacked our pants it's so good, etc'." **GTA: Vice City's little homage lines up one Edge staffer with a visit to the nurse**

E130 "**Edge** is not ashamed to admit that it enjoys the bear pit that is Pop Idol. Public humiliation is the best medicine for talentless celebrity-seeking individuals with delusions of grandeur, says **Edge**'s mum." **Imagine if they'd used the licence to make a good game. Of course we'd have bought it**

E131 "Kutaragi-san came to visit, and told me with confidence that this machine was going to rule the videogame industry! I asked him why he was so sure. And all he said was, 'Come on, we're Sony!'" **Enterbrain president Hirokazu Hamamura remembers being shown Sony's PlayStation by its biggest advocate**

E132 "I would like to say that I have a few rules when it comes to drink. Yes, I'm a little bit of a maniac! I drink almost every working day." **Ah, Toshihiro Nagoshi. Now we know why there's so much incidental detail in *Yakuza's* bars**

E133 "It's OK, they're terrorists: I like to feel I'm doing my bit for the 'Coalition of the Willing', the 'Special Relationship', and various other bogus rhetorical abstractions." **Stephen Poole likes *Time Crisis* – and puncturing Unspeak at the same time is just a bonus**

E134 "I have absolutely no embarrassment about how much money I've made out of *Tomb Raider*. If my picture is in the papers under the headline 'Lara's boy makes millions again', well, that's fantastic." **We wonder if Core man Jeremy Heath-Smith still has his SUV with that JHS1 number plate**

E135 "The sea caresses the beaches like a supernaturally attentive lover. The sky is powder-blue, the sea a living mirror and, emerging from it, verdant isle after verdant isle. It's all so perfect it seems a shame to pull the trigger and bring a heaving bag of violence to this unearthly paradise." **Edge gets a bit Jilly Cooper at *Far Cry's* beauty**

E136 "How to make a Nintendo ad: simply hire an overacting pensioner and ask him to gape at his grandchildren's 'space-age' new toy while a jaunty tune plays in the background." **Edge looks at how things were in the bad old days**

E137 "In a single step our [Spectrum] keyboard concept [took computer keyboards] from 200 components to one. That's amazing by any standards." **Rick Dickinson, Sinclair's industrial designer during the golden ZX era**

E138 "Needless to say, it's not so street. It's Prince Charles chatting to Jay-Z, it's a Tory MP dressed as Ali G, it's your dad telling you he likes hip hop and that it has a good beat. It's the sex ed lessons you had as a kid, when the teacher came round the front of the desk and half-sat on it to show everything was cool. It's not cool." **RedEye didn't think much of *The Urbz: Sims In The City***

E139 "When you get promoted to a certain level, you're expected to wear a suit and tie. For me, that's the end of the world." **Keiji Inafune, head of R&D at Capcom, still wears jeans**

E140 "When you see a Treasure game, you are pretty sure it is going to be quite an experience. 'Waaaaaaa!' In no time you're in front of the screen, screaming, reacting to the intensity. It is our trademark." **Treasure stalwart Tetsuhiko Kikuchi explains all**

E141 "The level system, which I introduced into *MUD* only after considering several alternatives, does not get the same degree of consideration in new virtual worlds. They think 'How many levels shall we have?' rather than 'Shall we have levels?' Yet a level system for a virtual world only really makes sense if there's an end to it – a point at which you can say you've won and stop playing it like a game." **Richard Bartle strikes RPG convention for 550 points of damage. Critical hit!**

E142 "To be completely candid – you know, it was a good idea to bring us to the pub. What Introversion do is sell Chris's games. And Chris is a complete bastard. He wouldn't last five minutes at EA." **Introversion director Mark Morris doesn't rate the chances of a long relationship with EA Partners**

E143 "Names to take and asses to kick? Well, yeah. [Hesitates] Well." **Reggie Fils-Aime when we ask him if he had any particular names and asses in mind**

E144 "At one time, marketing clearly asked: 'How do we get total strangers to play together?' I guess the answer is to build a great game." **Ed Logg, creator of *Gauntlet*, smacks down the beancounters**

E145 "Here's my favourite: 'We will not fund a prototype but we are happy to direct you while you develop it'. F.U.C.K. O.F.F. It's a take-the-piss kind of place, the games business." **Ninja Theory creative director Tameem Antoniades recalls pitching *Heavenly Sword***

E146 "[Leon] is only reacting to a hostile environment, and it is ultimately about self-defence. Of course, users don't think about self-defence while playing the game." **RE4 producer Hiroyuki Kobayashi would never make a game that was just about killing things for fun**

E147 "When I told Nintendo of Europe that I was coming for the DS launch, they didn't believe me." **We're surprised at Nintendo president Satoru Iwata's surprise**

E148 "The daughter of the landlord of the pub used to frequently visit in the afternoons. At first for SNES *Street Fighter* sessions – she was Chun-Li and I was Blanka – and, as things progressed with *Tempest*, as an unofficial gameplay tester. Her sister did pretty much the same thing during the development of *Llamatron*." **The enviable quality-assurance process at work at Jeff Minter's Llamasoft studio is revealed**

E149 "My friends, we are fucked." **Greg Costikyan begins his 'Developer's Rant' contribution on working practices at GDC 2005**

E150 "[The fate of] *Alone In The Dark* remains the trauma of my life. It sold two-and-a-half million copies. It made Infogrames tens of millions of pounds. And they couldn't show us some recognition for that?" **Frédérick Raynal reveals Infogrames' attitude towards the team behind *AITD*. Almost all left immediately after the project ended**

E151 "Convincing the luddites that I am really the father of videogames is another matter. I might as well tilt with windmills." **The quixotic Ralph Baer accepts that he's not as famous as Nolan Bushnell**

E152 "My guess is you can blame Star Wars. Why waste resources when you could make ten times as much money with a Star Wars licence?" **Ron Gilbert talks about what happened to Lucasfilm Games**

E153 "A lot of videogame developers really bitch about the long hours they have to do, and how other industries pay better and they don't have to do such long hours, and I'm reading this long tome – this is at home, of course! – and it's been written on some forum at three in the afternoon. And I think, well, that doesn't really add up." **Relentless' David Amor casts the first stone on crunchtime**

E154 "First of all, I never had a bad time during game creation." **Tomohiro Nishikado, creator of *Space Invaders*. Refreshing, no?**

E155 "For us, it may have been the cinema inadvertently stretching the ratio for the first five minutes, making Milla Jovovich's briefly glimpsed nipple around 24 inches long. For others, it was Collins meeting a slicy, dicy death at the hands of a mesh of lasers." **Do laser-mesh things have hands? Edge's reviewer hyperventilates about his standout moments in the Resident Evil movie**

E156 "You get enough money to buy a pond and when you buy a pond you can buy ducks and so on, so for women it's like crack." **Comedy writer/director Graham Linehan nails the appeal of *Harvest Moon***

E157 "Who should emerge from the crowd but Jeremy Beadle. He said: 'That's mad, that is – it plays just like Jimmy White!' He then pulls out this brick of a mobile phone and calls Jimmy's agent." **Archer Maclean, creator of *Jimmy White's Whirlwind Snooker*, recalls how much simpler celebrity endorsement used to be**

E158 "There are problems with the top people, with the business people, certainly. But even among the development staff, they don't have the creative ideas. It's all just routine stuff." **Keita Takahashi, creator of *Katamari Damacy*, takes no prisoners in his quest for creativity**

E159 "People ask how I got started as a game designer. I tell them I sat down in front of my computer, started typing, and said 'I'm a game designer'." **It just came easy to Sid Meier**

E160 "Lara Croft." **Eidos' head of brand management, Larry Sparks, lists everything that sets Eidos apart**

E161 "Personally, I think [*Far Cry Instincts*] is better than *Halo*." **Ubisoft's Cevat Yerli possibly takes the company line a bit too far**

E162 "[Mr Yamauchi] is the one person who really understood what is meant by the term 'entertainment' [and] was willing to spend the necessary amount of the budget. That means as well as giving me great opportunities he's also given me a lot of money. Although of course I had to spend the money on making games." **Shigeru Miyamoto, on the other hand, gets the company line just about spot on**

E163 "Get a new build of the game, test an area for hours, write up bugs, get a new build, regress your bugs, report failure/success… wash, rinse, repeat for months on end." **We don't think that Jai Kristjan is working as a tester any more**

E164 "We don't think it's an absolute no-no for us to use it. We intentionally avoided giving the Revolution a game machine's name, or a cool name." **Satoru Iwata says you can make all the jokes you want, because mum likes it**

E165 "It needed another six months, but it went out as it was, and everyone was pretty miserable to see it get mauled. But, to be fair, it did go on to sell over two million units." **Gavin Rummery looks at the bright side of *Tomb Raider: Angel of Darkness***

E166 "With *Formula 1* you have done great harm to Sega!" **How Kazutoshi Miyake, head of Sega Europe, guilt-tripped Bizarre Creations into making *Metropolis Street Racer***

E167 "Nah. I disagree with that fact anyway [laughs]. I'm sure there's some engine advertising going on there…" **Realtime Worlds' Dave Jones on the claim Gears of War was built with an average team size of 25**

E168 "The fact that Reservoir Dogs has come to share its name with this pitiful shooter feels like a betrayal. If developing it was supposed to prove that interactive media reduces emotionally charged drama to the realms of the purely disposable, this triumphantly succeeds." **Most readers saw the 3/10 coming from the first paragraph**

E169 "Maybe the most intriguing thing that FAQs suggest is that gaming is contagious – it infects everything it interacts with. With their bounty boards, competitions, rivalries and co-operation, the whole subculture of FAQs has become something that looks uncannily like a game itself." **And we try to skip the cheats-forum levels**

E170 "*Wii Sports* may well be the best launch title ever made, but that doesn't necessarily make it the best game ever made." **We're not sure how we forgot Super Mario 64**

E171 "For Amiga gamers in 1990 the world was oval, its core a rectangle. Time existed as 90-second intervals, each announced and punctuated by an electric buzz, a pneumatic hiss and the sound of 36 fists and feet converging on a steel sphere… "One day," promised *Speedball 2*, "all sports will be played like this." But somehow, come the day, none of them were." **Edge gets misty-eyed about the passing of a future-sports classic**

E172 "If people want to run our games on a Nintendo DS, well that's great, we're going to run them on a Nintendo DS, because we like customers more than we like vanity graphics showcases." **Ask Gabe Newell about high-end visuals and you deserve what you get**

E173 "I don't think that so-called 'Full HD' has any meaning in the game experience. What matters most for me is how to recreate a human smile or laugh." **A different angle, but the same perspective on technology from a more surprising source: Hideo Kojima**

E174 "Marcus Fenix is a 300-pound cliché whose grizzled chops and sports-metal beard identify him as the kind of person you'd inch away from at bus stops." **An Edge writer gets a little snooty about the lack of variety in game avatars. We love Fenix, really**

E175 "My dog could take his dog any day." **Peter Molyneux gets shirty about Miyamoto at GDC '07. We'd like to see that battle**

E176 "Most days we'd leave work at 7pm and go to the pub, then clubbing until 2am, then go back to the office to sleep under the desks… Paul McKenna used to keep a freezer full of pies and pasties… So, all in all, we rarely went home." **Stuart Fotheringham harks back to the four-man development of Odin's Nodes Of Yesod**

E177 "The real Nintendo hallmark has never been the Seal of Quality, or Mario's moustache, or Miyamoto's cheesy grin: ever since the launch of the NES it's been the yen." **Perhaps we should've said that it's been massive piles of yen**

E178 "My job helps me play games, and believe it or not, playing games helps me in my job as an infantry soldier." **We hope Pvt Pete Wilson of the British Army is on the front line when the aliens invade**

E179 "Activision could have remained more faithful to the film had it taken the entire shipment of this clumsy aberration and buried it in the Arctic." **Edge's reviewer's opinion didn't help the millions of consumers left disappointed by Transformers**

E180 "We are the new jocks, and this is our high school!" **Actor/comedian Jay Mohr warms up Blizzcon '08, with feeling**

E181 "For most of our history it's been a real effort to get the record companies to pay any attention." **Alex Rigopulos, CEO of Harmonix, speaks just before Rock Band's release, and the sounds of an industry waking up follow him**

E182 "The Orange Box is a perfect realisation of some staggering talent… In each part it excels and betters what has gone before; as a whole it is almost overwhelming in its depth, irresistible in value and certainly, unreservedly, brilliant." **Yes, we quite like Valve's games**

E183 "The kernel of a good board game is a good design idea. That's something that videogames could do more to follow." **Steve Jackson, who'd probably tell you to look up anything by Reiner Knizia**

E184 "Street Fighter II is like a bible. Every time I play it, it inspires me to strive and try harder." **Maybe this is the reason Yoshinoro Ono's Street Fighter IV is so good**

E185 "I think perhaps the bigger issue is shielding people from any form of violence." **Suda 51 responds to the need to 'censor' specific aspects of No More Heroes**

E186 "Freezing to death outside? That's what happens in the Antarctic." **William Latham responds to those who moaned about getting lost and dying in The Thing**

E187 "To me, as a film nut, there was something about GTAIII that just drew a line in the sand between games and movies, and it felt like: this is us taking over now. And it may be another ten years or 20 years until that really happens, but to me, I'm never going to be able to go back to, say, an action movie and watch it in the same way." **Sam Houser considers Grand Theft Auto's, and gaming's, future**

E188 "Look at Miyamoto – he's not actively building Zelda and Mario any more, he's a producer, so I envy him for that. But don't worry, I'm not about to create Wii Fit. As for Snake, though… that's it. It's over." **Hideo Kojima talks about leaving behind the series he'll always be known for**

E189 "Microsoft completely panicked. I think they just wanted the game to die, to go away… America's a very segregated society where racism is really quite rampant, so there's this ultra-PC sensibility – and it comes from white middle-class people who are talking on behalf of a perceived group or problem." **Tameem Antoniades explains how one wayward review and a lot of corporate back-covering killed Kung Fu Chaos**

E190 "EA sells our game once, maybe it sells out and maybe it gets some reorders. Then the company, as a publishing force, moves on to the next thing. So if we want our game to be a success in the long run, we have to do this for ourselves." **We wondered who was paying for Burnout Paradise's outstanding, and continuing, post-launch DLC. Criterion's Alex Ward clarifies**

E191 "You have to understand that we – no, I – had just about ¥30,000 (£142) to promote this title! I used ¥20,000 (£94) to get a mask made that I could use to go and promote the game everywhere! This mask was made by a true professional wrestler." **Tez Okano might not have had the budget for promoting Dreamcast game Segagaga, but he didn't skimp on quality of materials**

E192 "Microsoft wanted to call Munch's Oddysee 'Abe & Munch's Fun Adventures'. They actually proposed that. It was like: 'Well, can you be any less creative? Is that possible?'" **Lorne Lanning thinks back to the early days of Xbox**

E193 "Failure should be fun. In fact, it should feel like when you're a kid and making a huge sandcastle – what's the next thing you do but run up and smash it to smithereens?" **Lucy Bradshaw, executive producer of Spore, knows what we're like**

E194 "In [Spore's] defence, Will Wright says that he'd rather see the Metacritic scores and sales of The Sims 2 than Half-Life 2. Well, at least he's honest. But even looking beyond the planet-sized 'if' that hangs over its sales potential, Spore is a stark reminder that while greatness in this market doesn't always equal success, true greatness is almost seen as anathema to it." **It was still good enough to garner one of those coveted Edge 7/10s, though**

E195 "You can't deny that Lego Batman knows its limits. Unfortunately, those limits are 'Lego' and 'Batman'." **The magic of Travellers Tales' series had worn off by this point**

E196 "I have this big ambition for Wii Music, that it can eventually be something so influential that it might be able to influence what music means in the world." **Shigeru Miyamoto's has heard the criticisms, but they don't stop him dreaming**

E197 "People have been playing Tetris for 25 years, and they're still getting better at it!" **Jason Kapalka, co-founder of Popcap, reminds us where the power in gaming lies**

E198 "Vivendi's management get on the phone and go: 'We've changed our mind. We're not giving you any money. If you were better people then you'd just do this for free'. And they just demoralised an entire room full of Swedes who'd been working 60-70 hours a week." **Ian Stevens on the 'polishing' period for Chronicles Of Riddick: Dark Athena. The studio now has a different publisher**

E199 "That unmistakeable sound is of a righteous bandwagon heading straight for Capcom's front door, so let's leave before they collide." **Edge's Resident Evil 5 preview cues up the controversy that's probably kicking into overdrive about now**

"HE'S CUTTING THE RULE BOOK IN HALF"
BOB BALDINGER

MADWORLD™

KILLER ENTERTAINMENT

TUNE IN FOR MORE JACK ACTION AT
WWW.MADWORLDTV.COM

Review

New games assessed in words and numbers

Edge's most played

Street Fighter IV

Challenge mode, fight requests, icons, titles, colours, taunts, Ryu and Chun-Li and Ken. Oh my! If we seem a little tetchy this month, it's the lack of sleep.
360, PS3, CAPCOM

World Of WarCraft

God help us, the needle slips back in the vein so easily. Well, after an evening of installing, that is. The still-sane part of us wishes Blizzard would stop adding to it.
PC, ACTIVISION

GTAIV: The Lost And Damned

Even if it feels almost like an act of infidelity to walk the streets of Liberty City as another man, this slice of DLC reminds you just how much was achieved with *GTAIV*.
360, ROCKSTAR

Resident evil?

How do you solve a problem like Sheva Alomar?

In the latter stages, the enemies are more racially mixed, and there's an African supporting character who lends a hand to Chris and Sheva. By then, though, the seeds have been sown

R esident Evil 5 has a problem – and it's nothing to do with whatever strain of virus is doing the rounds. A game that's predicated on the player's fear of the unfamiliar, the unknown, has chosen the Third World as its setting. The first videos inspired a minor rumbling in the videogame community at large, which may have led to changes in the final game, but it's destined for much more criticism upon release.

Resident Evil 5 reinforces cultural stereotypes about Africa and Africans, presenting an atavistic, backwards society driven by mob rage, where the savage black men carry the white women off to their shanty houses. By the second chapter, you're fighting tribal groups with grass skirts, spears and warpaint. Sheva Alomar, Chris's partner, is African, but her skin tone is the milkiest coffee colour, while her slightly plummy accent is noticeably distinct from that of the other Africans. It is clear that she is a sop, and not a very convincing one.

Laid out like this, it looks like a damning charge sheet, but there will be plenty more implications teased out and details seized upon in the weeks following the game's

release. The debate will polarise prosecutors and apologists, but the really problematic thing about *Resident Evil 5* lies in the middle. It propagates stereotypes and portrays a region of the world in a negative light – but it does so largely through implication and clumsy hedonism. It would be wrong to call *RE5* a malicious game: racial slurs can be inspired by hatred or, as in this case, simple insensitivity. The increased profile of videogames in general, and the responsibility this brings, have put the medium under a level of scrutiny that goes beyond grimacing at gore and swearing.

The fact that *RE5*'s lazy conventions are exposed under this scrutiny shouldn't be glossed over. Capcom deserves to be criticised for ignorance and a lack of sensitivity – this is, after all, a product intended for a global audience. At a point when it has more international development partners than ever before – and while the Japanese game industry is contracting in size – Capcom's game is bewilderingly naive. In the insular world of videogames past, this kind of stuff was laughed at or dismissed. Nowadays, it can only attract negative attention.

Edge's scoring system explained:
1 = one, 2 = two, 3 = three,
4 = four, 5 = five, 6 = six, 7 = seven,
8 = eight, 9 = nine, 10 = ten

RESIDENT EVIL 5

FORMAT: 360, PS3 (VERSION TESTED) RELEASE: MARCH 13
PUBLISHER: CAPCOM DEVELOPER: IN-HOUSE
PREVIOUSLY IN: E193, E199

Running past enemies is still possible, but you're a little more prone to attacks. It's the movement of bodies that really needs work: post-*GTAIV*, you expect the mobs to react when you push past them. The next in the series may want to consider offering up Euphoria zombies. You can imagine the possibilities

The final stages of the game are a huge anticlimax, both in setting and mechanics – disappointing in the context of *RE4*'s closing pyrotechnics. On second and third playthroughs, the earlier stages stand up while the latter parts pall

With the fifth main instalment in a series that spans 13 console games, Capcom finally redefines the phrase 'survival horror'. The horror here is the survival of the past. Maybe it's that the finely detailed environments and Chris Redfield's sharply defined stubble clash with enemy animations that will be so familiar to players of the previous generation. Perhaps it's the enduring legacy of the controls, or the shambling return of monster X from *Resident Evil Y*. These are symptoms of a bigger dislocation, though, in a series in which nothing goes to plan.

The majority of *Resident Evil 5*'s lengthy story mode pits Chris and his partner Sheva Alomar against enemies that continually threaten to overwhelm in number. On normal difficulty the crowds can just about be herded, ammo husbanded and everything kept under control. On the hard setting, *you're* being herded – away from your partner, into blind alleys, on to roofs and through buildings, only grabbing ammo and shooting in brief respites. It's exhilarating and frantic but, as the core focus of the game, rubs the wrong way against that series fundamental: the control system.

Suggestions that the traditional tank-like *Resident Evil* controls render the game unplayable are absurd, but despite the option to increase turning speed, their essential

stop-and-shoot nature is strained under the extreme, fluid pressure that *Resident Evil 5* excels in pressing you under. Combat in previous entries was almost entirely forward-facing and slower-paced; *Resident Evil 5*'s assaults come from all sides and require different tactics. Constant running, turning, knife-wielding and close-quarters attacks (in which Chris and Sheva can alternate to deal three particularly weighty blows) keep the hordes at bay, but you will be blindsided and you will be wounded. Though on occasion frustrating, the control system is never worse than serviceable, but it's a baseline the game should surely have aimed beyond.

Like the controls, the camera system hasn't moved on much, but in this case the

shoulder-blade fetish presents all-new pleasures. It has discovered a love for Chris, and the player happily follows. His arms are like thighs, the delicate curve of their triceps an object lesson in eroticism. He barks commands in a deep baritone, and even the humble egg is an exercise in seduction, smoothly cracked on his leg before being swallowed whole. Raw, naturally. Presentation has moved on, however, with the game's dramatic zoom, depth-of-field and perspective effects for melee moves, which communicate Chris's punches as having the force of a steam hammer.

He's not the only one who's bulked up: the bio-organic weapons have been on a steak diet. Many enemies are beefier than

The sharp contrasts of bright African sun and dark shadow as you walk the narrow alleys of the opening shanty town show off excellent lighting effects. Disappointingly, this isn't the case with the rather dull water

> When the game has the confidence to simply put you in a layered, open environment, any problems disperse in the warm glow of gunfire and herbs

those of *RE4*, but no longer feel as if they're constructed from bone, blood, sinew and claw – especially when you're repeatedly blasting their lumpen heads with a shotgun. The only wars of attrition in previous games came against the odd Tyrant; in the latter stages here, they become pretty much par for the course. Most bosses are retrogressive and unsatisfying one-trick ponies, some being sad reappearances of *RE* bosses from time past, some simply over-spiced by the appearance of a special weapon to be rigidly used exclusively for their dispatching.

It's here that the uneasiness lies in *Resident Evil 5*. Its focus on intense combat and set-pieces leaves little room for much of an atmosphere, and the promising mystery of its opening swiftly turns into fan-fondling, a

The ammo-sharing system is better than the recent demo suggests: now, partners hand over half their stash when both have a particular weapon, or all of it when only one partner has the necessary shooter. It's still a little too fiddly, and exchanging items is unforgivably clumsy

stony-faced attempt to draw together disparate and nonsensical story threads from previous games that was doomed never to achieve coherence. Capcom desperately needs a proper screenwriter or, failing that, one who can manage basic dialogue. More than this, though, it's the dearth of imagination that disappoints. It's clear now just how confident and creative *Resident Evil 4* was, designing enemies for particular set-pieces and then discarding them, tailoring its environments to both titillate and terrify, and always aware of its own B-movie nature in both scripting and shocks.

Resident Evil 5 doesn't have much of this. And yet in its best moments the game is very, very good indeed – as good as *Resident Evil 4*. The basic combat, of resisting panic, picking targets and managing scant resources, is as finely tuned as ever, and its best levels are exquisitely crafted for open battles. When the game has the confidence to simply put you in a layered, open environment and throw multiple enemy types into the mix, any problems disperse in the warm glow of gunfire and herbs.

Above all of this is the decision to make the game co-operative. With a human partner, especially one in the same room, *Resident Evil 5* is raised from the status of merely good to great. Concerted fire destroying waves of monsters before they get close, harried pincer movements on the

larger threats and last-gasp saves are all present and correct. There could be a more elegant solution to resource-sharing than an unwieldy 9x9 box navigated by D-pad, and it's certainly weird that you can shoot through each other, but these are minor grumbles concerning an inspired addition.

If only there were more new things to talk about. *Resident Evil 4* was always going to be an albatross for its successors, but it's the temerity with which Capcom treats it that's really surprising. There's so much reverential reuse of ideas, from basic combat to the big set-pieces, that it's almost as if *RE4*

had a formula that could be copied. Even if it did, a trick never looks quite as good the second time around.

It's not surprising that *Resident Evil 5* was intimidated by its predecessor, and it's not surprising that it believes imitation to be the most sincere form of flattery. It's also not surprising that such reverence has created mechanical clichés, from barrels to chainsaws, as pervasive as item boxes ever were. It's not even surprising, despite all this, that *Resident Evil 5* is a good game. The surprising, and sad, thing about *Resident Evil 5* is that it feels old. **[7]**

Later in the game, series-customary puzzles crop up; this one manages the feat of being easy to work out but frustrating to solve, thanks mainly to the fact that the game reverses the controls when you try to turn objects

Mercenaries

If *Resident Evil 5* has one feature that makes it essential, it's the best iteration yet of Mercenaries mode. The roster of playable characters and environments has expanded hugely, it can be played in co-op, but the idea's the same: dropped into a sandbox-style environment filled with respawning enemies and a time limit, you have to kill as many, as quickly, as you can. There are time bonuses, combo bonuses, plentiful ordnance, each area is progressively deadlier, and there's the greatest pronunciation ever of the phrase 'nice bonus'. *RE5's* greater numbers of enemies and, freed from the campaign's constraints, its freedom to combine them at will in succeeding waves demands a level of ingenuity and husbandry with the combat system that is rarely required in the main game. If singleplayer mode won't quite stand up to repeated batterings in co-op, this will – and then some.

EMPIRE: TOTAL WAR

FORMAT: **PC** RELEASE: **OUT NOW**
PUBLISHER: **SEGA** DEVELOPER: **THE CREATIVE ASSEMBLY**

Whatever the form of combat, the advisor will generally pop up with one of dozens of bits of advice. Rarely repeating itself, it's worth keeping on just to hear the well-written snippets of strategy

t's little wonder the *Total War* series has an evangelical following. No other game takes on whole eras of combat with such a combination of respect and fetishism for the rules and wisdom of battle, and no series treats history like such a serious playground of possibilities, yet features such comic-book characters.

It's potentially daunting. But The Creative Assembly has been very deliberate about catering for the newcomer, and *Empire* is the most accessible game in the series. There's the usual friendly tutorial, and throughout the game, the advisor will tell you if you're making gross tactical mistakes – like pointing

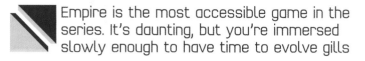

> Empire is the most accessible game in the series. It's daunting, but you're immersed slowly enough to have time to evolve gills

your artillery at cavalry, or shooting your own general. Then there's the story-led bridging campaign that introduces the world map, and takes America from its first scuffle with tribesmen to establishing independence, before you enter the grand campaign that spans the entire 18th century. Yes, it's daunting. But you're immersed slowly enough to give you time to evolve gills.

The *Total War* extreme close-up. Watching them fight is so distracting that you might forget to issue orders. The inclusion of randomised animations gives the whole battle an organic, human feel. You'll be tempted to give them all names

The most immediately obvious improvement is on the world map. For the first time, the visual feedback from the map gives you the real impression that your empire is building and your technology improving. That's thanks to a simple change – many of the developments that used to be stored inside your capital city are now spread across your land. Ports, farms, taverns and schools will all blossom into grand structures, and give you an instinctive global overview that was previously hidden away. It's such an improvement in terms of access, immediacy and intuition that it's difficult to imagine the older solution ever working.

Your agents, meanwhile, have been shuffled. Diplomats have been removed, with diplomacy taking place instantly. It might be artificial, but The Creative Assembly has never been a developer to let dogmatic

adherence to history ruin its gameplay. The rake replaces the spy and assassin, and the gentleman is a useful piece who will boost your research and can be used to dispatch enemy gentlemen without affecting the relationship between the nations. Meanwhile, placing missionaries in countries of other religions will slowly tip the belief of the populace, making them less likely to revolt when you topple their god.

The intelligence behind the new diplomacy has seen a moderate makeover, too. Apart from the absence of diplomats on the world map, alliances seem more stable. Perhaps that's because of the sheer number of countries: as well as the 11 playable major nations, the map is littered with minor states. A fickle approach to alliance in the previous games would lead to chaos, but relationships here are more fluid. If someone is making

The world map is fuller than ever, with much taking place outside the capital. New areas will pop up, as will new agents – depending on prosperity, growth and, in the rake's case, the number of bawdy houses

In fighting another ship, you can aim for its hull, or try to incapacitate it by firing chain shot at its sails. Alternately you can fire grape shot on to its deck, before attempting to board the vessel. Ships are expensive – stealing one from your enemy is a double boon

demands of you, that might be the first sign that they're viewing you as a less than valuable ally. It's another improvement – giving you a chance to respond tactically to a future threat.

There's a new win condition in the form of prestige, which allows you to claim victory on the basis of how wonderful everyone thinks you are. Abolishing slavery may make production less efficient, but it's a move towards enlightened government that will win you prestige. Of course, having a gigantic crushing army is another aspect of winning prestige, so it's not a complete get-out clause for woolly pacifists.

Empire's most dramatic addition to the game is its naval combat. As your ports grow into shipyards, you'll be able to 'recruit' brigs and sloops, and the world of saline skirmishing will open up to you. It's less

human than the land battles we're used to, but perversely the fact you're selecting one tangible thing – a boat, not 120 men – makes controlling the battle feel more intimate. And it's not easy. As the sides swell in number, it becomes as claustrophobic and chaotic as a game of chess in which both sides are allowed to move all their pieces at once.

Back to the newcomers – if you're not confident with the deeper nuances of management strategy, you can take advantage of the high level of automation that's open to you. The AI will never make the optimal choice, but it'll be good enough for all but the highest difficulties. Similarly, auto-resolving a battle might escape the fear of gross misjudgments, but you'll nearly always lose more units than you need to.

Playing like this, the suspicion will grow that you're only playing a part of the game, and you'll begin to forage in those menus. It's a case of tugging individual strands of the spider's web, to see if anything hairy jumps on to your face. If you are one of *Total War*'s newcomers, this is the process of strapping yourself into the machine, learning the personalities of the factions, how your generals pick up traits according to their experience, whether Sweden is trustworthy.

That's the true joy of *Empire*, and the whole series. It's the shared bad posture of a million squinting monitor-lit faces. Men filled with the concerns of emperors for whom going to bed seems like a mundane and unworthy decision. *Empire* is slick, intelligent, accessible and layered enough to bring this pallid fervour to a whole new crowd. **[9]**

Note the light shower of snow: weather can affect the tide of battle, and you should react to it. For example, the native American emphasis on melee is flattered by heavy rain, which will dampen enemy stocks of gunpowder and increase the riflemen's reloading time

Modified war

Empire starts out with 11 playable factions, and that's your lot. Unlike previous games, you won't unlock factions during play. However, The Creative Assembly admits that it's only a very simple change in a very accessible file to unlock all of the minor factions as playable. So, if you want to face insurmountable odds, force yourself into a more diplomatic trading game, or if you're simply a born tinkerer who hates the idea that things are there that you can't play with, someone will have discovered the 'unlock all factions' setting on the day of release, and you'll be able to play as West Tinystan.

A tip to those who would use nine-button QTE sequences for their melee combat: make the prompts big enough to actually read

SHELLSHOCK 2: BLOOD TRAILS

FORMAT: 360 (VERSION TESTED), PC, PS3 RELEASE: OUT NOW
PUBLISHER: EIDOS DEVELOPER: REBELLION PREVIOUSLY IN: E195

The wrong-est day

Now, where were we? Kill a few Viet Cong and the game moves 'up' a gear by unleashing 'the Infected', a horde of zombies that, depending on how the wind's blowing, will either jump or vomit on you. Missions, the objectives for which seldom relate to anything onscreen, often involve surviving wave after wave. And, no, you still don't get enough bullets. Thank God, then, for your machete, which at least unlocks an Achievement before it gets you killed. The game's debts to *Condemned* include an unusually tight FOV that works to tremendous effect… in *Condemned*. In an already horrible FPS, however, it makes even the smallest shrub a potentially lethal hazard, much like the game as a whole.

When the foremost face button of an FPS control scheme turns your torch on and off, you know you're in trouble. When the iron sight of your gun actually obscures the target – along with several other things for good measure – you know you're in for something worse. Worse than what, exactly? We're hesitant to say 'everything', but *America's Most Wanted: War On Terror* has never looked so good. A desperate bid to make easy money from the *Condemned* crowd, *Shellshock 2* is one almighty dung-heap of a game – and not just because of its sage advice: "You can't run from this. You'll only die shitting yourself in the jungle". Pass the Radio Times, we say – we'll take our chances.

The story is stick-thin, so we've had to fill in some blanks. You are Nate Walker, a rookie GI whose brother Cal has infected half

Jacob's Bladder, more like. Nate's hunt for his brother is communicated almost entirely by screens apparently written by the runner-up in an online competition

of Cambodia with a virus by the name of 'Whiteknight', leaving an army of undead soldiers in his wake. Stranger still, the local Viet Cong have apparently lost their marbles, unable to negotiate simple spaces and drawn like moths to exploding barrels. The bad news is that their bodies have become bulletproof from the neck down, and someone's mislaid all the bullets anyway, meaning that headshots are your only option. A shame, because Nate reloads in a kind of dreamlike stupor while the game around him asks itself whether there really such a thing as zero frames per second. Before playing this, we'd have said no.

John Merrick, the Elephant Man, could skip stones better than Nate throws grenades – with the added bonus that stones wouldn't emit the kind of flatulence that this game calls an explosion. The enemy seems equally unimpressed, even the RPG leaving many of its intended victims, at worst, a bit perplexed. The game merrily punishes you for reckless run-and-gun yet offers no alternative; you can crouch, protecting everything bar your head, neck, arms and torso, but the only real use of cover is a hideously protracted vault animation. Get shot, and a flash of dandruff along the side of the screen fails to tell you where from, the game as fond of precision as it clearly is of guns (see 'The wrong-est day').

No Vietnam game is complete without a giant man in a gas mask bursting through the door of a mansion before treating you to ten minutes of circle-strafing

Please, Rebellion, either stop making games like this or stop making the good ones, so that we know what to expect. *Shellshock 2* is a scandalous FPS made with no apparent knowledge of the genre, little but contempt for its audience, and few tools beyond a spluttering engine and a hammer. Its hope seems to be that there are people out there who, tired of *Killzone 2* or *FEAR 2*, want yet another shooter before the clocks go forward. For those people, there's always time for *Daikatana*. **[2]**

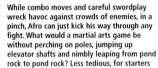

The distinctive character designs of the show are recreated here, and the lengthy – sometimes laborious – boss fights give you plenty of time to admire them all

AFRO SAMURAI

FORMAT: 360, PS3 RELEASE: OUT NOW PUBLISHER: BANDAI NAMCO
DEVELOPER: SURGE PREVIOUSLY IN: E197

While combo moves and careful swordplay wreck havoc against crowds of enemies, in a pinch, Afro can just kick his way through any fight. What would a martial arts game be without perching on poles, jumping up elevator shafts and nimbly leaping from pond rock to pond rock? Less tedious, for starters

Afro Samurai has but one motive: revenge. As a boy, he watched his father die at the hands of the long-nosed, three-armed gunslinger Justice. To avenge his dad, he's killed his master, watched his best friends die and suffered a bad dating streak – all to become ruthless enough to take Justice down.

Afro Samurai marries the stylish anime of the TV series with a bloodthirsty beat 'em up. Like the series, the game boasts a soundtrack by the Wu-Tang Clan's RZA, as well as stellar voicework by Ron Perlman and Samuel L Jackson, playing the sombre Afro and his wise-ass sidekick Ninja Ninja.

There's no HUD to block the splashy bloodshed and striking character design; instead, clues such as a bloody uniform and a glowing pendant provide effective status indicators. The lack of a HUD also smooths the transition between the cutscenes and the action – all the better to make *Afro Samurai* feel like an interactive cartoon.

While the game's script closely follows the plot of the series, the character arc has changed: in the player's hands, Afro becomes more tortured and more sympathetic, and the conclusion brings real closure to his story. Perhaps they weren't counting on a sequel. Likewise, Ninja Ninja – the imaginary friend who gives voice to Afro's suppressed emotions – is the perfect companion. He also plays the hero's conscience: the closer Afro gets to his goal, the more perceptive and more cutting Ninja Ninja's remarks become. In one chapter, love interest Okiku (Kelly Hu) narrates a tale of star-crossed love, but Ninja Ninja keeps piping in to break the mood, and to put Afro back in his place. After all, when would a stone-cold killer like him have the time to date?

But an engaging story masks an average, meagerly short hack-and-slasher. Afro wields one sword with no upgrades, and while his health and skills grow along the way, only a few combos are needed to get through the game. A focus mode jazzes up the fights by slowing down the action and letting the player carefully line up a strike. This is key to winning the witty minigame Body Part Poker, in which Afro racks up a winning hand in the form of severed heads and limbs.

While there's plenty of bloodshed, the action rarely thrills. The boss battles – particularly the final one – disappoint, as formidable foes hop around running through the same moves while the player slowly scythes them down. The platforming exercises and obligatory ninja wall jumps feel like make-work, and only a dizzying mid-air encounter with Afro Droid gives players a taste of the show's surreal violence. And while Afro's defined by his swordplay, his feet are deadlier: when in doubt, simply kicking an enemy to death will do the trick.

With its focus on storytelling, *Afro Samurai* is reminiscent of last year's *Star Wars: The Force Unleashed* – the hero's struggle resonates long after the gameplay is forgotten. The flash and the gore are toned down, and the henchmen never get any smarter, but that bond with the protagonist – and that investment in his salvation – make the game worthwhile. And more rigorous martial arts games such as the *Ninja Gaiden* franchise may have to explain why they couldn't reward their fans with a story this serious – or a 'road dog' half as memorable as Ninja Ninja. **[5]**

Focus mode slows the game's action and sets Afro up for devastating attacks and precise disembowelings. Achievements reward multiple deaths and outstanding atrocities

They named him twice...

"Ah, I see y'all came dressed as your favourite character: guy who dies like a bitch!" The game's true star is Ninja Ninja, enthusiastically voiced by Samuel L Jackson. Afro Samurai's constant accomplice and the walking embodiment of his id, Ninja Ninja is always on hand with clues, catcalls and praise. Instead of a mini-map, players can call on Ninja Ninja to appear in a cloud of smoke and help them find the next goal; naturally, insults about your helplessness follow. His running commentary also livens up the most repetitive battles: after a fight with a female adversary he cheers: "Damn, that girl puts both the 'asses' in 'assassin'!"

Whip Select, and those drab but essential icons, in effect (left). The visuals often fail to tally with the action, with soldiers not shown firing yet still damaging enemies

The acid-spitting crab beast here is the height of *Stormrise*'s visual invention. There are just nine units for each of the two sides, so you'll see everything in short order

STORMRISE

FORMAT: 360 (VERSION TESTED), PC, PS3 RELEASE: MARCH 27
PUBLISHER: SEGA DEVELOPER: THE CREATIVE ASSEMBLY
PREVIOUSLY IN: E194

This screenshot makes it all look very dramatic, but it's not an angle you'll ever see *Stormrise* running from – assigning Whip Select to the right stick means camera control is limited

Science friction

The plot? Two factions of humanity warring over ownership of Earth – the high-tech Echelon versus the mutants and psychics of the Sai. Grating dialogue and an apparently ad-hoc narrative accompany the campaign, the overall sense being it's a necessary but undesired evil. The Whip game first and foremost, clearly, and freed from the restrictions and irksome talking heads it becomes a more likeable affair. If *Stormise* has any future, it's one revolving around eight players transforming a map into a gauntlet of sniper ambushes and aircraft-guarded chokepoints.

If any scientists are reading, is it *definitely* the case that if Armageddon were to occur it would remove, as well as almost all life, all colour from the Earth? This sci-fi RTS, from the makers of the perennially acclaimed *Total War* series, is a startlingly ugly game, and that's to the detriment of its mechanics as well as its appearance and character.

Units are woefully indistinct from each other and their environments, which forces a reliance on selection via the similarly nondescript icons that float above their desaturated heads. This is future war played out in disorientating, unhappy sepia.

That *Stormrise* is such a graphical stumble wretchedly overshadows a clutch of very smart ideas intended to modernise a genre that so often rests on its laurels. The Whip Select system is an attempt to create an interface designed specifically for a gamepad, rather than the usual method (see *Halo Wars*) of assigning a thumbstick the role of a treacly mouse analogue. A nudge of the right stick in a given direction fires out a laser pointer of sorts; you'll instantly jump to whichever unit it passes through once you release the stick.

There's an element of the Wii Remote to this, in that it's a nearly-there technology – with broad gestures and precise familiarity with where you've left each unit you can hop around very quickly. Come the need for finer selection – such as picking one unit from a close cluster of others – it becomes a frustrating bunny-hop. It's certainly a noble attempt at reinvention, but it lacks finesse.

Similarly ambitious is an endeavour to make this a true 3D strategy world. Most RTS environments are little more than 2D worlds with a camera floating above them, but *Stormrise* offers building interiors, rooftops, tunnels and wide-open sky in which to place your meagre variety of units (a mere nine for each of the two factions). There's no fog of war to worry about – if you can't see an enemy unit, it's because none of your units can see it. Line of sight is essential here, requiring careful unit placement rather than simply commanding everything to conquer a given spot.

In theory, at least. This wants to be a game of stealth and ambush; in practice, the over-complicated controls and confusingly dreary art style mean it too often defaults to lurching pile-ons. While no doubt a few truly dedicated players will eventually master finer strategic thinking in online battles, for most it will be too much effort with too little reward. A seemingly arbitrary decision to restrict unit groups to a maximum of three prevents battles from becoming cheery all-out assaults, which renders *Stormrise* curiously inaccessible to the first-time console RTS players it so clearly hopes to court.

Despite coming from one of the most respected and skilled RTS developers of all time – albeit from its younger Australian arm rather than the main UK team – *Stormrise* feels peculiarly like something from a first-time European studio yet to match its high ambition with experience. It is a charmless mess, but underneath its disagreeable surface lurks an understanding that realtime strategy games have yet to truly embrace the third dimension. Perhaps it's best thought of as a glorified tech demo for The Creative Assembly's next step. Certainly, releasing it so close to *Halo Wars* suggests deliberate commercial suicide – that its genuinely progressive ideas will be ignored and lost as a result is a minor tragedy. **[4]**

In co-op, two players control a pair of squads each. You can afford to give each more attention, but co-ordinating all four becomes entertainingly fraught

The climax of the game's laughable plot is home to the few non-standard missions and the only major escalations of *Dawn Of War II*'s usually tight scale

WARHAMMER 40,000: DAWN OF WAR II

FORMAT: PC RELEASE: OUT NOW
PUBLISHER: THQ DEVELOPER: RELIC ENTERTAINMENT
PREVIOUSLY IN: E197

Though it might be histrionic of Relic to ditch so much of the realtime strategy template mid-series, there's plenty there worth ditching. Building a base and managing an economy have a place in mega-scale war games such as *Supreme Commander*, but they always sat awkwardly next to the bloody acrobatics of *Dawn Of War*'s squad-level violence, and yet more uncomfortably in the Warhammer 40,000 universe – a fiction whose tagline explicitly states that there is only war.

Dawn Of War II trades that set of ridiculous conceits for another, equally ludicrous set: *World Of WarCraft*'s. The missions that comprise the singleplayer and co-op campaign now entail ten men fighting their way through roaming enemy mobs to reach a boss who, on death, drops loot. Curious that a Tyranid Lictor should have been carrying a Space Marine-issue heavy bolter with slightly better stats than the one you're currently carrying. Curious, but fun.

Narrowing your jurisdiction to four squads of a few men means broadening their abilities and heightening their demands on your attention. Each squad leader has at least three superpowers – all are crucial and none can be automated. It asks a deftness with hotkeys that *Dawn Of War* never did, short

Defence missions offer the occasional break from the prevailing 'kill the boss' mission template, but sadly there's still precious little enemy AI in evidence

of competitive play, but only because these are tactics you never had to use in *Dawn Of War*. Now you're baiting commanders into killzones as a matter of course, jump-jetting over melee units to disrupt enemy firepower and thinking intelligently about who to suppress and who to grenade.

Dawn Of War II's strength is in the way it caricatures each unit's traits until their optimal use is obvious. A heavy weapons team is now so cumbersome as to be useless when moving, but so powerful when set up that the virtue of luring the enemy to it is immediately clear. The inability to create new units leaves you with nothing to focus on except the smartest way to employ the ones you've got, which is exactly what a strategy game – particularly a Warhammer 40,000 strategy game – should be about.

But for a game so widely lauded as brave, *Dawn Of War II*'s failings are all acts of timidity. Relic seems afraid to let any of its ideas meaningfully vary your experience, in

case the result isn't as satisfying as the scenario it has clearly tested so well.

You find new weapons, but the only functionally different ones are unusably weak. You choose where to pump points when each squad levels up, but only one or two attributes are relevant to each. You pick just four squads to take on each mission, but for most of the game you only have five to choose from. You can decide which mission to do next, but they're all tediously similar. Plus, while the beloved Tyranids have finally been added, in singleplayer you can only play as the Space Marines.

Relic's crisp engine and enthusiastic animations lend your soldiers' violence tremendous weight and the muscular feel of *Dawn Of War II*'s squad combat is its enduring appeal. But the hybrid genre that's been built for this series is half-formed, meek and muddled. That's surprising from a developer once so clear about what it wanted, and so right about what we did. **[7]**

A different wargame

Rather than make a competitive multiplayer game from the strong four-squad system that makes the singleplayer and co-op campaigns so smart and satisfying, Relic has sheepishly backtracked. *Dawn Of War II*'s multiplayer skirmish mode reinstates much of the pap that makes other strategy games so abstract and fussy: you have a base, with a tech tree, which builds units. Buying them, upgrading them and doing laps between the three victory points you must hold to win bears little resemblance to a war, and is accordingly unsatisfying. The default three-versus-three format ought to produce impressively grand kerfuffles, but the 12-minute average match time stops most games short of either a satisfying victory or convincing defeat.

50 CENT: BLOOD ON THE SAND

FORMAT: 360, PS3 (VERSION TESTED) RELEASE: OUT NOW
PUBLISHER: THQ DEVELOPER: SWORDFISH STUDIOS
PREVIOUSLY IN: E189

A problem shared

Along with its checklist of other must-have shooter features, *Blood On The Sand* has duly included a twoplayer co-op mode. It's online-only (disappointing, given how much fun we've been having with splitscreen *Resi 5*) and although it's technically sound it doesn't really add anything to the game. *Blood On The Sand* is so predicated on distraction and noise that you don't really need company, and the sequential slaughter-chamber design hardly supports advanced tactical thinking. It's good to have someone to fire the mounted gun in the must-have vehicle section, but otherwise it's an oddly vacant area of the game.

Hand-to-hand Counter Kills return from *50 Cent: Bulletproof*. They play out in slow-motion quick-time events with big, friendly response windows making it almost impossible to mess up whatever nasty combination of punch, stab and knee to the spuds Fiddy launches into

The unnamed and apparently unmotivated enemies 50 Cent and his crew plough through are often to be found standing helpfully near explosive barrels and on balconies with little or no cover. Implausible, maybe, but it keeps things moving

If the first *50 Cent* game was a technical disaster and a moral aberration – and it absolutely was – then what hope for the unexpected and frankly unasked-for sequel? Especially since that sequel relocates Fiddy and his rather well-armed entourage from their native New York to a thinly veiled model of Iraq, which on the surface is a suggestion so outrageous it barely seems plausible.

Against all the odds, though, *Blood On The Sand* isn't just fun to play, it somehow wriggles out from under the weight of moral indignation which ought to have crushed it. The key is not that it's a particularly exceptional game – the shooting is smooth but little more – but that Swordfish Studios has clearly come to terms with the kind of game it's making much better than did its predecessor Genuine Games.

For starters, it doesn't put major effort into innovation. There's an obvious comparison to *Gears Of War*, with a bulky, Unreal-rendered Mr Cent thumping into cover against cracked concrete barricades and walls. The controls and onscreen prompts are identical – 'X' to enter cover and again to break left, right or over the top depending on which direction is pressed. And the organisation of your mini-arsenal is essentially the same as *Gears'* D-pad arrangement, only with grenades separately mapped to R2. The shooting itself, though, has none of *Gears'* thunderous rattle, and owes more to *Uncharted: Drake's Fortune* – enemy machine-gun fire leaves white trace marks in the air, and the camera swings loosely but not impractically as you line up headshots on the rent-an-insurgent AI.

The effort instead goes into making the game a constant arcadey conveyor belt of flash and noise and reward. Gun down an enemy and a 'KILL' sticker pops up top-centre screen, with a succession of facts about the nature of the death – 'Indirect', 'Headshot', 'Snapshot' – which are translated into numbers and then added to your score, which ticks over continually in the top right corner. Chain kills together before a timer runs down and the scores are multiplied. Littered liberally in semi-hidden spots across the levels are boxes of gold which Fiddy kicks or rifle-butts to splinters, which can then be traded for new weapons, taunts and hand-to-hand finishers.

The effect is dizzyingly busy – a constant soundtrack of bumping 50 Cent tracks plays over headscarved gunmen spinning to the floor while piles of cash and jewellery literally fly *into* you, and your brilliance and deadliness is totted up in several different counters spinning simultaneously. And to make sure the pace never dips, entering new

Certain waves of enemies will trigger timed challenges that reward you with a short burst of extra-destructive ammo. Whatever you have to shoot, punch or blow up within the time limit is signposted in glowing red

areas frequently triggers a short timed challenge – kill two snipers in 40 seconds, say, or amass $4,000 in a minute. Succeed and you're rewarded with a short supply of special pistol ammo which either explodes on impact or consumes its target in flames.

It's this constant distraction that distances you from both the preposterous plot and 50 Cent's absurd macho posturing (by the game's end most inhabitants of the Middle East have been classified as either 'fools' or 'bitches'). In other words, it's very effectively designed, and while it's no technical marvel (there are too many routes blocked by cardboard boxes for that) it's thoroughly, thoroughly fun. A very guilty pleasure. **[7]**

Fig.1. Gamecube. 2002

Fig.2. Atari JAGUAR. c. 1994

Fig.3. Wii. 2006

Fig.4. dreamcast. 1999

Fig.5. SNES. 1992

Fig.6 Playstation 3. 2007

Fig.7. XBOX 360. 2005.

Fig.8. Sega MEGADRIVE. c.1990

An evolution in journalism.

EDGE has survived generations of consoles, outdated software
and pulped magazines to prove its staying power.

an.x would like to congratulate the EDGE team on their
consistent quality and originality over the last sixteen years.

The GeoEye satellite-mapped landscapes are, we're told, accurate representations of world cities. But wouldn't we rather have cities designed with an eye for their gameplay possibilities rather than geographical accuracy?

To add a frisson of topical flavour, the pursuit of money plays a large role in the game's plot – possibly paving the way for an upcoming *Rainbow Six: Wall Street*, in which you get to machine-gun evil hedge fund managers

TOM CLANCY'S HAWX

FORMAT: 360 (VERSION TESTED), PC, PS3 RELEASE: MARCH 6
PUBLISHER: UBISOFT DEVELOPER: IN-HOUSE (UBISOFT BUCHAREST)
PREVIOUSLY IN: E191, E198

The ingredients are all there: Clancy's paranoid brand of political and military hokum, some tub-thumpin', flag-salutin' American patriotism and a just-barely plausible vision of the near future (if you ignore Cold War-era jets carrying 100 missiles). So why doesn't it gel?

Well, for a start, fast jet combat is a hard thing to make entertaining in a game, since there is nothing of the twisting dogfights or seat-of-your-pants flying of the propeller age as seen in *Crimson Skies*. Ubisoft tries to recreate this by allowing you to turn off a lot of your jet's boring safety features (with a double-tap of the trigger Tom would surely approve of) in order to perform 'extreme manoeuvres', zooming the view out into distant thirdperson as you gracefully flip and roll to evade missiles and get a lock on fast-moving targets. This is something drummed into you in the training missions,

and is set up to be a major part of the game.

But you'll still spend a lot of your time flying round in a large circle using the chase-cam perspective, following a yellow arrow to your target. Once missile lock is achieved, A is pressed to launch, then Y to switch targets, then A, then Y then A until you've either destroyed them all or need to make another pass. The rebels and PMCs you'll be fighting are also surprisingly well funded, to the point of being able to take on the US Navy,

so you'll always have plenty to shoot at.

It's in the missions themselves where *HAWX* shows its major limitations. Escorting a large, vulnerable target is a sadly regular occurrence, while the main differentiator between stages is the number of enemies and the direction in which they originate. And the game pulls the occasional nasty trick, like disabling your missiles to force you into using guns. Later missions mix up the escort mission/air-to-air mission/bombing mission progression by getting you to do them all in quick succession

HAWX is a well-rounded package, with online co-op, a free-flight mode that lets you enjoy the satellite-mapped scenery, and an experience point system that unlocks extra jets and weapons in a similar vein to that seen in *Rainbow Six Vegas 2*. We can probably expect plenty of people online spinning a tooled-up F-14 around the skies while calling friends "Goose" as a result.

As an arcadey flight game it's just about on the enjoyable side of average, especially when compared to its still superior genre stablemate *Ace Combat 6*. But as a Clancy game, it tailspins feebly below the standard we've come to expect by failing to adhere to the standards of remote possibility those titles so consistently set. **[6]**

Zoom zoom zoom

The 'assistance off' zoomed-out mode is a bit of a gimmick, and while it can look extremely pretty, the majority of the game can be played perfectly well without it. Avoiding an incoming missile, for example, is just a matter of waiting for the warnings to start flashing an imminent hit, before holding the brake trigger and making a tight turn – something that's perfectly attainable with your safety features on using the chase-cam view. Zoomed-out mode also switches the camera angle depending on which target you've got selected, and can make it tricky to judge your height above the ground, leading to amusing bellyflops and collisions with buildings.

Your wingmen take forever to line up a shot, which makes the voice samples grate all the more as you order them to attack only to destroy the target yourself

TIME HOLLOW

FORMAT: DS RELEASE: OUT NOW
PUBLISHER: KONAMI DEVELOPER: IN-HOUSE

Just as Phoenix Wright can lose by asking the wrong questions, Ethan can drain the Hollow Pen by excavating the wrong portion of the screen. Waste too much and you'll need a chapter restart

In fairness, the plot does a good job of explaining the limitations of Ethan's pen. It transpires that he's less of a temporal vandal than a repairman

Were you to tell a tale about time alteration and the infinite possibilities therein, choosing the none-more-linear graphic adventure format as your narrative vessel would seem counterproductive. Playing as Ethan, a boy bestowed with a history-rewriting pen, the possibilities initially seem endless. Social faux pas can be undone, late homework unignored and deceased parents brought back from the grave.

However, just as you discover that Phoenix Wright is never destined to have a client's blood on his hands, you'll discover too that Ethan's future is just as predetermined, and that he actually has precious few powers to guide himself towards it. It turns out he can (by drawing windows to the past in a stylus minigame) only tweak a handful of timeline-defining moments, and aside from the odd occasion to help out his pals with optional meddling, the conclusion can't be rewritten; we are but page-turners in a predestined yarn.

Not that it's a bad story. Set in a school and its surrounding suburbs, *Time Hollow* eschews the grand anime melodrama that could have been spun from such a powerful Biro. The tasks are mundane enough – prevent a treehouse fire, for example – to add surprising dramatic heft when events of note do occur. Keep up with the complicated network of characters and forgive the odd paradox and the finale is actually quite poignant.

The game's writer, Junko Kawano, is not new to time tinkering. His PS2 adventure *Shadow Of Memories* reveals an ongoing obsession with the complexities of the butterfly effect – captured there with multiple endings. It seems we're left with one of two choices: branching gameplay through nine lesser plots or doggedly led through one superior tale. While *Time Hollow* fills a *Phoenix Wright*-shaped hole in our lives, we do prefer our chaos theory a little less tidy. **[6]**

DRAGON QUEST V: HAND OF THE HEAVENLY BRIDE

FORMAT: DS RELEASE: OUT NOW
PUBLISHER: SQUARE ENIX DEVELOPER: ARTEPIAZZA

Once again Square-Enix's deft translation work brings the world to vivd life, even if Sanchez's thick Spanish accent is a little over the top

Final Fantasy might aspire to the Tolkien fantasy epic, but *Dragon Quest*, by contrast, has always been happy as a simple fairytale. The fifth entry in the series, never before released outside of Japan, perhaps best exemplifies this confidence in identity. It tells the story of a mysterious baby who the player guides through boyhood, then adolescence and on through maturity in a series of sequential chapters. Seasoned with tragedy and humour, it's a poignant tale that courts cliché but which, thanks to its charm and creative twists on well-worn themes, represents one of the narrative high points of the series.

Employing the same engine that drove the recent DS update of its predecessor, this remake succeeds in maintaining the Super Famicom aesthetic despite its new 2D/3D hybrid styling. Characters are imposed on to fully rotatable 3D backgrounds and, with a fresh and careful translation, full of the regional dialects that enamoured many fans to the previous game, sprites have rarely felt so alive.

Dragon Quest V's wider significance to gaming is, of course, its monster hunting sub-mechanic, a system that begat *Pokémon* and its many imitators. In time, almost any monster encountered in the game can be recruited to your party and deployed into one of the four slots.

With their own development trees, even the lowliest slime can be built into a powerhouse with time, and the spread of team-building possibilities makes the party joyfully customisable.

However, there's no escaping the game's age, and the random battles that punctuate every journey across the game world are both traditional and simple. Characters gain new abilities only when they level up and you have no say in which ones they acquire. But they're also fast-paced and unfussy, lending this portion of the game a hypnotic edge.

But for those many players for whom JRPGs are stories as much as they are games, *Dragon Quest V*'s rather down-to-earth approach feels fresher than you might expect. A high point of both its series and genre, this is a game that achieves exactly what it sets out to, and whose western debut is very welcome for it. **[8]**

What the soundtrack (a CD was released for the original 1992 release) lacks in standout melodies it more than makes up for in evocative subtlety, tying together themes with careful creativity

RESISTANCE RETRIBUTION

FORMAT: PSP RELEASE: MARCH 20 PUBLISHER: SCEE
DEVELOPER: SONY BEND PREVIOUSLY IN: E199

CRYOSTASIS

FORMAT: PC RELEASE: OUT NOW
PUBLISHER: 505 GAMES, 1C PUBLISHER
DEVELOPER: ACTION FORMS PREVIOUSLY IN: E190

That Sony's PSP is a powerful device is in no doubt. But this has often been as much of a burden as it has a benefit to the system, with developers attempting to flex its muscle to deliver large-scale, tour de force games to compete with the home console experience, despite the limitations of its controls or the portability of certain genres.

Retribution's big-budget shooter action is another prime example. Conjuring technical marvels with its visuals, it resorts to using face buttons for aiming. Sure, Bend has eased the burden by including a generous auto-aim, but the decision is a mixed blessing: it minimises the awkward tapping required to target enemies but removes almost all of the challenge. The only way to avoid getting something locked in your sights is to turn your back on it. The result is to reduce what should have been active shootouts to almost passive experiences, as you watch an eager-to-please reticule jump from one Chimera to the next. The cover system, while beautifully implemented and intuitive, adds further to the problem. Its protection is so absolute that it devolves combat to little more than a timing-based minigame as you tap R1 to pop out and return fire between barrages of enemy bullets.

Adding further to the big-game-on little-console complex that Retribution appears to suffer from is some inventive but ultimately pointless PS3

Some of the bigger set-pieces offer a welcome change of pace – especially towards the end, when the basic shooting thrills begin to wane

connectivity via USB. PSP Plus enables you to play with a DualShock for… some reason. You can also 'infect' Retribution using a copy of Resistance 2 to unlock extra modes and weapons, but these are lost as soon as you switch either machine off.

If you can eschew such gimmicks, however, and accept the core game's superficiality, there's plenty to enjoy. Resistance Retribution might be shallow, but its good looks and refined controls lend a certain mesmerising pleasure to it nonetheless. **[6]**

Retribution's eightplayer multiplayer doesn't match its big brother's 30-man teams. But Sony Bend's PSP record is strong thanks to its work on the Syphon Filter series, so it should be an engaging diversion

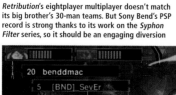

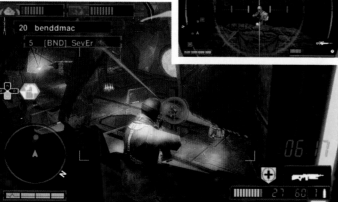

Visually, the game is functional, but not ugly, with calculated lighting design turning the cramped, bland confines below deck into spaces of indeterminate volume and danger. The heavy frost renders things dull, however, relying on flashback for colour contrast

'BioShock on ice' may be an easy reach for sloganeers, but whatever other assumptions it makes about Cryostasis it gets one thing right – the game's wrecked Russian icebreaker is exactly as cold as Rapture is wet. A British winter looks about as Arctic as a 99 Flake next to the blizzard which has claimed the ship as it founders on an iceberg.

A horror shooter, Cryostasis knits together various influences – among them principally Silent Hill, Doom III and, yes, BioShock – to imbue its sub-zero atmosphere with uncanny shocks and hackle-raising menace. Stumbling upon the hapless vessel long after its crew has fallen victim to the elements, or something worse, the player experiences the story of its trauma through flashback. It's adeptly written, and the fragmentary visions draw out an intriguing Faustian plot, as the captain of the ill-fated vessel struggles to maintain his command in the face of disaster and dissent.

Action Forms knows its horror, and delivers some chest-rattling set-pieces among the jump-scares that scatter its rigidly linear ride. A recurring feature is the ability to psychically re-experience the moments before a crewmate's death, allowing the player to take control and evade misfortune. Doing

The game's health system is entirely tied to the player's temperature. The sub-zero environment will continuously sap your heat, as will monsters' attacks, so it's necessary to huddle up against light sources or steaming pipes for a warm boost

so allows you to alter the environment in the protagonist's timeline and progress – successfully sealing a hatch before a cascade of seawater fills a cabin will empty the room of its ice blockade in the present, for example. The game exploits this effectively but too infrequently and, as it progresses, less time is given to puzzling in the creepy environments and more to combat. This is sadly leaden, often reduced to a matter of whose clip is larger. The reliance on implausible spawn-ins, meanwhile, rapidly tires.

The game squeezes as much out of its limited assets as it can, but the journey is inescapably padded by samey rooms, bulkheads, pipes and consoles. Nonetheless, Action Forms' moments of ingenuity and the sophistication of its writing demonstrate that it could do great and yet more terrifying things with a more intimidating budget. **[6]**

PUZZLE QUEST: GALACTRIX

FORMAT: 360, DS, PC, PS3 RELEASE: OUT NOW
PUBLISHER: D3 PUBLISHER DEVELOPER: INFINITE INTERACTIVE

HENRY HATSWORTH IN THE PUZZLING ADVENTURE

FORMAT: DS RELEASE: MARCH
PUBLISHER: EA (US), VIRGIN PLAY (UK) DEVELOPER: EA CASUAL

Puzzle Quest, it transpires, is Australian – a fact rendered noteworthy only because the series is so slyly anonymous, so studiously scrubbed of any kind of quirks, that's it's hard to imagine it coming from anywhere.

That, of course, is the point, as the game's success lies not with any single distinguishing feature, but with a careful absence of them. Infinite's quiet crowd-pleaser doesn't dazzle, and never tries to rock the boat. Instead, it presents you with the least threatening of make-believe worlds, throwing open its doors for as wide an audience as possible, and then politely refusing to let anybody leave.

Galactrix sees the series exchanging fantasy for science-fiction – a humourless, entry-level space opera with visuals that resemble the kind of thing the Mass Effect crew might use as clip-art in futuristic PowerPoint presentations. But nested within the new glossing of spaceships and aliens is the same anaemic RPG, and nested within that is the same Bejeweled variant standing in for every in-game action, from fighting pirates or mining, to upgrading weapons and hacking into computers.

As a mixture of genres, Galactrix remains basic, with the exploration reduced to the barest of point-to-point wanderings, and the puzzles threaded in with none of the quiet invention of Henry Hatsworth. There are a few changes along the way – the first

Resistance is futile: you know full well that you're being cynically manipulated by the game, and you're definitely going to do something about that – perhaps after just one more round

title's circular blocks have evolved into hexes, and there's a gravitational twist which sees the new pieces falling into the screen from the direction in which you made your last move – yet these are mild mutations, with little lasting effect on the game.

But while the structure remains uninspired, the title's hypnotic sway is as irresistible as ever. This is not a good game, then, so much as a supremely potent one, and it succeeds despite – or, perhaps more worryingly, because – of the brutal naffness that permeates its design. While the overall blandness means Galactrix is unlikely to truly thrill many people, it also means it won't exclude anyone either, and the ever-reliable pattern-spotting blends with the steady trickle of meaningless rewards to exert a pull on its audience that is truly Pavlovian. The videogame equivalent of knotweed, Puzzle Quest may be plain, but it's also tenacious, elaborate, and spectacularly tailored for survival. **[7]**

Build up your meter to unleash Tea Time as Tea Time has never been unleashed before: invulnerability mixed with a steampunk robot suit that trails a blur of Union Flag behind it

Somewhere in among the trivia quizzes and cooking recipes, are those secret things DS does best of all – rarities so gleefully warped that their designs simply wouldn't fit on any other hardware. That's where you'll find Henry Hatsworth, the videogame equivalent of an architectural folly: whimsical, surprising and with an unmistakable streak of stubborn resolve hidden behind its genial facade.

Both a platforming challenge and a puzzle game, Hatsworth's split personality is delivered in sweet-shop colours and covered in a brass-plated coating of antique Britishness. The platformer on the top screen is a surprisingly deep brawler with a healthy levelling curve, while the blocks that build up on the lower screen provide a chunky variation on the match-three genre. Tying both

pursuits together is a simple conceit: defeated enemies from the first game drop down to become playing pieces in the second, where they must be conclusively vanquished before they work their way upwards again. Meanwhile, sandwiched in between this is a mouth-watering muddle of gauges, special attacks and stompy power-ups that swiftly become logical and, ultimately, invaluable.

Rather than competing against each other, the separate challenges snap together like polished clockwork. Only one game is ever in play at a time, and it's a testament to the agile coherency of Hatsworth that travelling between modes never ruins the sense of flow. In fact, both interlock into providing a series of tactical choices, as you learn when to launch a prolonged attack on the top screen and when to harvest rewards and dead-head any lurking threats waiting below.

Apart from some punishing checkpointing and lengthy boss fights, this is a delightfully risky experiment, and the end result is pure alchemy: the blending of two fiercely traditional genres into something both unique and entirely natural. That's why Hatsworth is more than comfortable taking its place alongside The World Ends With You and Rocket Slime – colourful sparks of idiosyncratic brilliance that shine their light on the hidden face of DS. **[8]**

Yes, the AI still cheats, enemy aliens benefiting from a peculiar knowledge of the blocks that lay beyond the rim of the game screen, allowing them to chain together wave after wave of devastating attacks

Like Animal Crossing dubbed by Winston Churchill, the story is delivered in babbled chunks of stiff-upper-lipped grumpery. The EA logo looks entirely delightful encircled by a shiny monocle

PlayStation

PlayStation

PlayStation

PlayStation

PlayStation

PlayStation

PlayStation

PlayStation

PlayStation

PlayStation

PlayStation

PlayStation

PlayStation

PlayStation

PlayStation

PlayStation

PlayStation

PlayStation

PlayStation

PlayStation

THE MAKING OF...
PLAYSTATION

How Sony created the console
that redefined the game industry

FORMAT: **PS** PUBLISHER: **SONY** DEVELOPER: **SONY** ORIGIN: **JAPAN** RELEASE: **1994**

This is a story that isn't just about the design of an object made from silicon, plastic and metal. Nor is it just the story of the corporate politics that allowed the project to commence. It's also the story of sales forces and distribution systems, of marketing strategies and product evangelists, of a confluence of social, economic and technological circumstances that allowed it to thrive. It's about the vision behind the piece of hardware that pushed videogames into 3D and a veteran yet wide-eyed technology corporation into an industry that it would transform.

And it's a vision that rose out from the rubble of a very public disaster. At the Consumer Electronics Show in June 1991, Sony revealed to the world a videogame console on which it had jointly worked with Nintendo. This SNES with a built-in CD-ROM drive was a project driven by Ken Kutaragi, a Sony executive who had come out of its hardware engineering division. It was to be Nintendo's route into a brave new world of multimedia, and a way for Kutaragi to show his company how important the videogame industry could be. But the very day after Sony's announcement, Nintendo declared that it would be breaking its deal with Sony by partnering with Philips instead.

This humiliating turnabout enraged Sony president Norio Ohga, but though it seemed sudden from the outside, problems had been boiling between the two

companies for some time. The main issue was an agreement over how revenue would be collected – Sony had proposed to take care of money made from CD sales while Nintendo would collect from cartridge sales, and suggested that royalties would be figured out later. "Nintendo went bananas, frankly, and said that we were stepping on its toll booth and that it was totally unacceptable," explains **Chris Deering**, who at the time worked at Sony-owned Columbia Pictures but would go on to head the PlayStation business in Europe. "They just couldn't agree and it all fell apart."

But Ohga was dead set on remaining in the game. At the end of a July meeting to plan litigation against Nintendo, he declared defiantly: "We will never withdraw from this business. Keep going." And so Kutaragi went to work with strong support from the very top of Sony. "Ken brought together a handful of engineers that had come out of a broadcast and professional realtime 3D graphics engine called System-G," explains **Phil Harrison**, who joined Sony in September 1992 to start its European game publishing business, and would eventually go on to become president of Sony

"Nintendo went bananas, frankly, and said that we were stepping on its toll booth and that our proposal was totally unacceptable"

'Father of PlayStation' Ken Kutaragi, who joined Sony in 1975, initially to design LCD displays. The logo (left) was developed by Manabu Sakamoto

Computer Entertainment Worldwide Studios. System-G was a special-effects computer that broadcasters could use to augment live broadcasts with 3D images in realtime. "Technologically, that's not really a million miles away from videogames, but this was a super high-end workstation. And Ken's big vision was to take that, apply it in high volume and bring it into the home," recalls Harrison.

But the relationship with Nintendo wasn't quite over. It had indistinctly proposed that Sony could remain involved in 'non-game areas' of the project, though the move was probably just to delay any attempt Sony may have been making to enter videogames off its own bat, as well as sidestep the legal challenges Sony had made over Nintendo's breach of contract. Kutaragi was frustrated. Not only was he facing criticism and resentment from many at Sony who disagreed with the idea of Sony entering the game business, but the project's focus was also dissipating within the company. 'There is no consensus within Sony about why we are engaged in this business', he wrote candidly in his January 1992 business report. 'We are wasting time and missing opportunities while expecting too much from Nintendo and dealing with them in blind good faith'.

In May that year, Sony finally put a stop to negotiations, and whether or not it should retain the project was decided at a pivotal meeting chaired by Ohga on June 24. The great majority of those present opposed it, but Kutaragi nevertheless revealed that he'd been developing a proprietary CD-ROM-based system capable of rendering 3D graphics, specifically for playing videogames – not multimedia. When Ohga asked what sort of chip it would require, Kutaragi replied that it would need one million gate arrays, a number that made Ohga laugh: Sony's production of the time

PlayStation as it appeared in 1991, a Sony-built SNES with a CD-ROM drive. The project was a result of Kutaragi growing close to Nintendo after supplying the SNES PCM sound system

could only achieve 100,000. But Kutaragi slyly countered with: "Are you going to sit back and accept what Nintendo did to us?" The reminder enraged Ohga all over again. "There's no hope of making further progress with a Nintendo-compatible 16bit machine," he said. "Let's chart our own course."

And achieving that meant Ohga removing Kutaragi from Sony, fearing that the widespread internal opposition to the project might crush Kutaragi's resolve. "There was a huge resistance inside the company to actually being in the videogames business at all," explains Harrison. "The main reason why the Sony brand wasn't really used in the early marketing of PlayStation was not necessarily out of choice, but it was because Sony's old guard was

scared that it was going to destroy this wonderful, venerable, 50-year-old brand. They saw Nintendo and Sega as toys, so why on Earth would they join the toy business? That changed a bit after we delivered 90 per cent of the company's profit for a few years."

Kutaragi was moved with nine team members to Sony Music, a separate financial entity owned by the corporation, in the Aoyama district of Tokyo. There, he worked with Shigeo Maruyama, CEO of Sony Music and soon to become a vice president of the division that ran the PlayStation business, Sony Computer Entertainment International (SCEI), and Akira Sato, who'd also become a VP. Though on face value it hardly sounds significant, the involvement of Sony Music was fundamentally

the converging interests of the disc pressing divisions and Ken Kutaragi and Ohga-san they were truly well down the road to developing PlayStation."

The final two key players in PlayStation were Olaf Olafsson, who was president and CEO of SCEI's umbrella organisation, Sony Interactive Entertainment (and, incidentally, a writer who'd been nominated for the Icelandic Literature Prize), and Terry Tokunaka, who became president of SCEI and had come from Sony's head office. Tokunaka's vision for the project was simple, as Harrison explains: "It was that if we can be the creative choice of the game developers, and the business choice of the publishers, then those two together give us a chance of becoming successful.

Kutaragi's claim to Ohga about PlayStation's CPU power was not based on actual working examples but on Moore's Law. He was proved right, and also on his gamble over EDO RAM becoming standard

"The old guard was scared it was going to destroy the brand. That changed a bit after it delivered 90 per cent of Sony's profits"

important to PlayStation's subsequent success. "Music was huge business back then, and they knew you had to attract talent and that you have to spend money to launch things," says Deering. Sony Music knew how to nurture creative talent and how to manufacture, market and distribute music discs – with the move to CD-ROM, the mechanics of making and supplying games had become very similar to that used for music. "Sony made an awful lot of money pressing music discs," explains Deering. "Between

In order to be very successful you need both elements; you can't have one and not the other. I think this still holds true today for any company that wants to stay in the hardware platform business."

Harrison was among the evangelists who went out to scout for developers and publishers to create games for the platform, having joined PlayStation when it was finally greenlit in the summer of 1993. "We had to work hard to demonstrate our credibility, because bringing hardware to market is one thing, but being an

organisation to market and distribute and sell it is another," he says. With Sony's strategy distinctly different to that of Sega and Nintendo, it had a huge opportunity to change the console market, change that prospective publishers and developers were only too keen to happen. "A lot of the business questions related to what the business model was for a publisher, what the royalty rates would be, how we'd make and distribute the software," says Harrison. "That was set against the backdrop of the incumbent business models of Sega and Nintendo, which were at the time very restrictive. They've changed now, but at the time, publishing on 16bit Nintendo was an expensive and risky proposition."

One of the crucial points in the campaign to win hearts and minds came when Sony offered a solution to the problem that Japanese game publishers had no production capacity or supply infrastructure themselves. After all, under the Nintendo model, Nintendo would make and distribute their software for them. "All the publishers we worked with in Japan said that they loved the machine and were all super excited, but wondered how they'd bring their software to market," explains Harrison. "This was where the partnership between Sony Corp and Sony Music really came to fruition." Sony invited all the game publishers and developers to a hotel in Tokyo in 1994 and paraded on a stage the 40 direct sales people it had in place to distribute software. "It said: 'We know this is a challenge for you, so we've gone ahead and built our own sales force'," Harrison continues. "The net effect was that there were hundreds and hundreds of thirdparty publishers in Japan. Tonnes and tonnes of product being developed for PlayStation – with the resulting dynamic range of quality…"

Harrison found that developers began to allocate resources to

PlayStation long before they had publishing agreements that laid out their royalty rates. "That was an incredible demonstration of support and confidence, given that we hadn't even announced the formation of the company, just Sony Computer Entertainment in November 1993. And then throughout early '94 we hadn't announced the business model.

PlayStation's casing was designed by Teiyu Goto, art director at Sony Design Center, who modelled its central motif around the circle of a CD-ROM. His intention was that it wouldn't need changing, a principle that held until PSOne was launched six years later

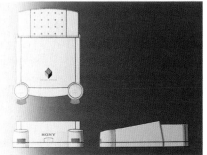

Sony's demos did much to sell the capabilities of the machine to prospective developers and publishers, including one depicting a camp phalanx of Gouraud-shaded fighters and, of course, the famous fully textured T-rex, whose head would later be featured on a demo disc supplied with every new console

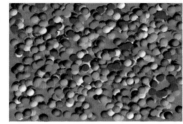

We hadn't a company, no leadership or executive team outside Japan – all that changed fairly quickly, but the key events were bringing in big companies like Electronic Arts in the west and Namco in Japan."

It helped that the demos for the new hardware were inspiring. Harrison recalls having a video FedExed to him that had been used to show Japanese publishers the capability of the machine. "I remember watching it over and over again and thinking that I

helped Sony's cause enormously. The first was that western developers and publishers were starting to move toward producing games heavy with full-motion video for CD-ROM on PCs, and experimenting with 3D. The second was that Japanese publishers were finding creating games for Sega and Nintendo expensive, risky – and slow. They were used to ten-to-12-week lead times for cartridges, meaning that they had to manufacture game cartridges according to forecasts

until early 1994. Though a weakness for Sony because it meant an almost complete reliance on external partners for PlayStation's early software, third parties saw it as an advantage because it meant less competition. But Sony wasn't entirely without capacity, having acquired Psygnosis in May 1993. It was a loose relationship – Psygnosis retained its publishing business, which released games for other platforms, but it played a vital role in creating PlayStation development tools that ran on PCs rather than the early kits, which were large, repurposed Sony NEWS workstations. "Psygnosis came to a large meeting at the Alexis Park Hotel in Las Vegas during CES 1994 – 11 months before the launch of the machine in Japan – with an early prototype of a working development environment that was far in advance of anything that had come out of Japan," says Harrison. Psygnosis, of course, would go on to make *Wipeout* and publish *Destruction Derby* for the

> ## "With the notable exception of *Ridge Racer*, there's no way you'd extrapolate the global success that happened from that first lineup"

couldn't believe it, that it was absolutely extraordinary. Just being excited, and also incredulous." In December 1993, it was his turn to show around 100 European developers and publishers what Kutaragi had been creating. Frontier's David Braben and Argonaut's Jez San were there: "Jez said he didn't believe it was running on the hardware and that it was on a Silicon Graphics workstation, and we had to take him to the side of the room to show him what it was running on."

Apart from the powerful allure of the hardware itself, two factors

and had difficulty reacting to actual demand. Sony offered an order system that was just seven to ten days. "It was a massive shift in the economics," explains Harrison. "The working capital requirement shifted massively in favour of the developer and publisher, and they could afford to put more money into product development and marketing, so it was a virtuous circle." The idea of a 3D-capable, CD-ROM-based console and a different way of doing business was a breath of fresh air for all.

Another major attraction for third parties was that Sony didn't have internal development studios

PlayStation's leading men (from top): Chris Deering, CEO of SCEE; Phil Harrison, who'd become SCEA's VP of thirdparty relations and R&D between 1996 and 2000; Olaf Olafsson, president and CEO of Sony Interactive Entertainment; Terry Tokunaka, president of SCEI

BUTTON CLASH

The iconography of X for 'no' and O for 'yes' is widely used in Japan, so it was logical for most Japanese software developers to widely use O as the main positive action button and X as the main negative button, even though the X button's positioning made it feel like the main one. The result was a global divide with western developers, who generally used X as yes and Triangle as 'go back' (because it was in the 'up' position and looked like an arrow). As a result, many games were initially rejected by SCEA thirdparty QA – a US-specific guideline demanded a certain interface standard. Developers in Japan were initially confused and subsequently furious – why should westerners tell them how to lay out their controls? Changes required more than a simple case of localisation, so many developers and publishers in Japan complained to the senior management at SCEI about the policy, which was quickly abandoned. Eventually, however, market forces would do what the policy couldn't: the global standard became X for 'yes' when western hardware sales began to dwarf those of Japan.

European launch lineup in September 1995.

It was Namco's *Ridge Racer* that stood out by far among the Japanese launch games. Visiting Namco's Yokohama tech centre, Harrison saw the finished game a few weeks before the December 3 release. "I'd seen an earlier work-in-progress build a couple of months before, but they'd done the port from the coin-op remarkably quickly. I remember realising that was going to be pivotal piece of software for the west in particular." But then he saw one of the pieces of software that would help define the console's later success. "It was almost an afterthought. One of the men demonstrating it asked, since I was there, would I like them to show me another game they're working on? 'Yeah, sure', I said. 'What's it called?' 'It's called *Tekken*'."

The rest of the launch games were rather less memorable. "With the notable exception of *Ridge Racer*, there is no way you'd extrapolate the global success that happened from that first lineup," concedes Harrison. And that's including Kazanori Yamauchi's *Motor Toon Grand Prix*, a title he made before forming Polyphony to create *Gran Turismo*. But the 100,000 units Sony made for Japanese launch day sold out all

the same. "It was an incredible undertaking from all manner of perspectives," says Harrison. "Manufacturing, financial, buying the components, getting the distribution infrastructure in place to ship them – we started manufacturing probably around October to hit the launch date."

Another 200,000 sold in the console's first 30 days on sale. This was at a price of ¥39,800 – which at the time translated to $390, or £245 – compared to Sega's Saturn launch price of ¥44,800 the month

before. Though instrumental to PlayStation's success, price was a contentious issue at Sony, because, against all corporate tradition, PlayStation would be sold at a loss. While Kutaragi had initially forecast that memory prices would go down, the truth was that, ten months before launch, they were going up – and they'd stay high all the way up until late 1995. The trend was principally due to booming PC sales, but, ever resolute, Kutaragi stuck to his guns, declaring that they would

certainly come down over time, and that every competitor was in the same position. And besides, the PlayStation business was to be quite different from Sony's conventional appliance business, which depended on direct profits from hardware sales, because in games, profits could instead be gained from software sales. The policy was still hard to reconcile with Sony's old guard until Kutaragi dropped certain hardware features, such as the original model's S-Video port.

This pricing policy allowed SCEI to severely dent the fortunes of Sega's Saturn in the US. Famously, Saturn was surprise-launched in the US at $399 during E3 on May 11, 1995, but the timing allowed Sony to immediately get the upper hand. Harrison was at Sony's E3 press conference shortly afterwards: "Olaf Olafsson was doing the spiel about growth in the industry and droning on – it was deliberately staged that way. I can't remember a single thing about his presentation, but he did say that he'd like to bring on stage the president of Sony Computer Entertainment America to share with you an important piece of information. Steve Race went up to the microphone, just said '299', and sat back down again. The room erupted." But staff at Sony's corporate headquarters

INPUT COMMAND

Ohga closely supported Kutaragi throughout PlayStation's development, but there were two notable disagreements between them. The first was over the PlayStation controller, which was designed by Sony engineer Teiyu Goto, who also designed the console's casing. Ohga, who was at the time in his 60s, had requested that it should be comfortable for older people's hands, and Goto wanted to make something more ergonomic than traditional, flat pad designs. Ohga immediately liked the sculpted, 'horned' result, but Kutaragi didn't: along with other team members and game developers, he felt that it was too removed from recognised pads. But Ohga was clear about his decision. "Stop arguing and adopt this design," he said. "I'm the president, so you must do as I say. Otherwise you are all fired!" But Kutaragi got his own way in another dispute, in which Ohga insisted that PlayStation CD-ROMs should be supplied in protective plastic caddies. Kutaragi insisted that this would make them, and the machine, more expensive to make. Ohga eventually backed down, but only after demanding that PlayStation's discs should be differentiated from other CDs. Kutaragi's team came up with a solution in the form of black discs.

The launch controllers for PlayStation in its home territory were around 15 per cent smaller than the western and European versions. It wasn't until Sony introduced the Dual Analog Controller in 1997 that all controllers became the same size globally

Since PlayStation was Sony's first console, Goto designed all products and peripherals himself because there were no internal precedents

weren't amused. "It was properly agreed, but word had not made its way back to Japan and there were parts of Sony scratching their heads in shock," says Deering. "I think Tokunaka got in trouble. It was a scary thing for them."

But we're getting ahead of ourselves. Shortly after the Japanese launch, plans started for the European and US launches. Deering was initially asked to head up US operations, but turned down the role in favour of the opportunity to direct the more challenging but more interesting cultural patchwork of Europe. "They thought I was pretty crazy, actually," he remembers. "The European market is only 60 per cent the size of the US, they said, but I said, 'Right now it is, but that's only because it's handled in a dilettante fashion'. Europe was almost exploited by Japanese

console makers in demanding high minimum orders from distributors." After all, the usual focus for a Japanese console maker was always the US after the home territory. "Sony Japan really didn't understand Europe at the time, or pay much attention to it. Which is why we got to manage in an unencumbered style."

Steve Race, a long-time executive for such companies as Sega, Nintendo and Atari, hired many ex-Sega employees for SCEA. "They went by the handbook of the old Sega business," says Deering. "They limited the number of thirdparty releases, drove hard bargains – there were a lot of rough edges in treatment of thirdparties [see 'Button clash']

and had even been rough in approving products by Konami and Namco." Race also played rough, as Harrison recollects: "At the Alexis Park Hotel in January 1995, where Sega held their CES party, Steve Race organised for every napkin to be printed with 'PSX welcomes Sega to CES'! That was a fun moment, because these napkins were everywhere. [Sega Of America head] Tom Kalinske went totally nuts and demanded that all the napkins were purged from the hotel, quite reasonably so, but legend has it that later on in the party he was handed a beer with one of these napkins around it, and he exploded."

A larger sticking point, however, was PlayStation

much ended the debate." In Europe, at least: the US nevertheless went ahead with early trade promotion, calling it PSX, and had even come up with its own mascot, Polygon Man.

SCEA's marketing company was Chiat/Day, the LA-based agency that had produced the famous Apple '1984' Super Bowl advert and had come up with the Energizer Bunny. Its consumer research had said that the golden age was 17, in that a 12-year-old wants to be 17, and a 25-year-old wants to be 17 again. So SCEA wanted to aim its message at that age group. "Polygon Man was going to be this iconic brand that would talk in various media to consumers as this kind of next-gen type spokesman," says Harrison. With shades of Sega's anarchic Pirate TV campaign in the UK in the early '90s, it was far from SCEI's minimalist vision for the brand. "It upset the Japanese because they thought it was fighting the PlayStation brand," says Deering. "But we knew it was to dodge it."

"I remember walking onto the E3 booth in 1995 with Ken and seeing the Polygon Man design on the side of the booth. Ken just went absolutely insane," says Harrison. Kutaragi's problem was that SCEA was investing a limited budget in an alternative brand. "But the thing that really upset Ken was that the Polygon Man design wasn't Gouraud shaded, it was flat shaded! So Polygon Man was taken out into the car park and quietly shot." Other parts of the US launch campaign were

> ## "I remember walking into the E3 booth in 1995 with Ken and seeing the Polygon Man design. Ken just went absolutely insane"

Early marketing activity emphasised PlayStation's power, while the hapless Polygon Man attempted to speak to SCEA's 17-year-old target demographic

branding. SCEA hated the name and wanted to change it to PSX, a contraction of the project's codename. "This was actually a huge internal battle, to the point where there was research done among consumer groups," says Harrison, who, having seen various youth groups reacting badly to the name PlayStation, had his own fears about it. "I remember thinking, 'Oh my God, the name is bombing and everyone is going to hate it'. I shared the information with Tokunaka-san, and he said, 'Oh, that's nothing, you should have heard what people said about Walkman'. And that pretty

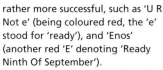

rather more successful, such as 'U R Not e' (being coloured red, the 'e' stood for 'ready'), and 'Enos' (another red 'E' denoting 'Ready Ninth Of September').

Race would leave SCEA just six weeks before the big launch – rumours flew as to whether such marketing disagreements had anything to do with his decision. Nevertheless, the US PlayStation launch was a massive success. All 100,000 units sold out in September, and by Christmas PlayStation had sold 800,000 in the region compared to Saturn's 400,000 since May.

PlayStation launched in

Europe on September 29 at £299, across many more countries than Sony had intended. "They were quite upset with me – they really only wanted us to launch in the UK, France and Germany, because of possible advertising expense," says Deering. "I said that it'd go elsewhere anyway, and there would be other issues, and leave it to me. So we went everywhere except Scandinavia, which we didn't get to until November or so." By the end of the year, his team had shipped 600,000 units, using Deering's experience with and contacts in Sony's film and music publishing businesses. SCEE eventually covered Russia, India and the Middle East.

By the end of March 2007, Sony had sold 102 million PlayStations. Sales between SCEA and SCEE were almost equal, demonstrating the importance of Europe to the global game market. And it was

a game market transformed by a new way of doing business and given new legitimacy by the presence of such an internationally respected company as Sony. PlayStation was the product of a confluence of the right technology at the right time at the right price, but it took Sony to create it. Indeed, it's hard to imagine any other company than Sony, armed with the combined experience and capabilities of its hardware, software and entertainment divisions, producing a story like PlayStation. All those different divisions were galvanised by a single vision, however. Kutagari's constant insistence that PlayStation was a gaming machine, not some multimedia device, focused a sprawling organisation into unity.

Today, PlayStation 3 is the result of anything but focus, and Nintendo has regained the position as the leading console maker that Sony took from it. And with what? A console driven by the most coherent vision of its generation. Perhaps St Augustine was right and there is only one story: of creation, fall and redemption. In PlayStation's case, we're now waiting on the latter.

Depending on territory, launch titles included (clockwise from top left) *Ridge Racer, Destruction Derby, Battle Arena Toshinden, Wipeout* and *Motor Toon Grand Prix*. Some early games exposed the console's texture warping problem, something often addressed using careful art fixes

24 MONTHS LATER

PlayStation's launch was promising, but it took the push that started in 1996 to seal its success, and it needed a price cut to do it. SCEA chief Steve Race said from before the console's US launch that the price had to start with a two in first year, a one in the second and be under $/£100 in the third, and Kutaragi followed the plan precisely. But the first price drop took place in May 1996, rather earlier than expected. "I don't think the rest of us expected the first cut to come before Christmas," remembers Deering. "'But we're out of stock, Ken, we can barely keep up with demand at £299 – what are you doing?' we said. And he just said: 'Fashion and scarcity'. He didn't mind if it was out of stock." Time revealed that Kutaragi was anxious to take PlayStation to an installed base of three million. "I think he'd made some deals with SquareSoft to get *Final Fantasy* away from Nintendo by making sure there was a huge installed base, and he had targets for Christmas that we thought were in the moon. And darned if I don't say, we ended up shipping those numbers."

Codeshop
Tracking developments in development

Facing up to the future

It's been used to reverse Brad Pitt's ageing, but in gaming terms Image Metrics' performance-capture tech makes characters more believable

Michael Starkenburg,
CEO, Image Metrics

www.image-metrics.com

What connects Brad Pitt, Nico Bellic, Nathan Drake, Tom Hanks, Helghast leader Scolar Visari, Richard Burton and Jack Bauer? Aside from a masculine overload that surely says something about the alpha male domination of massmarket entertainment, this collection of living, dead and fictional characters have all been facially animated thanks to the computer vision smarts of UK-headquartered Image Metrics.

Its technology is easy to describe: get some video footage of an actor's face in motion; perform a rough pre-processing step to define areas such as the eyes and mouth; check the mapping to the CG facial rig you want to animate; and then put the footage into Image Metrics' black box. Out the other end comes the

Worried about the quality of the output? Go and watch the first part of The Curious Case Of Benjamin Button. Alongside some other capture technologies, Image Metrics was used by special effects house Digital Domain to create the facial animation for the elderly but child-sized Benjamin Button from the facial movement of the 45-year-old, 5'11" Brad Pitt.

"Two years ago, we didn't have a meaningful film business, but now we've done a couple of things that are really great," explains **Michael Starkenburg**, a software entrepreneur and venture capitalist who became Image Metrics' CEO towards the end of 2008. "Benjamin Button is going to kickstart a lot of attention for us, but games remain 80 per cent of our business. We did 400

Games require more facial animation than they used to. Publishers used to get away with hiding faces behind helmets

sort of industry-standard animation curves that would cost a rather hefty fortune to produce any other way.

The trick is what happens within that black box; that's where the company's technology analyses the subtle physical movements of the face and generates an output that recreates the performance of the original actor.

minutes of cutscenes for *GTAIV*, and we've also done another 55 minutes for a very high-profile console game we can't talk about yet. What we're now seeing is that games require much more facial animation than they used to. Publishers are trying to differentiate them using character and story. They used to be able to get away with hiding faces behind helmets, but not any more."

It's a significant point that highlights a wider trend that certainly seems to be complementary in terms of expansion of the company's business. Still, surprisingly perhaps, Image Metrics has been working with high-profile clients such as Rockstar and Sony since 2002. Until recently, though, it was more focused on research and development rather than building up its sales momentum across the industry.

This balance has shifted, however, with one of the original founders leaving

Shown at its most basic form, Image Metrics' performance-capture technology enables you to use video footage of a facial performance to drive the expressions of a computer-generated character

One experiment attempted by Image Metrics, along with the ICT Graphics Lab at the University of Southern California, was Real-Time Emily. In this, they replaced HD video footage of the presenter Emily O'Brien with her facial animation to see if viewers could tell the difference

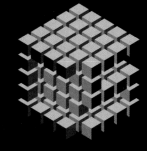

Image Metrics has worked with Epic Games to create facial animation for characters in games such as *Unreal Tournament III*, including broadcast marketing materials

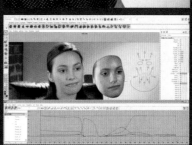

One of the high-profile games to have used Image Metrics to drive its in-game cutscenes is Rockstar's *GTAIV*. In total, 400 minutes of content was processed

to spin-off medical-imaging company Optasia, while Starkenburg, previously the chief operating officer, has stepped up to the CEO role. Other measures to kickstart future growth include a hard-won round of investment, which raised $6.5 million, as well as the hiring of sales and marketing staff with previous game experience from the likes of middleware and tools companies such as Havok, Emergent and NXN Software.

"The games business is a very structured sales process. You have to pound the pavement, know the status of every game in development and talk to every producer," says Starkenburg. "We were lucky early on with Rockstar because it has quite a centralised command and control structure, so we're being used in the majority of their games. Most publishers aren't like that. In the film business it's completely different too. We don't work with the film studios, we work with the special effects houses. There's only about 60 of those and we know who they are."

Another issue for games is timing. Starkenburg describes this as a case of either getting into the development process early enough to provide the maximum efficiency benefits, or late enough that customers are freaking out. "We've had a couple of cases where

complete their games compared to their deadlines and started thinking about what they would have to cut. We're a real alternative because of the speed and scalability we can offer," he explains.

Of course, all technology comes with its own strengths and weaknesses. With enough time, money, animators and composition talent, you can use Image Metrics to create the photorealistic motion required in Benjamin Button. In contrast, for *GTAIV*, most of the facial animation was applied to standard-resolution game-quality models and used to drive in-engine cutscenes.

It's this sort of divide that's seen Image Metrics launch what it calls its four service levels. The cheapest option is Value, which it defines as being around half the cost of standard facial animation and is designed to generate large volumes of facial animation for secondary characters or pre-visualisation purposes. The next level is Pro which is for in-game cutscenes and provides for the capture of more subtle facial movements, while Premium provides for the 'pore-level analysis of facial movement'. The final option, designed for those triple-A movies, is Elite.

"The bottom line is, we provide a huge amount of efficiency over hand animation or facial motion capture.

either do more animation at a set level of quality or you can do a higher level of animation for a set quantity," states Starkenburg. "In the past our biggest impediment has been getting people to know about what we do, but those days are over." And guess what? He's smiling.

Making it as easy as possible

One of the founders of Image Metrics still with the company is **Kevin Walker**; indeed his Ph.D in computer vision was part of the basis on which the company was formed in the first place. Growing from what effectively was an academic startup out of Manchester University into a service-driven company also took a lot of thought.

"Obviously facial animation was around long before Image Metrics. People would create it by hand using tools such as Maya and 3DS Max, so a key part of our process has been to ensure we operate in the same format that animators are used to," he says. "Not only does this mean the cost of integration is low, but it has the additional advantage that you're giving back the data in a form that people can make changes to if they want to."

Described in this way, Image Metrics' technology seems to be about as seamless a process as could be imagined. What does impact the development process is the quality of video that's analysed by its system. Technically the resolution or lighting doesn't have to be great – for example, Image Metrics is working on a webcam option – but the performance of the facial actor needs to be expressive.

"Sometimes you'll find publishers have cast a brilliant voice actor, but their face might be deadpan," Walker says. "We can use our technology to amplify performances, but if we don't get a good performance it'll affect the animation."

The other important factor that determines the quality of the output is the facial rig the final animation curves are used to drive. "The rig can be a bottleneck, so we've had to become experts at creating good rigs in order to be in control of our own destiny," Walker says. "This expertise extends to the process of re-targetting the animation to the rig too. It's not usually difficult if the actor and avatar faces are roughly the same, but it can become more problematic when human facial animation is being applied to a dragon, an elephant or the multi-celled Zgfdger beast from the planet B'bbrn.

"That's where providing the flexibility to allow the artist to change the interpretation is important," Walker explains. "You could automate the process, but enabling control is an important part of not being a disruptive process."

Studio profile

■ Like Top Trumps, but for game dev

■ NAME: Media Molecule Ltd

■ DATE FOUNDED: January 2006

■ NUMBER OF EMPLOYEES: 34

■ KEY STAFF: Mark Healey (creative director),
David Smith (technical director), Alex Evans (technical
director), Kareem Ettouney (art director), Siobhan Reddy
(executive producer), Chris Lee (business director)

■ URL: www.mediamolecule.com

■ SELECTED SOFTOGRAPHY:
LittleBigPlanet (and subsequent DLC packs,
including the recent *Metal Gear Solid* pack)

You can't be reading this magazine and be unaware
of Media Molecule's *LittleBigPlanet*, first announced
at the 2007 GDC. The company won the Studio of the
Year award at the Spike Video Game Awards 2008

■ LOCATION:
Guildford,
Surrey, UK

■ CURRENT PROJECTS:
As yet unannounced

■ ABOUT THE STUDIO:

"Once upon a time a small group of
Lionhead veterans worked together on
what turned out to be a cult indie game
called *Rag Doll Kung-Fu*. Inspired by this
experience (and possibly slightly mad
ambition), they believed that they could
see a way to make great games for
consoles with a small team of talented,
committed and passionate people.

"Talented, committed and passionate
people were duly enlisted and Media
Molecule was born.

"The thing that binds the molecules
together is a mutual love of collaborative
creation, using the process they like to call
'jamming', where everyone contributes
their own vision but follows along with
the music.

"In November 2008, drawing on the
collective industry experience of decades of
pain and pleasure releasing rather a lot of
great games (including *Black & White*,
Fable, *Burnout*, *Dungeon Keeper*, *Ratchet
& Clank*, *Rome: Total War*, Home,
EyeCreate, *Crackdown* and of course *Rag
Doll Kung-Fu*), Media Molecule released
their first title, *LittleBigPlanet* on PS3.

"The adventure continues…"

This red door in Guildford hides Media Molecule's studio. Inside, staff continue to work
on adding new functionality to *LittleBigPlanet* which will be revealed throughout 2009

CONGRATULATIONS EDGE TEAM!

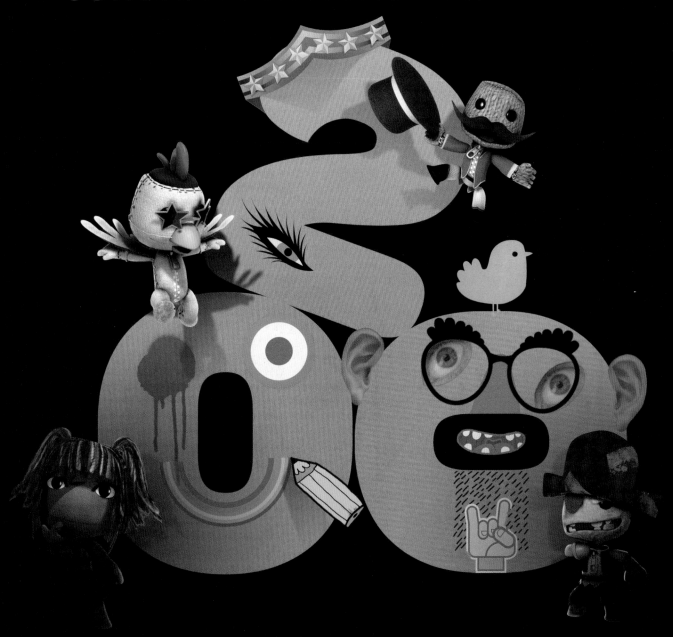

And while you're reading if you're:
a tools programmer, a level designer,
a community manager, a lead QA technician
or a physics/gameplay programmer
we'd love you to join our own little gang.

HIRING NOW

realtime worlds

PERMANENT & CONTRACT POSITIONS AVAILABLE

www.realtimeworlds.com

NOW HIRING PROGRAMMERS

ALL SHAPES AND SIZES

AI, GAME, CONSOLE, RENDER, ONLINE, PANDA, UI...

jobs.ioi.dk

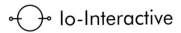 Io-Interactive

Work with us.

FRONTIER™

www.frontier.co.uk

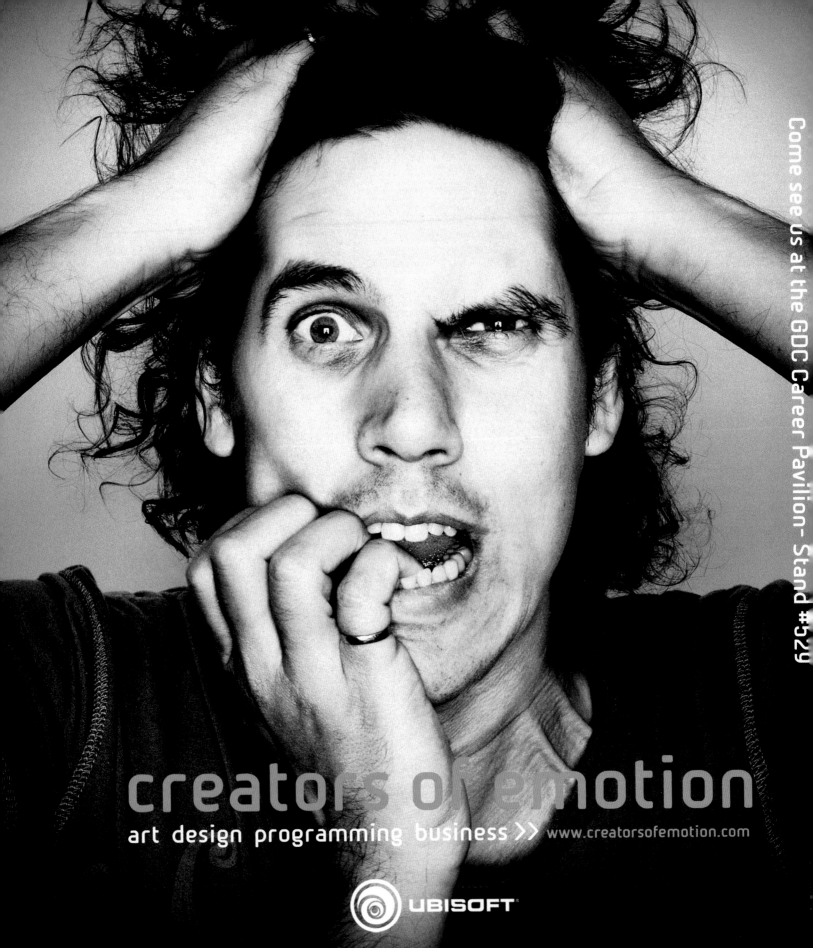

YOU THINK YOU KNOW US?

THINK AGAIN.

With a well-deserved reputation for bringing excellent and innovative games to all types of players from all over the world, and a massive investment into developing powerful new technology... there's never been a better time to play at Codemasters!

With over 60 no.1 titles in the trophy cabinet, and more to come... we're a leading force in the games industry. Be it action, fantasy, driving or war-based gaming... there's something for everyone. Combine all of this with Codemasters Studio's powerful EGO™ Engine technology and we are making a whole new unstoppable generation of games.

So, with our investment in people, technology and quality, it means that we are built to win! If you want to be part of the fastest growing studio in the UK, take a look at the many positions available.

to find out more go to:
www.codemasters.com

or email:
TheEdge@codemasters.com

codemasters™

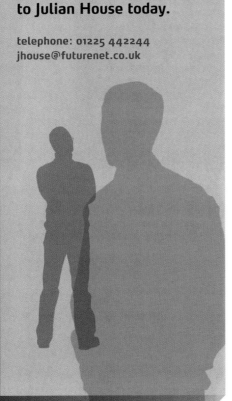

University profile

■ Like Top Trumps, but for universities

■ **INSTITUTION NAME:** City University

■ **NUMBER OF STUDENTS:** 23,000

■ **URL:** www.soi.city.ac.uk

■ **CONTACT:** pgenquire@soi.city.ac.uk (020 7040 0248)

■ **KEY STAFF**
Andrew Tuson (head of department, computing),
Chris Child (lecturer, computing), Dr Darrell Conklin
(reader, computing), Dr Tillman Weyde (lecturer, computing)

City University's MSc in computer games technology is a new course that builds on the BSc in the same subject. It has a project component, which gives the opportunity for an extended piece of work in either an industrial or academic context

■ **LOCATION:**
London, England

■ **COURSES OFFERED:**
MSc computer games technology;
BSc (Hons) computer science with games technology;
BSc (Hons) computer science with music technology

■ **INSIDE VIEW: ADAM LEGGE** STUDYING: BSC (HONS) COMPUTER SCIENCE WITH GAMES TECHNOLOGY

The school of informatics benefits from state-of-the-art premises in City University's building

"I have always had a passion for videogames, yet was at a loss as to how I could carve out a career in this notoriously competitive industry. I was impressed by City University London's high employment rate and the BSc in computer science with games technology, so decided to apply.

"After studying on the course, I have already gained insight into all aspects of computing, as well as the skills to get my foot in the door of the games industry. The university even helped me find a six-month placement with a successful London-based games development house. Here, I was given personal tuition on games programming

(gameplay and tools) and involved in design meetings, where my ideas were included in the games. I was then put into a small team to develop an MMO as a lead programmer!

"This was a hugely rewarding and valuable experience that I am sure will help me secure a job once I've completed my degree. In fact, my placement company has already asked if I'll come back and work there full-time.

"All in all, City University London has been a fantastic resource for me; for knowledge, support and a degree that the growing games industry takes notice of."

Computing lecturer Chris Child

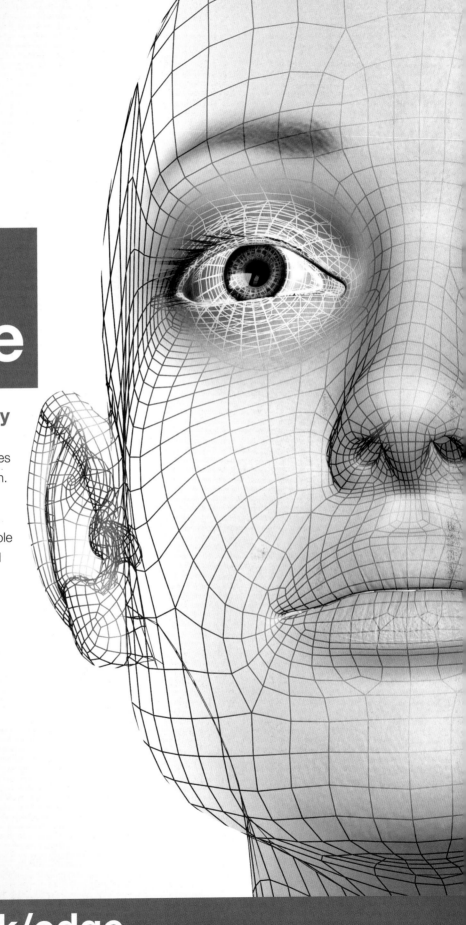

CITY UNIVERSITY
LONDON

Get ahead of the game

MSc in Computer Games Technology

If you're looking to build your career in the games industry, and are considering how best to develop your skills in games technology, you should be looking to City University London.

Conveniently based in Central London, we are offering a MSc in Computer Games Technology. The course is available in both full-time and part-time formats. This new course will complement our respected undergraduate courses in Games Technology and Music Technology*.

To find out more, visit www.soi.city.ac.uk/edge or call us on 020 7040 0248. Alternatively, email pgenquire@soi.city.ac.uk

www.soi.city.ac.uk/edge

*City University London ranks fifth in the UK for graduate employment

Welcome to part two in a series about Fun, why some games should focus on being Not Fun instead, and what about our artform makes that so hard to accomplish. Last time we described a formula that started with a dark topic and gave it a heavy, serious treatment. Imagine a game about running a hospital during hard financial times. You deal with the poor and homeless, the insurance companies, untimely deaths, conflict between your doctors and shortsighted budget cuts. You make the tough decisions and try to do what's right. Let's say magically we also accomplish the really hard part of the formula: we've described the drama of the hospital in algorithmic terms so that every player winds up crafting a unique story particular to the actions they have taken but which always portrays deep, poignant observations about the difficult topics. The stories this hypothetical

name of Mihaly Csíkszentmihályi. He deconstructs the concept of optimal experience, of being in the zone, an ascendant state achieved by great composers, athletes and the like. Your whole being is absorbed in your work, time melts away, and you use your skills to their utmost. Attaining flow involves a balance between ability level and challenge, clear goals and direct feedback. The origins of this theory are decades old, but it sure reads like a modern textbook on videogame design. It's like our platonic ideal. Think *Tetris*.

So games have this amazing ability to reproduce a rare transcendent human state, which is a fabulous public service we provide and can help justify all those hours you logged in *EverQuest*. But that doesn't mean we have to do it all the time, for every game, not any more than every shot in a film must have the most harmonious composition and steadiest camera,

like a system that leads to flow. Players will strive to understand the rules and optimise. We specifically don't want them zipping around the depressing hospital adjusting knobs and scheduling doctors thinking, 'Man, I'm good at this! I'm winning!' Instead of something that's as fun to solve as a big soup of game mechanics with clear goals and direct feedback, we could provide our players with a different type of interaction, for example choice and consequence. Suppose the play cycle in *Hospital Director* is based around a little anecdote or situation, like a scene in a movie, and always ends with a difficult choice to be made. Instead of rapid pattern matching, players are given novel situations to contemplate, which will cause them to slow down and absorb the emotional weight of their decisions.

That sounds like designer-authored content, a glorified Choose Your Own Adventure book, which we don't want. But remember under the hood it really is a game system, the imaginary one we generated in following the formula, so the difference is just that we deliberately obfuscate the dials and meters. Instead of constant small inputs and behaviours, the algorithm spits out a less frequent, larger chunk of content and some procedurally generated affordances so the player can express their decisions. Yeah. No problem.

So our Not Fun game has dark, serious material covered in depth by a game system whose interactions we've now tuned to avoid the natural tendency to be inherently fun of their own accord. But we haven't answered all the questions, such as: are players ever really going to care about the hospital patients? Why would players make a choice that makes them feel bad about themselves, and why would we want them to?

> ## Games have this amazing ability to reproduce a rare transcendent human state, which is a fabulous public service we provide

game produces could be ported straight to a high quality, Not Fun film.

That would be an amazing accomplishment, but would it guarantee an entertainment experience that is valuable without being fun? Or would it, in fact, be fun? When we say a film is 'fun', is it the same kind of fun we mean when we talk about a game? How about this: do you ever have trouble breaking away from a game that is kind of lame because it's too easy to keep playing? What is it about interaction that can make even weak experiences gratifying?

A focus of modern game design is tuning interactions according to formal theories of fun. One example is 'flow', which comes from a Hungarian psychologist with the impossible

not any more than every piece of prose must be grandiloquent and have proper grammar. Flow is one of the tools of our artform that we should use deliberately to create targeted effects and aesthetic responses. No matter how dark the story is, if a game flows too well the interactions themselves are going to engage you and be gratifying of their own accord, and you won't really connect with the material emotionally. It's like a mortician who takes so much pride in his work that he always has a good time with it. His brain tunes out, and he's just in the groove.

What were you imagining for game mechanics in the hospital director game? It could be an RTS or sim, with different sliders to tune and meters to monitor, but that sounds

Randy Smith is the co-owner and game designer of Tiger Style, a new indie studio with an unannounced game in the works

illustration: tstokes

152

With all the guff surrounding the coming of President Barack Obama, it was easy to overlook one thing: that he had declared war on videogames. "The time has come," he said in his inauguration address, "to set aside childish things." He then outlined a vast programme of console destruction, with videogames to be replaced by enforced listening to Brahms, and communal readings of the Federalist Papers and Goethe. America needed to grow up, because playing with virtual soldiers on your Xbox inevitably makes you want to play with real soldiers and send them en masse to attack far-off countries – which had been, after all, one of the many lamentably childish habits of the outgoing administration. Dick Cheney, watching from his wheelchair, muttered, "Go fuck yourself," and then tilted the giant calcified potato of his head back downwards to continue his game of

awful lot of videogames, I'm afraid, *are* childish, in the sense of that word that conveys disapprobation: immature, simplistic, illogical, given to irrational tantrums and unjustified outbursts of violence.

Many of the most childish videogames, in fact, are those targeted precisely at older adolescents or adults. Most games of 'realistic' warfare or fantasy ultraviolence are no more sophisticated than a children's game of cowboys and Indians, and less interesting in their intersubjective phenomenology. I recently tried playing the PSP *God Of War* and, after 30 incredulous minutes, I decided I would rather be reading Harry Potter (and when I had tried to read Harry Potter I decided after 20 incredulous pages that I would rather be reading something for grown-ups.) A childish videogame's idea of novelty is: 'Hey, now you can slice off the limbs of your enemies one by one!' Psychopaths who

granted. Similarly, *World Of Goo*, *Phantom Hourglass* or *Professor Layton* are childlike not because of their warm 'n' fuzzy cartoony aesthetics but because of the opportunities they provide for joyful experimentation. More naturalistic games can also be childlike in this sense: for example, *MGS3* or the best *Tomb Raider* levels.

The stunning art direction of *LittleBigPlanet*, meanwhile, seems itself to be presenting a subtle visual argument about the relationship between the childish and the childlike. A priori, it seems a childish thing to construct make-believe games from scraps of cardboard and fabric. But once those materials can be realistically simulated, we are ushered into a second-order realm where it is possible to reflect pleasurably on the cutely juvenile physical resources that are being replicated, at the same time as we marvel (in properly childlike fashion) at the ingenuity with which they have been combined, and attempt to solve (with gleeful childlike fearlessness) the puzzles they present. During a recent session of *LBP*, in which a friend and I played through the co-op parts, we were both giggling like six-year-olds when a bomb went off too near one of us and he got covered in soot; but we weren't being childish, we were being childlike. It would have been substantially more childish, I propose, for us to have watched some TV show in which men in tight jeans tell a mooing audience how brilliant it is to drive cars.

Instead, in *LittleBigPlanet*, we were working out strategies, experimenting and discovering things. And it is that childlike potential that is among the the most important virtues of the form. Every child, it has been said, is naturally a scientist. The best videogames enable us all to practice science as pleasure.

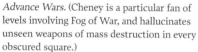

> The best games are not childish, but they are likely to be childlike, in that they invoke a sense of innocent wonder and experiment

Advance Wars. (Cheney is a particular fan of levels involving Fog of War, and hallucinates unseen weapons of mass destruction in every obscured square.)

Oh, all right then, that wasn't exactly Obama's message. By 'childish things', Obama really meant Beltway bickering. But it has long been a criticism of videogames, too, that they are childish. The normal response of the videogame industry is to intone the latest demographic statistics (the average age of a videogamer is now 76), or to point to 'mature' themes treated in videogames, such as neoliberal interstellar economics. (One awaits the first videogame about a galactic recession.) Both responses, however, miss the point. An

enjoyed pulling the legs off spiders in their youth no doubt rejoiced (along with Dick Cheney). But it is clear that *Dead Space* is a much more childish videogame than *Zelda: Phantom Hourglass*, even though the latter is drawn in a more apparently child-friendly style. Similarly, *Far Cry 2* is more childish than *World Of Goo*; and *Fallout 3* is more childish than *Professor Layton And The Curious Village*.

The best games are not childish, but they are likely to be child*like*, in that they invoke a sense of innocent wonder and experiment. It is always meant as laudatory when it is said of some fantastic doddering old genius in science, philosophy or art that he maintained a 'childlike' attitude towards the world, taking nothing for

Steven Poole is the author of Trigger Happy: The Inner Life Of Videogames. Visit him online at stevenpoole.net

Cartoon Network made a AAA in-browser MMO. What will you make with Unity?

WORLD OF CREATIVE POSSIBILITIES DOESN'T HAVE TO COME WITH
BIG PRICE TAG. THE TOOL THAT CARTOON NETWORK AND OTHER
DUSTRY LEADERS AND INNOVATORS USE CAN BE YOURS FOR $1499.
BEGGING, NO NEGOTIATION, NO HASSLES.

COME SEE US IN BOOTH #5110 IN THE NORTH HALL AT GDC
FIND OUT MORE AT UNITY3D.COM

PLAYING IN THE DARK ...because people refuse to see

The eye of the beholder

One of the most overused words in the videogame writer's lexicon is the word 'realistic'. I'm as guilty of it as the next person, but I always feel slightly, um, guilty whenever I use it, especially in reference to graphics. Because even those titles which are widely seen as exemplars of game realism, be they *Crysis* or *Mass Effect* or *Grand Theft Auto*, are themselves stylised in some way. So what is it that we mean when we say that a game is realistic? Are we talking about verisimilitude? Detail? Atmosphere? More interesting to me are the conventions that games have amassed over time – from double-jumps to infinite depth of field to lens flare – that end up creating a type of videogame reality that we rarely have reason to question. Until some development comes along that forces us to do so.

I had a moment like that when I first received my Xbox 360 review unit in 2005 along

gap between what I'd come to understand as 'videogame realism' from the previous six years of games and what I was now playing. But after several months of playing Xbox 360 titles, followed by those that launched with PlayStation 3, I became accustomed to this generation's adjusted standard for videogame verisimilitude and never looked back.

I shouldn't have been surprised when *Killzone 2* elicited a similar sense of visual disorientation. After all, when I went hands-on with the game's opening mission at E3 2007, I distinctly remember feeling as though there were something oddly unnerving about the texture of *Killzone 2*'s imagery, only to have Guerilla's leads explain how each of their post-processing techniques could help take what looked like a sunny mid-afternoon and transform it into an environment that looks as though all of the hope has been leached out of

large appealing to the eye. That's because for all of the additional graphical details that *Gears* may have when compared to last generation's titles, people still expect to derive a certain amount of visual pleasure from the games that they play, whether it's *Halo 3*'s gleaming green-purple-chrome colour palette or the saturated deep blues and nightvision greens of *COD4*.

Killzone 2, by contrast, consistently denies us those pleasures. Yes, its graphics engine is unquestionably stellar. Yet based on the creative and technical art direction for *Killzone 2*, the guiding principle for Guerilla's PS3 debut must have been 'decrepit ugly'. Helghan's grimy environments clearly weren't much to look at before the Vektan invasion, but the way that the war has chewed them up further isn't helping matters. All of this is subtly reinforced by Guerilla's penchant for supplying a single hint of beauty – lapping waves on a beach; the barest glimmer of sunlight peeking through Helghan's thick cloud cover – that only serves to augment the game's overall gloom.

It might be churlish of me to say so, but I'll do it anyway: Guerilla may have succeeded in its aesthetic aims a little too well. For while all of its visual effects are impeccably implemented, in contrast to the clumsy attempts at the start of this generation, I could have done with the suggestion of devastation instead of a meticulous recreation of it. I'd have preferred a more distanced, iconic representation of Helghan's scorched surface rather than the flawlessly dismal illustration in the finished game. Four holidays into this generation's titles, the last thing I expected was that I'd find myself clinging so hard to my long-held assumptions about what defines videogame reality. But if wanting a little more beauty in my games is wrong, I don't want to be right.

N'Gai Croal writes about technology for Newsweek. His blog can be found at blog.newsweek.com/blogs/levelup

> **People still expect visual pleasure from games, whether it's *Halo 3*'s gleaming colour palette or the night-vision greens of *COD4***

with a slew of launch titles from various publishers. From *Perfect Dark Zero* to *Condemned*, from *Project Gotham Racing 3* to *Need For Speed: Most Wanted*, each game made me feel as though my eyes were being overwhelmed by the sheer amount of onscreen visual detail. It was as if I didn't know where to look, or even how to look at what I was seeing, so different did those titles seem to me from their last-generation counterparts.

In hindsight, a good deal of this is probably due to overdone, poorly implemented effects like normal mapping and depth of field, and in fairness, it takes developers time to master their new tools. But what I blamed at the time on 'too much realism' had, in fact, been caused by the

it. But at the events leading up to E3 as well as E3 itself, I all but ignored *Killzone 2* to focus on other titles that were making their debut at the show. So it wasn't until late last autumn and early this year, while playing the first 30-40 per cent of the game, that I had the chance to reflect on the various ways in which it calls into question our notions of what constitutes videogame realism.

Cliff Bleszinski described one of *Gears Of War*'s aesthetic premises as 'destroyed beauty,' the way that the environments combine the splendour of Seran architecture with the detritus of the planet's ruins. *Gears 1* and *2* have their share of slimy surfaces and gruesome killings, but the images themselves are by and

Powered by

Wwise®
audio pipeline solution

Divinity II
Larian Studios

"For years we'd been looking for a complete solution that removed the hassles of managing audio resources, from both a coding and audio engineer perspective. Then we discovered Wwise, with its rapid iteration times, ease of integration, and good results. It's everything we needed!"

Swen Vincke - CEO - Larian Studios

DIVINITY II
EGO DRACONIS

audiokinetic®

dtp
entertainment
AG

www.audiokinetic.com

Inbox

Issue 199

After reading the **Edge** verdict on *Killzone 2* (**E**199), I felt that, as with many other games before, there was something wrong with the score. Not that it was given a 7 rather than a 9 or 10, but rather that a score had to be given at all.

I have often wondered why so many publications and websites still use five-, ten- or hundred-point scales. I'm doubtful the conclusion of a thorough review can be adequately reflected in a simple number. How does a reviewer decide where the boundaries lie, where

But beyond simply being outmoded, I feel that these ratings could, in some cases, be indirectly damaging to gaming as a whole. The *Killzone 2* 7, once loosed upon the internet, was seized upon as flame-bait, any attempt at genuine debate drowned by angry cries of bias and 'it's just attention seeking'. Can we expect readers (and developers) to take note of valid points when obscured by inane rants and spiteful bile? How can consumers be confident of a game's merits and faults when honest but critical reviews attract such negativity?

Letter of the month wins a DS Lite

It's one thing for a game to make cheerful nods to Asimov and Clarke, quite another for it to share the same title as a bona fide literary classic

7 becomes 8, and which factors take precedence? At what point does an enjoyable experience of a game outweigh notable technical shortcomings? Can quality be a substitute for innovation and imagination, or vice versa?

For example, I adored *Dreamfall* for its story, dialogue and characters. However, I am well aware that the actual 'gameplay' left much to be desired. As a result such a game becomes a dichotomy that is difficult to reconcile; whether you mark it high or low, it would do a disservice to the game, the review and the reader.

I don't doubt this is a subject that has been discussed many times. However, I think it's becoming increasingly difficult with each generation. 'Triple-A' titles become increasingly complex every year, with reviews having to cover far more ground — single — and multiplayer, technique and artistry, presentation and intentions — combined with ever-increasing hype and expectations.

Expecting rationality on the internet is most likely futile at the best of times. Still, I can't help but feel that if *Killzone 2* (and, before it, *MGS4*) had gone reviewed but unmarked, then maybe a smaller, quieter but still impassioned debate may have followed. Even with a more straightforward 'good or bad' game, surely a concise summary paragraph could be of infinitely more benefit. A score tells us so little about a game yet proves an easy target. Maybe it's time to ditch them once and for all.
James D Rutterford

Scores don't convey much nuance, no, and it's really quite fortunate that we print them alongside words that do. Ignoring those words? Bad idea.

On your Incoming games preview page in **E**198 (in reference to EA's *Dante's Inferno*) you speculate whether the real Dante was much of a fighter. If you want to know how and when Dante took to the sword you need only read Barbara Reynolds' excellent biography.

However, I do realise that this really isn't the only point of concern.

Seeing as *Rise Of The Argonauts* scored so badly in the same issue, it's tempting to suggest that games developers should stay away from adapting literary texts. It's one thing for a game to make cheerful nods to Asimov and Clarke, or to wear its Conrad inspiration on its sleeve; quite another for it share the same title as a bona fide classic. The academic elite will demand that the essence of their beloved text has been translated well and not been butchered by poor implementation or reduced to a juvenile artist gimmick.

It's easy to be cynical and I must point out that I do applaud such ambition. Let me ask you this: can you imagine what would happen to the industry if a developer took a classic text for the basis of their game and got it exactly and utterly right?
Andrew Venables

Do tell us if you come across a brilliant shmup based on The Canterbury Tales for your new DS.

In years gone by, many **Edge** readers have lamented the fact that gaming was perceived by the mainstream as something that was for kids — or adults who should know better. We gamers demanded that our pastime be regarded by the public as a legitimate form of interactive entertainment that covered a wide range of ages and cultural demographics. Now in 2009 this wish seems more of a reality than ever due mostly to the seemingly unstoppable Wii, and it seems that the gaming 'hardcore' feel betrayed.

When the N64 was competing against the PS1 many felt that the N64 was the true gamers' choice, and that the PS1's outstanding commercial success was due to flashy FMV intros and licences that appealed to casual gamers and women (not to mention rampant piracy and the fact it was a CD player). Now the situation is the exact opposite. The Wii is regarded by 360, PC and PS3 users as a 'couples console' or something that appeals to overweight 40-somethings who define themselves as real gamers.

male anti-social tech heads more concerned with how many polygons our consoles come move than simply enjoying the experience of gaming? I would like to think not, but a quick check of any internet forum might indicate otherwise. Of one thing we can be certain: the future of games and the people who play them is more unpredictable than ever.
Trevor Byrne

Us, anti-social tech heads? But we do voice chat and everything!

 I'm one of **Edge**'s subscribers from Thailand. I really love **Edge** — it's awesome. However, in **E**198 I found incorrect information in the [Codeshop] article 'Modelling for world domination'. The opening sentence of the article reads: 'The Japanese boardgame of Go has often been used as a metaphor for strategic business activity'.

Do we really want the mainstream to fully embrace our medium? Are we comfortable to play against grandmothers online and potentially lose?

The question I am asking is do we really want the mainstream to fully embrace our medium? Are we comfortable to play against grandmothers online and potentially lose, or are we exactly what they said we were: a bunch of predominantly

Go is not Japanese, it originated in China more than 2,500 years ago. Some time later it spread to Japan and other countries. It should be 'The Chinese boardgame of Go' if the author wants to specify its country of origin.

I speculate that the author of this

Is this really *Dante's Inferno* or EA's? Andrew Venables welcomes games which find themselves inspired by literary classics, but wonders if wholesale adaptations set themselves up for a fall

Send us email (**edge@futurenet. co.uk**), using 'Inbox' as the subject line. Or send a letter: Inbox, **Edge**, 30 Monmouth Street, Bath BA1 2BW

Rob Moir gets a little hot under the collar about Steam, having refused to use it since *Half-Life 2* required him to connect online

article might have got confused by the strong Japanese Go community or because Japanese comics make reference to Go.
C Keereeto

Apologies for the error. The author of the piece has been reprimanded with a rolled-up portrait of Hiroshi Yamauchi.

I have to say that I was a little surprised at the Steam article in **E**199. I hope they paid you well for it because frankly it read like one of those multi-page testimonial style adverts rather than an article that actually took a proper look at the technology.

I've not had Steam on my computer since I first purchased *Half-Life 2* years ago and it promptly 'infected' my computer, with apparently the sole intent of making it very difficult for me to play a singleplayer game offline quietly by myself. In other words, in the manner that I personally choose to enjoy my gaming.

I don't miss it in the slightest. I've not seen a single game that requires Steam and regretted my choice. At the end of the day, this sort of technology has more benefits for the publisher than the customer — it puts more obstacles in between me and starting a new game, all for the sake of making it easier for the publisher to push out patches at their convenience instead of mine.

You enjoy Steam. I'll enjoy being able to do what I like without getting Valve's permission.
Rob Moir

Yes, that pesky Valve, making it easy for developers to release critical patches! In seriousness, many important questions remain about Steam but, like it or not, it's going to be a big part of a future that is online, all of the time.

F

Topic: Love and marriage
Usually we only encounter significant others in games in the form of kidnapped girlfriends or murdered spouses. I'd like to see family explored more as a theme between player characters, especially since there's so much more in the way of games with multi-character campaigns nowadays.
JB

I guess the problem with families and kids if that they have to be settled in a certain place, which I can imagine would limit a lot of kinds of gameplay. If they weren't, their continued survival might seem implausible.
EvilRedEye

The Sanderson family in *Chibi-Robo* are wonderful. Mr Sanderson has been turfed out of the bedroom and is now sleeping on the sofa and, as the game plays out, you discover Mrs Sanderson is completely fed-up because of her husband's laziness and lack of job prospects. Their daughter Jenny is caught in the middle of this bickering, and as a result has resorted to locking herself in her own world and dressing up as a frog. Family breakdowns and financial troubles are the last thing you expect from a title wrapped in a *Toy Story*-inspired world.
Lerxst

***Fable* has not been mentioned here. I had a threesome with my complicit wife in this game. More of this, designers.**
regmcfly

When done badly emotional attachments are a nuisance. I hated the Dom's wife subplot in *Gears 2*. I wanted to blow up monster brains, not care about my sidekick's marital problems.
-sigge-

Just what was the relationship between Pac-Man and Ms Pac-Man?
Tinglefan117

Friends with benefits, surely?
-sigge-

To celebrate the 200th issue of **Edge**, when you subscribe today we'll send you a special postcard collection of all 200 covers

- Get an exclusive pack of 200 **Edge** cover postcards
- Save 30% on the cover price
- Pay by Direct Debit – only £10.23 per quarter
- Delivery direct to your door
- Never miss an issue

ONLINE: www.myfavouritemagazines.co.uk/edg/P134
CALL: 0844 848 2852 (quote ref P134)

Offer available to new subscribers only. You will receive 13 issues per year. Your subscription will start with the next available issue. Minimum subscription term is 12 months. If at any time during the first 60 days you are dissatisfied in any way please notify us in writing and we will refund you for all un-mailed issues. The gift is subject to availability. In the unlikely event of stocks becoming exhausted, we reserve the right to substitute with items of a similar value. Offer ends: April 9 2009. Order ref: P134.

GIVE **YOUR GAMES** THE EDGE

SHARP CREATIVE CAMPAIGNS THAT CONNECT WITH YOUR MARKET

:eye-d
C R E A T I V E

OVER TEN YEARS EXPERIENCE DELIVERING HIGH QUALITY PRINT, DIGITAL AND
MOTION COMMUNICATIONS FOR THE INTERACTIVE ENTERTAINMENT INDUSTRY

CAMPAIGNS / KEY ART / PACKAGING / POINT OF SALE / PRINT ADVERTISING / ONLINE ADVERTISING
TV ADVERTISING AND IDENTS / TRAILERS / EMAILERS / MINI APPS. / WIDGETS / FLASH PRESENTATIONS
FLASH GAMES / SCREENSAVERS / EXHIBITION MATERIAL / PRINT MANAGEMENT

INFO@EYE-DCREATIVE.CO.UK   +44 (0)20 7407 1440   WWW.EYE-DCREATIVE.CO.UK

Next month

Edge 201
on sale April 9